THE WAY OF A SEER

REFLECTIONS FROM A NON-ORDINARY LIFE

PETER L. NELSON, PH.D.

EMPIRICUS PRESS

NEVADA CITY, CALIFORNIA

Empiricus Press
Nevada City, CA 97520
www.wayofaseer.net

ISBN: 978-0-692-20686-7

Cover design: Ann Lowe, GraphicDesignforBooks.com
Waterfall picture: Pedro Antonio Salaverria Calahorral, Dreamstime.com

This book is dedicated to my teachers:

Alice—for her love, superb guidance and incredible patience

Stanley Poulton—for a wonderful demonstration of what is possible

Trixie Allingham—for facilitating the discovery of my potential

Dr. Lloyd T. Delany—for opening my eyes to the unconscious

Dr. Haridas Chaudhuri—for guiding my first steps in meditation

Shunryu Suzuki, Roshi—for offering me a moment of clarity

Tarthang Tulku, Rinpoche—for his demonstration of vigor and compassion

...and to the memory of

Dr. Andrew J. Singer

Note

In this book, out of personal preference for stylistic simplicity, I use the pronoun "he" when speaking of a person who could be either male or female. This has nothing to do with a gender differential with regard to *seeing*. I could have as easily used "she" throughout.

Contents

Acknowledgments

My first attempt to write this book started over 35 years ago but was soon abandoned. A couple of other starts were made over subsequent years only to be quickly dropped as well.

Long overdue and with my life-clock ticking with less certainty, it was finally picked up again and completed, not least because of the encouragement and insistence by my wife, Virginia, that it was worthwhile. To her I am eternally grateful for both her belief in the project and her practical support—offering suggestions for organization and doing the final edit and polish.

The first draft of this opus needed considerable editing to make it a more accessible book. This task fell to Carolyn Bond, whose know-how regarding book-craft helped to shape it into a more readable text. I thank her for her good work.

Also, my heartfelt thanks to Michele Kelly, who asked many useful questions and contributed to the final proof reading.

I'm deeply indebted to Susan Fassberg, for her steadfast belief in me and encouragement of my work as a *seer*. She was around from the very early days promoting, connecting, and pointing direction, even acting as my interpreter when I spent time in Freiburg, Germany teaching and mentoring.

And, finally, my gratitude to all my students and teachers whose lives and wisdom informed my outlook and the content of the pages that follow.

Introduction

This book is the story of personal transformation and a journey into the realm of the *seer*, someone who can perceive beyond the curtain of everyday reality and straddle the border between the worlds of ordinary and non-ordinary perception. The story begins with my birth in New York City in 1943 and continues some seventy-odd years later where I am now. Along the way it covers the encounters and "rebirths" that have enriched my life with awakenings and realizations that deepened my awareness and broadened my perspective on what the satiric writer Douglas Adams calls "Life, the Universe, and Everything."[1]

In a way, this is really two books in one. The first tells how I was "called" to the path of becoming a *seer* and the impact that encounter had on me. In this sense consider it a type of memoir, though many events in my life are left out in order to focus on my development as a *seer*. Most of the non-ordinary experiences recalled in this narrative, and in other parts of the book as well, are from the earlier chapters of my life as a *seer*, because they represent pivotal moments in my development and therefore stand out in memory as intense, first encounters tend to. As time went on, however, similar events became commonplace—therefore standing out less in memory—as *seeing* became thoroughly integrated into my daily life.

The second book-within-a-book outlines what being a *seer* is all about—how *seeing* works as a technology of consciousness and attention and how it produces the larger experiences and daily awarenesses I have had as a result of this unique way of paying attention to the world around me. It includes reflections on the scientific, psychological, and philosophical issues that I believe need to be addressed by anyone who accepts science and rational thought, as I

---

[1] D. Adams, *The Hitchhiker's Guide to the Galaxy* (London: Pan Books, 1979), p. 170.

do, but who also realizes that there is more to the world than what scientific materialism suggests. Together, the narrative of my transformation and the exposition of its process comprise a case study that maps my *seer's* world and, hopefully, will give you an opportunity to make better sense of your own—ordinary or non-ordinary.

This book is not a neat or simple story with a clear beginning, middle, climax, and resolution—nor is it a morality tale, suggesting a correct way to live. Even less is it a self-help manual, though it does unpack some of the methods behind *my* way as a *seer*, including what I have learned as a psychologist and social science researcher. Think of it as an insider's view of one *seer's* development and understanding of *seeing*, which I define simply as the art of living with attention continuously on both the ordinary and non-ordinary streams. Please be aware that you do not have to reproduce what I have done to become a *seer*, for mine is not the only way to enter into this way of knowing.

Culturally speaking, I am a twenty-first century American, raised and educated in the scientific worldview so it should be no surprise that I have attempted to unite the realms of science and *seeing*. Impossible, you might say, since they seem to be practically at war with each other. For a long time I struggled to reconcile these apparently opposing ways of knowing, but once I relinquished the religious-like dogma underpinning the ontological claims of many members of both camps, any conflict between the two evaporated. In reading this book, therefore, I urge those on all sides of this divide to keep an open mind.

Because of my deep commitment to the scientific worldview, this book is a major step out of a self-imposed closet into the full glare of the criticism levied at anyone who insists on the veracity of non-ordinary perception. It represents my decision to publicly face the wall of denial dominating most of Western society in relation to the world of non-ordinary knowing.

I. Beginnings

For each soul there is a time and a place, and an end of time and place. When the body dies, the borders of its soul subside in favor of the psyche, the soul of the longbody, and its larger space. When the longbody dies, the psyche is absorbed in Big Mind. Each body and soul is emplaced in its own realm of time and place, the larger encompassing the small, the small often unaware of the larger. Nothing disappears, only the vision expands and contracts.

– William Roll
My Search for the Soul

1. FIRST INTIMATION

From my earliest years I can remember sensing things that other people could not. I perceived energetic fields emanating from living things and places around me and I was acutely aware of people's intentions, even when these contradicted what they said and what others picked up about them. Sometimes I even saw visions in the form of images and scenes playing out in my mind's eye, though I could not understand what they were.

My world was multi-layered and multi-dimensional. At first I thought this was normal and then, in 1951, I found out otherwise through a traumatic event that changed how I thought about everything and that altered the course of my life.

It was the beginning of summer vacation. I had recently turned eight and my favorite uncle had just arrived with my aunt and cousin for a visit at our suburban home in Long Island, New York. They were planning to stay a few days and then take me to their house in Connecticut for a week.

I was very excited to see my uncle. He was what I can only describe as a "kid magnet," drawing children to him because of his natural kindness, gentle eyes, and an ability to give special attention to a child's world. A quiet, wiry man, who by occupation was an electrician-handyman, he worked jobs ranging from repairing light fixtures to climbing power poles in order to hook up houses to the grid. Although I was fascinated by anything electrical and hung around him whenever he worked on our house, the really irresistible draw for me was the radiance of his gentle presence and his melodious singing voice. He often hummed and whistled as he worked.

Moments after his arrival, as we stood in the living room exchanging greetings, I remember gazing up at him with my usual love and admiration but as he smiled back at me, I saw something that surprised and disturbed me.

For just a few seconds, in place of his face, I saw a beating heart. At first I couldn't make sense of the image but as I continued to stare at his face, once again I saw a living heart appear and disappear. The image seemed to be in my mind and outside of me at the same time, as if I was watching a movie projected on an invisible screen. With it came an overwhelming feeling that something was wrong, and, while I could not verbalize my feelings, I felt a compelling urgency to do something, so I darted into the kitchen where my mother was preparing dinner.

For a few minutes I hung around her, saying nothing. Then, in an off-handed way I later realized was unusual for an eight-year-old, I asked her if there was anything wrong with my uncle. She looked down briefly from what she was doing and said, "Don't be silly, he's fine." But this did not reassure me as I got the sense she was just avoiding the issue. Not knowing how to question her further, however, I let the matter drop, though my uneasiness remained.

Two days later, it was time to make the drive to Connecticut. By late morning my uncle, aunt, father, mother and I had gathered around the Steinway baby grand piano in the alcove off the living room. We were singing Stephen Foster songs. I can still hear my uncle's soft, clear tenor voice above all the others in the group, as he then took the lead in the last song of that morning—a traditional Scottish folk tune.

> Tell me the tales that to me were so dear
> Long, long ago, long, long ago
> Sing me the songs I delighted to hear
> Long, long ago, long ago
> Now you are come all my grief is removed…

About an hour later we were preparing to leave. While the others finished packing, my uncle and I stood by ourselves in the living room waiting for my aunt and cousin. I was impatient to get on the road and buzzed around him in anticipation like a little fly at a picnic. As usual when I had him to myself, I barraged him with questions and chatter typical of an eight-year-old, and he responded with the patience that always made him such a hit with children.

Then, suddenly, as I prattled away, I felt an eerie stillness descend over the room. The very air seemed to thicken and solidify, enveloping us in a shroud-like silence. I abruptly stopped talking and looked up at my uncle. What I saw shocked me.

His usual relaxed expression had changed into one frozen with pain. All the color had drained from his face, which was now a pale, greenish hue. As he stared out as if at some unknown horizon, he broke the silence with a terrible groan that seemed to well up from the depth of his being and with that he dropped to his knees. At the same moment I felt a sensation in my own body that can only be likened to a ripping or wrenching apart of some inner, vital fabric. There was another pause as he remained kneeling in front of me, still transfixed on that distant horizon, then, keeling over onto his side, he became perfectly still.

I bellowed for my mother. She and my aunt came running from the bedroom as I bolted out the front door and down the street to a doctor who lived a few houses away. I remember running straight into the doctor's house shouting that something terrible was happening to my uncle. In my child's mind I thought that he was having overwhelming pain from the ruptured spinal discs that had plagued him in recent years.

The doctor grabbed his bag and followed at what seemed an agonizingly slow pace. I shouted at him to run, but he ignored my panicky implorations. I burst through our front door soon followed by the doctor, who immediately kneeled at my uncle's side and, after examining him briefly, quickly filled a large syringe and injected it into his chest. CPR had not yet been invented, and as I later learned, other than a shot of adrenaline directly to the heart, nothing could have been done. Unfortunately, it had no effect. My uncle was dead from what was later revealed to be a massive heart attack.

When my mother and aunt realized what was going on, they panicked and yelled at me and my cousin to get out of the room. Reluctantly we retreated to a nearby bedroom to wait and watch. An ambulance arrived, and we peeked out to see the paramedics remove his body. Left behind was a gaping void that I could barely comprehend and an atmosphere of profound shock that encompassed my entire family. My uncle was only 46 years old.

In the early hours of the next morning, after a deep and exhausted sleep, I awoke with a start. My bedroom door had been left ajar, and as

I stared into the dark I saw a translucent, glowing ovoid shaped figure about my uncle's height and build slide into my room through the narrow opening. The dimly luminescent figure moved—or I should say floated—to the end of my bed. I sat bolt upright, my heart pounding, but the apparition came no closer. It remained hovering at the foot of my bed for a brief time and then began to fade away. Once it had gone, I ran to my parents' room to tell them what I had seen, but, to my surprise, they did not seem alarmed. Instead, they told me I had been dreaming and after a bit of comforting, I was sent back to bed.

Over the next few weeks the figure reappeared several more times and though these visitations terrified me, I never again told my parents about them. I was sure I was not dreaming. Indeed, I was fully conscious at each of these sightings. Typically, I would awaken in the pre-dawn hours tense with anticipation. Sometimes nothing happened but when the apparition did come, I would become very frightened and sit up in bed, pressing my back against the wall and dreading what might happen next. Eventually, it came no more, and after several months I began to sleep through the night again.

Whatever I feared during these encounters never transpired. Years later I realized that my fear had been a typical reaction to the unknown—in particular, the occurrence of highly improbable events. All humans carry templates of what it is possible to perceive to ensure that we experience only what we expect to experience. Most of us find it disturbing when phenomena that are not part of our internal map of beliefs irrupt into our awareness and we respond with forceful attempts to reinstate the world as we believe it to be. In my parents' case, either they did not want to know about the apparition—a kind of denial—or it was so far out of their range of experience and beliefs that they assumed what was happening to me could only be a dream. Most likely it was the latter.

The most important result of that dramatic encounter with non-ordinary perception was that, despite my fear, I learned to remain steadfast and allow events to unfold. Because I believed that my parents could not help me since they did not accept what I was experiencing as real, I had to hold my fear in check and manage it on my own. It was my determination not to allow myself to fall apart that kept me afloat. This lesson would prove vital to my development as a *seer*, for one of the most important things to be learned on the *seer's* path is that terror and panic are blinding and prevent us from fully experiencing what is occurring in the moment, whereas acknowledging them allows us to be who we are and still attend to whatever we are witnessing.

Another result was a key life decision. Although I did not articulate it to myself at the time, I committed, first and foremost, to testing my own perceptions and trusting my direct experience rather than believing what others said. That decision, too, proved crucial as I became a conscious *seer*. In fact, being a good perceiver takes a capability to strip awareness down to non-judgmental witnessing as well as a willingness to allow events to unfold without attempting to manipulate perception in the service of one's needs or beliefs. It is my contention that non-judgmental attention is basic to being a reasonable human being, whether one is a *seer* or not.

In later years I came to realize that, without knowing it, I had spontaneously used my innate capacity for *seeing* to connect to my uncle's *bio-field* (for an explanation of *bio-fields* see Chapter 15), which led to my vision of his beating heart and then, to seeing his *bio-field* "remains" for some weeks after his death. Because the culture in which I grew up did not acknowledge *seeing* as a reality, it offered few constructs and little language for talking about it. Being an untutored *seer*, without a conceptual roadmap to guide me, I could not make sense of what I was experiencing much less understand what to do with what I *saw*.

I assumed at first that everyone was aware of what I was perceiving and I was perplexed when they did not seem to acknowledge it. As a result, I felt isolated and different—an outsider—without knowing what that meant other than it was a bad thing to be.

Wanting to be accepted as a normal, average child, I kept this sense of being different sufficiently in the background, trying to ignore it for the most part. However, that protective bubble burst when my uncle died. From age eight onward I had to grapple consciously and continuously with a wrenching, gut-level awareness of life, death, and eternity together with the ongoing consciousness of a level of reality that everyone around me seemed to deny.

In looking back, I realize it took a great act of will not to reveal my imagined "flaw" to others or to fall to pieces in front of adults and ask for what I intuitively knew would be wrong guidance. Yet in spite of my efforts to blend in with those around me, in a fundamental way I knew that I was never going to tread the same path as my peers. Accordingly, I made an effort not to be noticed, because, in my child's mind, being noticed meant that I would be recognized as "other." Hiding in plain sight became my *modus operandi*.

The strain of maintaining integrity in the light of my radically different awareness often made me a "difficult" child for parents and teachers, and I seemed strange to other children too—a loner. Although I was warm and outgoing by nature, if anyone said or did something that exacerbated my feelings of difference, I would react by retaliating verbally and physically. As a result, it was not long before I developed a reputation for being unpredictable and, generally, I was left alone by my peers.

For most of my childhood I felt fearful about being discovered as different—not belonging. The discrepancy between my perceptions and those around me continually highlighted my experience of being different. When, in my teen years, I became interested in neuroscience, I developed a theory to explain all the extraneous information that seemed to flow through my awareness, postulating that faulty neural networks in my brain—defective circuits if you like—were generating a cognitive and emotional stream of "noise." This stream seemed to have little to do with my personal perceptions and cognitions and was unconnected to my ordinary internal dialogue (self-talk), memories and chain of personal associations.

As a youngster I could not tie these extraneous perceptions and cognitions to my day-to-day life and wanted to turn them off. In my mid-twenties, however, when I answered the "call" to become a *seer*, I discovered that the source of my "other awarenesses" lay in another kind of knowing given by my capacity to *see*. I call this type of awareness the *second stream of attention*.

2. MY ORIGINS

I was born in the Bronx, New York, the second son of a couple with immigrant backgrounds. My father, who was born in Belarus, was just eight when he landed at Ellis Island in August 1921, under the gaze of Lady Liberty. He was accompanied by his mother and grandmother who, a year earlier, had fled the strife torn Soviet Union with him in a horse-drawn sled during a Russian winter. Near the Polish border, which was closed at the time and heavily guarded, they were chased by Soviet troops and fired upon. During their dash to freedom, the sled overturned and his mother broke her arm.

After escaping into Poland and finding a doctor who would treat her, they made it to Warsaw, where they remained for about a year while obtaining the necessary papers for travel to America. Their intention was to join my grandfather, who had emigrated to New York seven years earlier. From Warsaw they traveled to Antwerp and then on to England where they boarded the *Aquitania* and sailed for New York. Upon arrival, however, they discovered that my grandfather had met another woman and had divorced my grandmother. This rejection by my grandfather eventually led to my father changing his last name to Nelson, taken from Katznelson, a name from my grandmother's side of the family.

My father was small for his age but made his presence felt at school because of an exceptional academic ability. He first attended a religious school, but by the time he was ready for university he had opted for science over religion. He began his studies in chemistry at the City College of New York in 1931, during that institution's heyday. The influx of talented and bright young immigrants and their children filled the college with many who would go on to make significant marks in science and medicine. Graduates of CCNY in the 1930s included Jonas Salk (Nobel Prize for developing the first polio vaccine) and other

Nobel Laureates: Julius Axelrod (medicine), Herbert Hauptman (chemistry), Robert Hofstadter (physics), Jerome Karle (chemistry) and Arthur Kornberg (medicine).

Graduating in 1935 *magna cum laude*, my father went on to graduate school in chemistry, but, with the Great Depression at its height, after a year of study he left to join a chemical company. Like most of his generation, he believed that financial security was more important than academic success. Later, in his forties, he returned to postgraduate study in mathematics at New York University, where he completed a master's degree (he had a special affection for integral equations).

***

My mother's family arrived in New York from Budapest, Hungary, nine years after the turn of the century, and she was born in New York in 1914. Her father was a violent alcoholic, and my mother soon made her mark in her family as the only one of six children who would stand up to him. Quick-witted and resourceful, she usually escaped his wrath. According to family rumor, my grandfather left Hungary because of an incident during his service in the Austro-Hungarian army in which his fiery temper landed him in serious trouble.

If my father was the scientist and intellectual in the family, my mother was the "people-person." Her great passion in life was working with young children, and she did this first as a preschool teacher and then as a director of preschools in Nassau County, New York. She was involved in establishing the Head Start program in her home county and, in her fifties, she completed a masters degree in early childhood development. Later in her career, she became an expert witness in court cases involving the welfare of young children.

After her retirement, people would sometimes approach her on the street or at shopping centers and with warmth and affection they would tell her: "You saved my child," or "You made a real difference in my life." When she died, a 60-year-old woman wrote in response to her obituary, "Your mother was my nursery school teacher about 56 years ago and I still remember loving her." Although my relationship with my mother had a rocky start, by the time I was in my early thirties we had become good friends, and we remained so until her death at the age of 95.

***

While I inherited my mother's interest in people which later contributed to my work as a social scientist, it was my father who introduced me at a young age to the world of science and mathematics. Through his encouragement and guidance, science as a practice and as a way of knowing became central to my life from then on. By the time I was 13, I had become fascinated with mammalian physiology and consumed any book I could find on the topic. Understanding the dynamic interactions and mechanisms of living organ systems became a passion. I pondered the questions: What is life and how does this highly complex system of biochemistry, tissues, and organs produce and sustain it? When I wanted to install a colony of lab rats in my bedroom so I could run my own experiments, my father backed me against my mother's strenuous objections and, by the age of 14, my bedroom had become a makeshift laboratory complete with test equipment and animals.

In my first controlled experiment I tested a "fact" I had read in one of my precious physiology textbooks: if a mammal lost a paired organ, such as a kidney, the remaining one would compensate by taking up the function of the lost one and, in the process, would grow in size. Accordingly, I surgically removed a kidney from each of a group of rats and measured and weighed the excised organs. Having established basal metabolic rates (BMR) for the rats beforehand, I continued to measure their metabolisms post surgery and discovered that the book was correct. Then I made my own discoveries on the effects of surgery and kidney loss on BMR, which led to my first scientific paper: "The Effect of Unirenalectomy on the Metabolic Rate of the Rat." In another set of experiments, I conducted a study of the effects of induced diabetes on a rat's metabolism and then did a joint project with some friends to try to integrate an electro-mechanical servo-mechanism with a rat's nervous system.

Soon I was winning ribbons in the biology division at local and state science fairs and at 15 I was awarded a National Science Foundation summer research grant for high school students to work at the

Waldemar Medical Research Foundation. That summer I wrote my first scientific literature review ("The Hyperglycemic Glycogenolytic Factor in Mammals"). The following year I was given an equipment grant by Tektronix Corporation to aid my electro-physiological studies, and after that, I became the first high school student admitted on a summer research assistantship at Rockefeller University, where I worked on the bio-assay of synthetic tri-iodothyronine (thyroxine) that had been developed in the laboratory to which I was assigned.

Through these experiments and explorations I became a competent small animal surgeon and saw myself as a budding mammalian physiologist. Not only did I operate on rats and mice, children in my neighborhood brought me wounded wildlife to treat. I worked on several birds including a crow I later named "Houdini" because of his miraculous escape from death. He became a much loved pet and because of his inability to fly more than short distances, I kept him. About a year later I donated this ever-watchful, sleek black companion to a zoo, where he lived out the rest of his life.

For me, science was like a religious calling as well as a career path, and it claimed me early as its disciple. After high school, I studied physics and mathematics at Columbia University (the path recommended by my mentor at Rockefeller University). However, after a year and a half there, I dropped out and became a computer programmer apprenticed to a team at New York University Medical School that was attempting to develop software for doing neurological diagnosis by computer.

Later I studied psychophysiology in California, New Mexico and Denmark but, thanks to a string of unusual circumstances I will reveal in the next part of this book, I was ultimately forced to question my religious-like scientific beliefs. This did not lead me to abandon science, however. Rather, it helped me to appreciate it in a different light. Ultimately I would come to see that the scientific approach, when unfettered by the dogma of materialist ontology, is a beautiful and clear searchlight that can illumine many dark corners in the creation of human knowledge.

The mid-1960s saw me leave New York and move to the San Francisco Bay Area. I lived in and around the Haight-Ashbury, attending

San Francisco State University while working at the University of California, Berkeley, doing odd-jobs as a freelance computer programmer for academics and the computer center.

Every film and book I have seen or read describing the 1960s seems to ignore what I understood to be the core *Zeitgeist* permeating that era—an exploration of consciousness and ways of knowing. True, the sixties were also about free speech, ending segregation, stopping the Vietnam war, women's liberation and a general liberalization of American politics. However, what is never addressed—only alluded to—is that this period was the center of a revolution in our understanding of ourselves both psychologically and spiritually. This fundamental reorientation in self-awareness has continued, long after the Vietnam War ended, the Civil Rights Movement entered a more mainstream, developmental phase, and women's studies courses became the established norm on American college campuses.

Of course, all that upheaval and change in the second half of the twentieth century represented, in various forms, a reorientation in our understanding of our values and the workings of social and political institutions. But underpinning the specific foci of these movements, a fundamental shift in the very way we perceive and know our world also was occurring—a change in consciousness itself. This was most evident in the psychedelic movement as well as in the growing migration of white, Judeo-Christian Americans into Eastern religions such as Hinduism and Buddhism.

At the time it seemed to me that individuals were breaking through the traditional epistemic boundaries that circumscribed what they knew as well as what they would allow themselves to know. In my view however, little attention was paid to what had been revealed by these breakthroughs about the deconstructive-constructive processes of consciousness in framing perception, knowledge and belief. It appeared to me then, and still does now, that as quickly as their new encounters with their boundaries of knowing revealed a deconstructed view of the cultural givens of their lives, those views were reconstructed, and along only slightly revised social and political lines.

From my perspective, the 1960s was about expanding awareness, though the framework I brought to this period was a narrow, self-assured and absolute belief in science as the one true way to understand "life, the universe, and everything." Observed from my current perspective, most scientists appear to defend their rationalist bastion with a passion akin to religious zeal. Indeed, based on the definition of religion posited by the philosopher, Ninian Smart,[1] this dogmatic and unquestioning devotion to science can be thought of as a religious movement: "scientism."

I also believed that technology was the solution to problems and the one true path to what I conceived of as "progress" at the time. I was not attracted to political activism, however, mainly because I did not see violent confrontation or armed struggle as methods that would create genuine social justice, which always has been the issue for me.

During the sixties I was aware that I was taking part in a great social experiment being conducted by none other than those participating in it. What that experiment did was to make me cognizant of a broader range of possibilities.

Despite this and my success with science, throughout this period I remained stuck with my childhood sense of being fundamentally "flawed". It underscored everything I did and every social interaction. This feeling of "otherness" often left me isolated, like some kind of interloper. Although I enjoyed the eccentricity and sheer variety of lifestyles of the Haight-Ashbury in the 1960s, even there the feeling persisted.

In a way, the sixties "revolution" set the stage for the shift in consciousness I was about to experience even though nothing could have prepared me for the shock of that change as I embarked on the path to becoming a *seer*. In some ways, I can say I have never fully recovered from the ontological earthquake that struck me in 1969.

---

[1]N. Smart, *The Religious Experience of Mankind,* 2nd ed. (New York: Charles Scribner's Sons, 1976), pp. 16–24.

II. Initiation

The bird is fighting its way out of the egg. The egg is the world.
Whoever wishes to be born must destroy a world.

– Hermann Hesse

Damian

3. THE CALL TO ENGLAND

When I first arrived in the San Francisco Bay Area in the summer of 1963, I thought I had found the Promised Land and after a few months, I began to imagine it as my permanent home. However, by late 1968, I was having doubts. By then, the ethos of consciousness experimentation that pervaded Bay Area life at the start of the decade had morphed into a degenerate drug scene, including more than one murder in my neighborhood, the Haight-Ashbury.

In 1966 I had begun studying for an undergraduate degree in psychophysiology at San Francisco State University. During that era of strident student unrest and brutal police repression I managed to finish my degree and then commenced a masters program in experimental physiological psychology. On any given day during that time, I did not know whether I would be able to cross the main quad and enter the psychology building to get to my lab, or if it was even safe to appear on campus.

I was also spending progressively longer days in the lab, and my wife back then, whom I had known since I was 19 and to whom I had been married only a year, was showing herself progressively less willing to be a partner to someone so dedicated to scientific work. After I learned that she was becoming involved with someone else, it dawned on me that I had married the wrong person, and with turmoil and discord in my personal and professional life, I realized it was time for me to leave the Promised Land. As my Buddhist teachers often said: all is change and nothing remains the same, no matter how much we want it to.

After discovering that the psychology department at the University of New Mexico would support the research into the neurophysiology of arousal and states of consciousness I wanted to pursue, I applied to and was accepted into their doctoral program. So it was that in January

1969, together with my German shepherd dog, Bhakti, I left for Albuquerque, driving south on Route 1 in my newly acquired 1956 Ford. Just south of San Francisco I picked up a couple hitchhiking to Los Angeles. They insisted on sitting together in the back seat with my dog. That seemed a bit odd until I realized that they wanted the back seat because they were methamphetamine addicts and were helping each other shoot up as the dog looked on quizzically. Those two were the closest things to zombies I have ever met. I dropped them off somewhere in the San Fernando Valley seven hours later, much relieved to no longer be the driver of a "speed hearse." A few days later I arrived in Albuquerque.

The disparity between the urban San Francisco environment and the isolation of the high, empty valley surrounding Albuquerque was disorienting. New Mexico was like an ocean of land. The beauty and power of the landscape were matched only by a vast, yawning silence in which all human activity was swallowed whole. From the incantations of ancient Native American ceremonies or the detonation of the world's first atomic bomb—all seemed suspended in a kind of existential aspic.

I enrolled at the university and found a place to live that I could afford—a large, permanently mounted trailer located in an agricultural grazing area not far outside the city limits. However, it was not many weeks before the spring winds began to storm across the high plateau, howling with unrelenting ferocity through the seams of my trailer home. For the first few nights neither the dog nor I slept much.

Classes commenced, and I quickly entered into the life of a doctoral student. To my surprise, I did not long to return to San Francisco, perhaps because there was nothing there for me any more. This was confirmed a few weeks into the semester—while I was sitting in an advanced statistics lecture—when I was served with my divorce papers. My last link to the Bay Area was broken. "So be it," I thought.

Around the same time, my supervisor, the head of the department, gave me an unpublished paper to read. Authored by a military associate of his, the paper described a mathematical model, derived from empirical data, of the behavior of an individual sensory neuron. I found that by algebraically manipulating the model, I could derive a more complete form of an experimentally established principle of sensory perception, dating from the nineteenth century, called the Weber-Fechner law. My neurophysiological modification of the law demonstrated that the relationship between perceived and actual stimulus intensity was encoded at the sensory receptor stage, without any need for additional processing by the brain and spinal chord. My preliminary calculations (done laboriously with a slide rule since there were no electronic calculators or personal computers yet) showed that my revised model could also account for observed effects, particularly hysteresis, seen in the graphical plots of data produced in later research on the Weber-Fechner law.

At the next advanced neuropsychology seminar, I enthusiastically presented my newly created mathematical model, hypothesizing how this view of sensory encoding might relate to the role of the brain's ascending reticular activating system in creating arousal and possibly states of consciousness. The presentation was greeted with dead silence. None of the other graduate students said a word but sat around the seminar table looking at me with the eyes reminiscent of stacked mullet in a fish market. Even the professor offered no substantive comments. Instead, he chided me for taking 11 minutes for my presentation since professional conferences allow only 10, adding that I should be mindful of this in the future.

I took the lack of response—not a word of critique or debate—to mean that no one in the room grasped what I had said. The professor told me I should present this work again sometime in the future because the other students needed more time to digest it. I believed he was actually talking about himself. After only a month in this department, I was already beginning to feel inappropriate for the program and, once again, I found myself in the all too familiar position of being an outsider.

It was also during my first month on campus that I began to formulate my views on science being an epistemic method without any innate capacity to allow its practitioners to make definite ontological ascriptions. In other words, I started to see science as a way of generating operationally derived knowledge that was repeatable to a certain degree, yet lacking a basis for making definite statements about what actually exists. This uncertainty regarding what we can know was becoming apparent to me not so much from my coming in contact with the ideas arising from quantum mechanics (later, books such as Fritjof Capra's *Tao of Physics*[1] would take up that theme), as from Einstein's description of riding on the end of beam of light and the relativity of the measurement of space and time.

As a result of these reflections, I often found myself in the library reading physics and philosophy more than neurophysiology. I eventually concluded that all knowledge derives from human experiencing and, therefore, can only be considered as human knowledge, not a direct apprehension and knowing of a "thing-in-itself."[2] The philosophy of Kant came alive for me, too, as I realized that the study of the human brain as an attempt to understand how we know reality is no more than a description of the human experience of "brain-ness." In other words, the depiction of the model of the nervous system as a communication network of neurons using frequency-modulated nerve impulses and the production, uptake, and re-uptake of neurotransmitters is a story based on human experience. It is not a description of "what is" out there in the "objective world," offered to us as human-free, context-stripped knowledge pointing directly at an absolute, external reality that exists apart from the knower.[3]

It was during this period, while I was wrestling with the disconnect between my approach to neuropsychology and that of others in my department, formulating my views on science, and trying to get some sleep in my wind-tossed trailer, that I had two very vivid dreams. In the first, I found myself standing, a bit awestruck, in front of Albert Einstein. Realizing that I had some questions about relativity theory I wanted to ask, I requested permission to do so. Politely he answered each one—my last question being whether the special theory of relativity was actually a theory of mind rather than of matter. He hesitated for a

---

[1]F. Capra, *The Tao of Physics* (Boulder: Shambhala, 1983).

[2]I. Kant, *Critique of Pure Reason*, trans. N. K. Smith (London: Macmillan, 1929).

[3]Later I came across William James' wonderful essay "Radical Empiricism," which delineated to a finer degree what I intuitively understood at that time: W. James, *Essays in Radical Empiricism and a Pluralistic Universe* (Gloucester, Mass.: Peter Smith, 1967). Also see: T. Reason and J. Rowan, eds., *Human Inquiry: A Source Book of New Paradigm Research* (New York: John Wiley and Sons, 1981).

moment and then said: "That question is for you to answer," whereupon the dream ended.

I awoke somewhat bewildered but still awed by my experience. Although a sense of Einstein's presence lingered, meeting him as a symbol in a dream did not seem that unusual, since he was a cultural icon and had been a personal hero of mine from childhood. What intrigued me was that he seemed different in personality from the warm and kindly old genius Santa Claus figure I usually imagined. In my dream he seemed a bit cold with a diffident, slightly sardonic edge in the way he spoke.

I wanted to check out the answers he gave me in the dream, so I went to the university library the next day and got hold of a copy of his lay lectures on the theory of relativity.[4] I was struck by the tone of his writing, which I found similar to the way the Einstein of my dream had expressed himself. Then, to my great surprise, I discovered that the information I received in my dream—which I had not known before— was indeed in the book, down to some of the same phrasing and tone.

If I was already feeling suspended between worlds due to the recent personal and geographic changes in my life, this experience heightened it. Nevertheless, I plunged further into my pursuit of understanding consciousness and physics neglecting my real duties: multivariate statistics and the advanced seminar in neuropsychology.

In the second dream, which occurred a few days later, I found myself flying, unaided, above a landscape of rolling green hills dotted with clumps of trees and occasional small groups of houses and farm buildings. The color and vividness of the dream experience were intense. I was entranced by the soft, velvet green beauty of the scene, especially in contrast to the open, semi-arid landscape around Albuquerque. As I scanned the scene below me I was engulfed by a powerful and inexplicable nostalgia. I had no idea where this dream place was—it was nowhere I had seen before—yet it was so familiar, inviting, and real.

---

[4]A. Einstein, *Relativity: The Special and the General Theory*, trans. R. W. Lawson (New York: Bonanza Books, 1961).

I awoke with a start and looked at my bedside clock. It was still the middle of the night. In an anguished state, I lay there feeling an intense sense of separation and sadness, combined with a longing to return to that unknown place. But how could I feel nostalgia for somewhere I had never been? Did it even exist? As I thought about it the next morning, I could not interpret the dream in terms of the psychotherapy and analysis I had been through in the past, and the feelings that accompanied it seemed completely irrational, so I decided simply to try to ignore it.

That evening I went with some acquaintances to see the just-released animated Beatles film, *Yellow Submarine*. The first showing was a short travelogue about Devon in the West Country of England. I was only half watching it until what appeared on the screen suddenly caught my full attention—an aerial sequence of rolling green hills dotted with clumps of trees, much like I had seen in my dream the night before. Again, for no apparent reason, I was overcome by intense feelings of nostalgia, this time accompanied by an irrational desire to go there.

For a graduate student with barely enough money to survive month to month, picking up and flying to Britain appeared as remote as flying to the moon. Yet during the days that followed, that picture of England and the associated nostalgia recurred with increasing frequency and intensity. I found myself battling a crazy impulse to just take off and go, oblivious to the contingencies of cost and career. Confused, worried, and ever more distracted from my studies, I quietly wondered if I was "losing it" psychologically.

About a week after I saw the film, my dog, out of boredom, attacked the insulation under our trailer and made a mess that the owner discovered before I had time to fix it. As a result, I was summarily cast out and had to find accommodation in a hurry, so I moved into a converted garage in town. I was just settling into my new "digs" when I met Ruth.[5] She dressed better than most of the impoverished students I knew, drove a fairly new car, lived in a small but very nice adobe house in the stylish Old Town section of Albuquerque, and, as a part-time

---

[5]Not her real name.

student with no job, she seemed to have time on her hands. There was an instant mutual attraction, so we started to date.

The nagging nostalgia and "pull" to Britain continued to grow in the background of my awareness, though I considered it too crazy to mention to anyone. Instead, I started complaining to Ruth about the department and the quality of the graduate program. One evening, after listening to my usual litany of gripes, she asked in a somewhat detached manner: "What would you do if you could do anything you wanted?"

I thought for a moment and replied, "Travel." When she asked where to? I groped around in my mind and, purposely bypassing the obvious choice, said, "Hawaii." A friend from my San Francisco years had lived in Maui for a time and spoke of it glowingly as a magical place.

"Well," she said, "let's go."

"Don't be ridiculous!" I retorted. I was a very broke graduate student and, therefore, not going anywhere. I expected the subject to be dropped, so her response surprised me: "I have independent means and I'll take you, if you really want to go."

I felt embarrassed at the offer and wondered if she was playing with me, yet she repeated it again in a manner suggesting that she could and would do it if I said yes.

Sitting on my small army-cot bed, I fell into a whirlpool of thought, trying to imagine myself abandoning my graduate studies and taking off for Hawaii, yet my mental efforts produced only more inner conflict as each thought arose and fell away under its own weight. The proposal of Hawaii, I realized, had been an empty statement offered up to avoid confronting the raging battle within. I was about to say "forget it" when a picture of the West Country of England sprang vividly into my mind's eye.

Hesitating to reveal myself and caught in the push-pull of my continuing ambivalence, I groped around looking for something else to focus on when, before I could stop myself I blurted out: "Not Hawaii, but if you want to take me somewhere, let's go to England."

Ruth reflected for a only moment and then said, "Sure, let's do it." She had been there many times before. She was particularly enthusiastic about Europe because she liked the island of Ibiza, off the coast of

Spain. "After a couple of weeks in England," she said, "we can go and have some real fun in Spain."

Still unsure, I said I would think about it, and the subject was dropped for the time being.

The next day was the start of monkey surgery week at the lab. Under the scrutiny of our professor, graduate students were to implant electrodes in the brains of living monkeys to aid his research project for the US Air Force. Although I had performed small animal surgery as part of various physiological research projects in high school and college, vivisection was becoming abhorrent to me. The animals were starting to seem too alive and sentient to be treated as experimental objects.

Worst of all for me were surgical experiments on cats, called spinal preps. The animals, virtually awake but paralyzed by the drug curare, had their spinal cords surgically exposed while graduate students probed through the bloody mess with stimulating and recording electrodes to trace the poor creature's spinal roots. This was not a matter of scientific discovery—these neurological pathways had been well mapped many times in the past—but merely a heuristic device for graduate students to gain firsthand experience of neuroanatomy and electrophysiology.

The cats were provided by the local animal shelter, so they faced either the shelter's decompression death chamber or experimentation in our lab. However, I started to find it difficult to accept the suffering these animals had to endure before being dispatched. They were housed, five to ten at a time, in a small room at the back of the lab which had been set up as a cage. One day, standing in front of this prison, I noticed several were in good condition and apparently they had good temperaments so, quietly, I began to canvas my friends to see who might be willing to take one and, after finding a home, I would return to the lab at night and "liberate" a cat.

This caper did not last long, however. I was caught, and, after a major chewing out by the professor, I was forced to stop. Of course, this only widened the gap I perceived between myself and my colleagues, who were now starting to view me as squeamish and not up to being an "objective" scientist.

When it came to the first surgery day for the monkeys, the graduate students usually worked in pairs. One acted as surgeon and the other as anesthetist, and then the roles were switched for the next animal. I was the first to act as surgeon. The internal conflict of recent days had been playing havoc with my concentration on my studies and lab work. Trying to keep my mind on task, I placed the first electrode into the stereotaxic device—a piece of hardware attached to the monkey's skull designed to guide the electrode to its appointed place in the animal's brain. However, as I started to turn the screws to lower the electrode into the hole in the animal's skull I inadvertently bent the electrode, rendering it useless. At that moment the professor arrived in the operating room. Seeing what I had done, he exploded into a tirade of abuse and expletives about my supposed incompetence. Feeling helpless against his onslaught, I said nothing in my own defense but just stood there as he raved.

After enduring his lambasting, in spite of my confusion and shame, I found another electrode, and, after various electrophysiological tests, my partner and I completed the first monkey in time for lunch. Instead of going with the others to eat, however, I slipped off down the corridor to the changing room, stripped off my surgical garb, donned my street clothes, and left the lab, never to return.

I headed back to my garage-home, called Ruth, and told her that if her offer was still open, I wanted to go to England. She thought that was great, so that evening we planned the trip. A few days later, I drove out of town with her, heading east and away from my long-dreamed-of career as a neuroscientist without so much as a good-bye to the department or even officially signing out of the university.

***

In spite of having jettisoned many years of academic work, the decision left me feeling relieved and liberated. We took the northern route back east so we could visit my brother, Steve, outside of Boston before going to Washington, D.C., where we would stay with Ruth's parents while we made our travel arrangements and I got a passport. I was more than a little apprehensive about my brother's reaction to my sudden change of direction. He had two Harvard graduate degrees after all, but when we arrived, I was relieved to find that he seemed pleased to see me.

At the time, Steve was producing rock and roll concerts at a venue he created called the Woodrose Ballroom near Springfield, MA. The Velvet Underground was playing that night. The pre-punk, art-scene music of groups like the Velvet Underground did not appeal to me much in those days. Nevertheless, Ruth and I went to the Woodrose because it was the only thing to do. While the first act was playing I wandered backstage and found Lou Reed, the leader of the Velvets, sitting quietly by himself. Although I expected him to be a bit of a bizarre, kinky character, it was clear, as we began to chat, that he was a kind-hearted, humble man. Although we talked about trivia, impressions about him began flooding into my consciousness, though I tried to ignore them as I did most of the "noise" that impinged on my awareness in those days.

From what I recall, one of these impressions was a picture of him alone and isolated—an outsider but in a way quite different from his public persona of the twisted, sexually deviant bad boy. I knew that his sense of being an outsider existed from childhood, and that he carried sadness combined with stoicism about having been born into circumstances where he did not fit. Playing at being the outsider in his pop image was a game that amused him and one he did not take too seriously. I realized that it was a fabricated image, sardonically intended.

Two days later Ruth and I were off to New York, to see my parents who did disapprove of my plans, and I noted that my mother seemed ill at ease with Ruth, too. The next day we left for D.C. where her parents lived. Their home was a large neo-colonial mansion, a genuine antebellum imitation. Her mother seemed to avoid me, but her father, a successful builder and land developer, was friendly and offered to "read" my palm—a hobby of his. He told me that I was about to find my "true career." I thought that was unlikely. If anything, I believed I had just destroyed my true career.

The preparations for the trip went smoothly and surprisingly quickly. Within a week I had a passport and Ruth had purchased our tickets and some traveling clothes and accessories for me. She also gave me a black leather travel bag that had belonged to her ex-husband and in early May 1969, we took off for London.

Irrational as it seemed, the moment I stepped out of the plane at Heathrow and breathed England's faintly coal-tainted air, I had the overwhelming sensation that I had come home. I had never been interested in British history or culture, but this place seemed familiar. Apart from the slight disorientation of jet lag, I felt excited and strange— a kind of euphoria and sense of being a bit "spacey" as if on a mild psychedelic drug.

Straight away, Ruth took charge, since she knew London from previous trips and I had no idea why I had asked her to take me there. After we spent a few nights in a bed and breakfast near Russell Square, she decided that we should take a "bed-sitter" apartment, since I was insisting, for no reason I could explain, that we stay at least a month in London. We looked in the newspaper and found a room in a teacher's house in Clapham South, but after just a week, we began to quarrel. She was anxious to get to Ibiza, while I insisted that we stay on.

After a few days of bickering, she decided to fly to Ibiza for a couple of weeks while I got my "fill of London." I agreed and saw her off a couple of days later. She flew to Spain and out of my life. As abruptly as she had appeared, facilitating my leap across the Atlantic, she departed. I felt grateful for the ride but quite confused by the whirlwind speed with which I had been picked up in the US Southwest and dropped in London.

So there I was, in England, destination of my choice, a place for which I felt an inexplicable nostalgia, with only a couple hundred dollars in my pocket, a return ticket to Washington, a small black leather suitcase, and a great deal of time on my hands. As I turned my psychoanalytic searchlight inward to explore the possible symbolic meaning of such impulsive behavior, a cold dread spread through me. I did not know why I was there or what I was going to do. Feelings of regret and loneliness began to engulf my optimism of previous days. Perhaps my leap across the Atlantic had been some kind of crazy "acting out," I pondered.

I tried being a tourist for a few days, visiting some of the standard historical landmarks, but I soon became bored and even more anxious.

The sense of having "returned" did not go away, but it had no focus and I quickly ran out of things to do. For several days I roamed the streets of Central London just listening to voices, watching people, and breathing that coal-tainted but strangely familiar smelling air.

4. An Unusual Encounter

One morning not long after Ruth had departed, as I sat in my small, rented room south of the Thames River, a thought popped into my mind as I struggled to decide what I should do. I had read that England had an active scientific community interested in parapsychology, the formal study of non-ordinary experiences. My interest in the subject had developed during my San Francisco years when I came across the statistical research done by J. B. Rhine into card guessing and had always wondered whether the phenomena associated with those experiments were real.

Still feeling anxious about my situation and desperate for something useful to do, I grabbed a telephone directory from the shelf below the phone in the living room and searched for organizations having anything to do with parapsychology or psychic research. I located two entries: the College of Psychic Science and the British Society for Psychical Research. I decided I should visit one to see firsthand what it was about, so mentally I flipped a coin, and it came up in favor of the College, in South Kensington.

Just before noon, I walked to the Clapham South underground station and caught the Northern Line into Central London to connect to a train to South Kensington. I arrived at the College about an hour later to find it closed, though a sign posted on the door announced a demonstration of clairvoyance would be held at 7:30 pm that evening. My curiosity was piqued despite my skepticism as to whether such phenomena actually existed.

My attitude toward this topic was due to the poor thinking and credulous approach endemic in most of what I had heard and read on the subject, and I wondered how paranormal phenomena could exist in that they seemed to violate the laws of physics. Nevertheless, the chance of witnessing a specific demonstration was too good to miss, so, after telling myself my interest in the topic was "purely intellectual," I decided to attend. In retrospect it seems strange to me that I had not yet related my own experiences, such as those surrounding my uncle's death, to the topic of psychic phenomena.

For the next few hours I visited the Natural History Museum, followed by a leisurely dinner at an Italian cafe. Then I returned to the College where a receptionist told me the demonstration would be held in a small lecture hall at the rear of the building. This turned out to be a fairly narrow, florescent-lit classroom with a lectern in front and about 25 to 30 folding chairs neatly laid out. As a precaution I sat with my back against the wall next to the exit at the rear of the room. If the whole business proved silly or stupid, I could leave with minimum fuss, I reasoned. Pretty soon, about a dozen people trickled in and chose seats around the room. No one spoke. Shortly after 7:30 pm, a middle-aged, conservatively dressed woman entered, announcing that she was the clairvoyant and the demonstration would begin. I was unimpressed. Although I did not have an expectation of what a clairvoyant should look like, I was disappointed by her apparent ordinariness.

She started out by giving the group some instructions, telling them that she would pick people as instructed by "those on the other side" and relay any messages given to her from the "spirit realm." If we were chosen, we were to respond in one of three ways: "yes," meaning we understood and the statement was correct, "no," indicating the message was incorrect or not applicable or "I don't understand," in which case she would attempt to clarify what she was trying to convey. She asked if we understood with only a flicker of response from the group as a few nodded their heads in assent.

Her first choice was a young couple sitting toward the front. As she quietly gazed into the distance she made a series of statements to them, beginning with, "You know an elderly woman who has recently passed over." The young woman said "yes," and the clairvoyant continued in a similar vein for about five minutes, eliciting mostly positive responses with a smattering of negative ones. The episode reminded me of listening to one side of a phone conversation. It was not very interesting, and the quasi-religious tone of the clairvoyant's statements made me uncomfortable, so I decided it was time to leave.

As I perched on the edge of my seat, waiting for an appropriate moment to exit, suddenly she looked across the room at me and said, "You, in the back, don't leave. There's an elderly man standing behind you wearing a Tyrolean hat. He was in his mid to late 60s when he passed over." Behind me? My back was against the wall, and I did not know such a person or even what a Tyrolean hat (worn by men in the European alpine region of The Tyrol) looked like. She continued: "He has an important message for you: 'It's the other place you want, not this one.' Do you understand?" She repeated, "It's the other one, not this one." "Yes," I found myself replying.

Her voice, gesture, and attention, which was focused squarely in my direction, shot the message, arrow-like, across the room with some force, which I would later understand as *intentionality*. The message appeared to penetrate right through the miasma of the room, the people and the florescent lights, into some deeper recess of my being like a trumpet sounding a wake-up call. "Hey you," it seemed to say, "don't ignore this." Instantly I knew what the "other place" meant from my search for parapsychological organizations in the phone book that morning. It was the British Society for Psychical Research. Surprised and dazed, I slid out the door shortly afterward, leaving the demonstration to other recipients of calls from the "other side."

After catching the underground back to my rented room south of the river I felt strangely disoriented yet elated. I had received my "message" and knew what to do next. If my adventure that evening had been a made-for-TV movie, music from the *Twilight Zone* would have been playing as the scene closed.

***

Next morning, on one of those rare blue-sky days in London, again I caught the underground northward, arriving about an hour later at the Society, located at Number One Adam and Eve Mews just off Kensington High Street. London mews are narrow lanes that in earlier times gave access to horse stables but in recent times most had been converted into dwellings and places of business. After I pressed the button on the intercom a woman's voice answered and asked: "May I help you?"

I replied: "I am from the USA and I'd like to learn about the Society and its work."

The latch buzzer sounded and I entered. The dim lighting and creaky floor boards of the entryway seemed in stark contrast to the brightness of the day and my upbeat mood. A woman in her early thirties stepped into the hall and greeted me. She said she was the librarian for the Society and would be pleased to help me. In fact, she seemed more welcoming than any other librarian I had known in my various sojourns through the halls of academe and, compared to the reserve of most of the English I had met up until then, she seemed positively warm, although in a low-key way. For a moment I wondered if she was coming on to me but then, as I noted her conservative appearance—her dark suit with its regulation white blouse, her hair neatly pinned up in a bun—I decided probably not. It was yet another incongruity in weeks of unusual events.

She ushered me into a room that was lined with glass-fronted bookcases from floor to ceiling. An old, dark-stained wooden conference table dominated the middle and a small librarian's desk faced the outside wall in a corner next to the only window. Straight away I began to peer into the bookcases, trying to ascertain what the Society was about from the volumes it kept. At this point she told me her name was Alice and she offered to answer any questions I might have regarding the Society and its work. I responded that I did not have any questions at that point and I continued my tour of inspection.

After about 15 minutes she interrupted my search through the bookshelves. "I have some notes dictated by a trance medium that I think would interest you," she said. I turned and looked at her quizzically.

"A what?" I asked.

"They were dictated to me by a trance medium 10 years ago," she repeated.

At this point I had no idea what a trance medium was, but to my scientific mind it sounded pretty hokey, even ridiculous, and definitely not anything worth thinking about. The image being conjured up in my imagination was a woman with a scarf around her head, a crystal ball and 13 or so smelly cats. "No thanks," I answered, "I'm not really interested." I continued my search among the books, still not sure why I had followed the clairvoyant's instruction to go to this "other place."

A short time later I was reading a fascinating section in a book called *Perception, Physics, and Reality,*[1] by the late Oxford philosopher C. D. Broad, when her musical-toned voice again broke the silence. "I am sure that you'd be interested in these notes," she insisted.

After growing up in New York and spending a number of years in San Francisco's Haight-Ashbury district, I was used to people who thought they had the answers to life's "great mysteries" and who were on the lookout for sympathetic ears to receive their wisdom. My ears had been sympathetic too often, and I now felt only annoyance when someone seemed to want to facilitate my salvation so, with growing irritation, I said "No thanks," and returned to my reading.

After only a few more minutes she brought up the topic once again. Out of growing irritation with her repeated request, I announced that I was leaving, which seemed to worry her. Reacting to her disappointment and before really considering my response, I said I would come back the following day, at which point she appeared to be relieved.

As I left the building and stepped back out into the mews and then onto the brightly lit high street, I noticed I was feeling a bit disoriented, as if I had not accomplished what I had set out to do, even though I was unsure what that task actually was. I had been given the message to go to the "other place," so I did. However, nothing much had happened, except for meeting an overly friendly librarian with some unknown truth to sell. Despite my annoyance with her, however, I could not help feeling that I had missed something and I was surprised to discover that I was looking forward to my next visit. I wondered why I had offered to come back, when the whole event had seemed rather pointless, but I was unable to come up with an answer, just a feeling that I should return.

That evening I ran into a young school teacher who lived in one of the other rooms in the house where I was staying. She must have spotted the "helper" in me, because within a matter of minutes she was

---

[1]C. D. Broad, *Perception, Physics, and Reality* (Cambridge: Cambridge University Press, 1914).

weeping and telling me all her troubles, including her fear and hatred of Indians and Pakistanis. To her the smell of curry signaled the presence of evil. That was my first taste of the ugliness of British racism. After excusing myself and returning to my room, I spent the remainder of the night in recrimination about dumping my graduate studies and coming to such a strange place for no apparent reason. I felt very much alone, with no one to turn to and no way out but to go back to the US and work out what to do with my life. The night did not offer much in the way of rest.

When I returned to the Society's headquarters the next afternoon, Alice seemed both pleased and relieved to see me, though she maintained her usual reserved demeanor. It did not take her long, however, to once again raise the issue of her notes. Again I refused, this time firmly stating that I was not interested in trance mediums, whatever they were. I simply wanted to get on with my research, I said.

It was then I noticed several neat stacks of books on the central table. These were organized into categories that all turned out to be of interest to me. In my excitement, I did not stop to consider why the librarian had gone to so much trouble. Instead, I started exploring and reading, pleased about the wealth of philosophical material in front of me. By this stage, I think I simply wanted to immerse myself in work to provide a break from the questions that were nagging at me: why I had come to England, why I was staying in a house with a disordered racist and most of all, why I was visiting an institution for psychical research, trying to fend off offers of notes dictated by a "trance medium" 10 years earlier. What kind of activity was this for a serious scientist, I asked myself?

After about half an hour of reading I heard the librarian's melodic voice yet again break the silence: "I am sure you'd find these notes interesting," she insisted.

With exasperation I turned toward her desk where she was picking through a box of index cards and said: "For the last time, no, I am *not* interested."

She stared at me, and for the first time I really noticed what she was like. There was a vague sense of familiarity that I could not identify. Her pale round face and broad, open forehead were topped with dark brown hair pulled back into its customary bun. Her eyes, also dark brown, stared at me with an impassive patience I had never before experienced from friend or teacher. I sensed that she was not angry with me, she was just patiently waiting.

I put down the book I was holding, and as I did, she began to speak to me in an offhand way. It was English "small talk" at its directed best, the purpose of which is to create intimacy with another person without verbally acknowledging it—a cultural style that leaves neither party open to interpersonal compromise. After a while I noticed that she was very good willed and for some reason I felt a sense of connection to her that I could not explain. Her presence seemed to generate a feeling of well being in me.

Dropping the issue of the notes entirely, she started to tell me that she lived in a part of London called Hampstead, and after further chat about its history and some of the interesting people living there at the time (including Yehudi Menuhin and Peter O'Toole), she invited me to visit her on Saturday afternoon for tea.

"How English," I thought. "I am being invited to tea. "

She described Hampstead a bit more, saying that the open common, known as the Heath is a wonderful place to walk on a nice afternoon. She added that if I wished to come, she would meet me at the underground station and we could go straight up there, weather permitting.

The invitation was offered in a calm, matter-of-fact way, but underneath there was a distinct pressure for me to respond positively—a "push," if you like, but without it appearing needy or demanding. I thought about this for a moment and then—unusually for me at the time—I agreed to meet her on Saturday. Again, I did not know why, but for some reason I just felt I should not refuse.

5. An Invitation to Become a *Seer*

Early the following Saturday afternoon, Alice and I met outside the Hampstead underground station as pre-arranged. The sun was making another of its guest appearances in London, and there, at an altitude of 300 feet, the air was fresher and cleaner than in the central part of the city, which is below sea level.

From the tube station on Hampstead High Street we turned left onto Flask Walk and made our way toward the Heath. Alice started to talk about growing up in London's East End during World War II and her life at home, first with her grandfather and mother while her father was at war, then with both her parents in the post-war years. After surviving the terrible bombings of her neighborhood during the war she had to endure her parents' turbulent marriage and its unhappy consequences. To me it sounded like a typical dysfunctional family scenario, yet I was surprised, given her reserved nature, that she was willing to divulge so much.

Briefly I wondered if, like the racist school teacher, she had unconsciously spotted me as a "helper" and was about to unload her entire life story. However, when I responded to her account of her troubled family in my usual helper manner, she ignored my efforts and abruptly changed the subject to the Heath and its history. Such a comeback was disconcerting, and I was not sure how to react for she did much more than simply change of subject or ignore what I was saying. Some kind of palpable force, that I was unable to resist, stopped me from continuing in my helper mode, as though the power of her presence somehow pushed me to redeploy my attention away from her. So I gave up and decided to just be an observer rather than a participant. At worst, it would be an afternoon wasted, I thought.

In the midst of her story about the war and the bombing of East London, Alice also mentioned that in 1943 she had a dream that made a big impression on her. She found herself "transported" to a distant location where she saw people being herded into large concrete rooms that had shower spigots along the walls. She could see the doors being closed and bolted behind them, followed by mass panic as the people began choking and trying to escape. Many beat on the door and clawed the walls, but in a matter of minutes they were all still, lying dead on the floor. She recalled that, as they were overcome and dying, the panic she experienced coming from them reminded her of thousands of trapped and terrified birds. The feelings that emerged from them were like palpable entities that rose up and ascended through the ceiling into the air above the building, from where she was witnessing the scene. After the chaos and fear dissipated upward, an awesome silence and peace descended. At that point she woke up, she said.

As a six-year-old she did not realize what she had witnessed, but after the war, in 1945 and 1946, when she saw pictures in newspapers of the Nazi concentration camps in Germany and Poland, she recognized the rooms she had seen in her dream as gas chambers where hundreds of thousands of people had been put to death.

I found myself intensely interested in what she was saying and began questioning her about her experiences. She said she only occasionally remembered her dreams, but when she did, they always turned out to be remote perceptions of real life events elsewhere in time and space. Later I learned that when she was very young her grandfather introduced her to certain aspects of *seeing* and, therefore, she regarded non-ordinary events, including recognizing the content of a dream several years after it occurred, as normal.

In telling me all this, she was quite matter of fact, making no attempt to aggrandize herself or exaggerate the importance of her experiences. This was in marked contrast to the hyperbole and self-proclaiming I had witnessed in California by those who claimed to be psychics. My initial perception of her as possibly a fanatic with something to sell was beginning to crumble as I became aware that I was in the presence of a person of extraordinary depth and strength of character who understood much more than she talked about.

We left the duck pond, where we had been standing, exited the Heath at the top of Well Walk, and made our way back to her flat. It was time for tea.

Shortly after our arrival, as we sat down to drink tea, she again raised the issue of the notes. I felt a bit trapped, in that I had accepted her hospitality and the situation was more personal than it had been at the library, so I acquiesced. "Okay," I said. "Let me see these notes."

She handed me seven pages of standard letter paper covered with her calligraphic-style writing. As I took them, she told me that her medium friend, Stanley, had dictated all but one of the pages 10 years earlier. The last page had been recorded around the same time from an elderly woman, another medium who died not long afterward. On the first page, dated May, 1959, I read:

> You will meet Peter through your job in the second or third week in May. He is an American about 26–27 years old, has a high forehead, curly hair which tends to stand up on his head.

> When you meet him he will be in a great deal of turmoil about his career, which he has just thrown over. He is, at this time, trying to find a direction....

> He had a very unhappy childhood and, as a result, he feels that the best method of defense is a good attack....

> He will introduce you to his friends Frank and Ian as well as Andrew, a long time friend of his and a very determined man...

> You and Peter have met in dreams twice before.

> You are his teacher on the emotional level and he is yours on the mental level....

And so the notes went on. The last page, dictated by the old woman, referred to me in the first sentence as Peter Elson. It was as if she had simply misheard my name, as the aged tend to do as they become hard of hearing, by missing consonants.

I was stunned and confused and it did not take long for these feelings to turn into fear. My mind raced, seeking a rational logic that would contain this moment and nullify my growing sense that I was somehow a pawn being led to a series of appointments that I had not consciously made. I imagined a collection of CIA-type files on me, and a series of bizarre plots swept through my mind, each crashing, in turn, as its absurdity became obvious. I imagined I was being "set up" but then why would someone want to do that, I wondered? I had no money or property, nothing, in fact, that anyone would want.

My response to all this was not well thought out. In my confusion I accused Alice of making it up, I accused her of lying. But how could she know about Frank and Ian, I wondered? I had only met them recently in London and not mentioned them to her, nor did I mention my close friend Andrew nor anything about my current situation for that matter.

Then, as I reread the first couple of pages, including the section about having met her twice before in dreams, an intense memory bubbled to the surface. I recalled that, one night, when I was 15, at a time when I was experiencing a great deal of unhappiness at home and school, I had a vivid dream in which I experienced myself getting out of bed and leaving the house. I exited as usual through the front door and proceeded down our street to the local country club about half a block away, which was the social hub of our middle-class community. The action in the dream and the quality of events seemed just like ordinary waking life, and I had the same sense of volition associated with being awake. (Many years later, I recognized these characteristics as the markers of a lucid dream.) The only difference was that the events were taking place in daylight while I knew, even as I dreamed them, that it was currently night.

As I walked up the grassy knoll behind the club's back fence, I saw a young woman sitting on the ground, her knees drawn up to her chest with her arms wrapped around them. She had long, dark, fine hair that wafted in the soft breeze. I walked over and sat down at her left side with our backs to the fence. We talked for a while, and as we did, a deep relaxation and reassurance came over me, accompanied by a sense of relief and well being. After a while, in my dream I knew it was time to leave, so I stood up and walked back to my house.

The next morning when I awoke, I remembered few of the specifics of the conversation I had with the woman. All I could recall was her face and hair and the soothing feeling I had in her presence that eased my sense of loneliness. Over the following days the dream came back to me many times but I was puzzled about seeing, in such detail and clarity, a person I had never met and whose picture I had never seen.

Emerging from my reverie, I looked up at Alice in her Hampstead flat. While I had been leafing through the notes, she had taken her hair down from its usual bun, and immediately I recognized the same long, dark hair and the same face of the woman in my dream 11 years earlier. Now I understood why she had looked familiar to me when we met. This dawning realization threw me into deeper confusion.

"What's going on here?" I demanded. I wanted to know how I had come to be in England.

She said simply: "Your overself guided you here."

I did not know what that meant; it sounded more like religion than science, so I immediately rejected it as meaningless.

She added that Stanley had told her not to expect me for 10 years, and that we would meet at an organization involved in psychic work. Although she had worked as a research librarian at a British government department for many years, she had left that job to have a break for a few months before my arrival. Then, a few weeks before the deadline for me to turn up, she had seen a job advertised for a librarian at the British Society for Psychical Research and *saw* that it was the place we were going to meet, so she took the job, she said. The Society was quite pleased to have a librarian of her caliber for their modest organization.

Her tone and attitude remained matter-of-fact and calm. I scanned through the rest of the notes, which contained many details about me and my life, as well as a suggestion to her not to show me the notes too soon after our meeting. Stanley warned her that I was prone to paranoia and would become hostile and distrustful if presented with the information too early.

That was exactly how I felt—paranoid. I still could not dispense with the idea that there was some plot behind it all. My response, as predicted in the notes, was hostility.

It was then she looked at me and said: "You're here because you're a psychic and need to be trained," as if that explained everything. It did not. Nor did I know what it meant. The term psychic was, for me, as bad as "trance medium" back then. No matter how much I had experienced with the psychedelic movement in San Francisco, I still regarded those kinds of phenomena as dwelling on the far edge of reality and perhaps beyond it.

With my "leap" to England and this meeting, I was beginning to realize that I had entered into another dimension of perception and action. It was starting to look as though my life was being run by forces outside my control, that I was merely pacing back and forth, figuratively speaking, while waiting for various appointed "buses" to arrive and take me to the next stop. The magnitude of the existential shift required to comprehend my life this way was too great. I bolted from my seat and shouted, "What are you up to? What are you trying to do to me?"

In spite of my outburst, she remained impassive and started to make small talk again, which at first was infuriating, though it had the paradoxical effect of defusing and calming me. Then in the middle of it, she invited me to leave my bed-sitter in Clapham South and stay at her flat for the rest of my time in London.

Although I was bewildered by what I had encountered up to that point, I felt impelled to stay and I was drawn to be near Alice's emotionally steadying presence. The notes also had remarked that I would have a strong feeling that I had "come home" when I arrived in England. This was true and especially when I was around her. There seemed to be an inexorable pull to enter the door being opened for me and stay the course, in spite of my impulse to bolt and run.

I returned the following day with my meager belongings. I told Alice that I needed time to think, so I decided to rent a motor scooter and drive through the West Country the following week while she was at work. Because of my dream and the travelogue I had seen in New Mexico, Devon was my first destination. The trip was pleasant but nothing out of the ordinary. The countryside was just as I had *seen* it in my dream and it still seemed familiar, yet my connection apparently was to London and this unusual woman.

My first questions on returning to her flat in Hampstead were: "What does all this mean? What's the purpose of my being here?" She looked directly at me but said nothing. As I look back at that moment, I remember that I felt I was gazing into a deep, still pool. Everything about her implied a hidden knowledge that would be revealed if one could only penetrate its depths. But I didn't even know the right questions to ask.

Throughout the days and weeks I stayed with her, no matter how often I asked, she still said nothing directly about my arrival and what it signified. On the occasions when she did respond to my questions, she would relate an anecdote from her life—she would tell me a story. For example, in response to my inquiries about becoming a *seer* she talked about Stanley and his difficulties when he first realized he was a psychic. He had not understood what was happening to him. She had taught him how to manage his ability to perceive across time and space and how to deal with the people who pestered him night and day for help.

Early on, I found her stories quite annoying. I felt I was being handed non sequiturs instead of direct answers. Eventually, however, I understood the stories to be illustrative of the difficulties I would have to face as a *seer*, with each one offering a solution. For example, she related how Stanley finally learned a method of regulating the people who came into his life so he would not be emotionally inundated and psychically drained. Years later, I found myself implementing a similar strategy when I discovered that the demands on my time had gotten out of control.

Several years on, as I came to understand the events of May through August of 1969, I realized that I had entered into them as an unknowing member of a conspiracy of ignorance, one that insists that such experiences do not happen and that people who claim to have them are self-delusional frauds or lunatics. Nevertheless, there I was, enmeshed in the very kinds of events that science insists are impossible, even as they were undeniably impinging upon my life. I had *seen* a place before arriving there in physical time and space, and I had kept an appointment I had never consciously made—a meeting that had been predicted in detail 10 years earlier. I was overwhelmed by the immensity of it all. How could real life work this way, I wondered?

6. FURTHER CONFIRMATION

After about a week at Alice's flat, I felt a desire to revisit the College of Psychic Science—the starting place for all these weird events that had transpired so far. It was part of an effort on my part to make sense of where I was, how I got there, and whether what had happened to me was real or some kind of hoax or self-delusion. Alice as usual remained unperturbed in the face of my relentless questioning, so with her encouragement, one evening I returned to the College on my own.

When I arrived, I learned that a well-known English psychic, Trixie Allingham, would be conducting the demonstration of clairvoyance that night. Trixie was a big draw, and many people attended. Her presentation began in a similar way to the first demonstration I had seen there. After engaging in a supposed dialogue with the dead on behalf of someone in the audience, Trixie turned her attention on me: "You have a friend who committed suicide a couple years ago—he shot himself," she began. "He was only 21 or 22 years old at the time. Another person connected to this young man's suicide is named Jackson." The statement hit me like a rock. Indeed, I had a friend, Tom, who committed suicide in 1967 aged just 21. Trixie must have noticed my reaction, as she seemed to try to ameliorate its impact by saying that he now regretted his actions, and then she added the usual banality about him being at peace.

My friend Tom's face had arisen in my mind's eye with a wave of terrible poignancy. He and I had met in the summer of 1966, when he worked for the Marine Biology Laboratory at Woods Hole, Cape Cod while I was employed at the computer center of the Oceanographic Institute. We had become good friends, and he later visited me in San Francisco during one of his vacation times while he was studying at Amherst College. I vividly remembered the phone call about 18 months later that brought the news that he had shot himself in front of his family. The married name of the young woman with whom he had been in love at the time was Jackson, although in all likelihood she was not the reason for his suicide.

My next awareness as I came out of my reverie was Trixie's voice: "You are a psychic and should be trained—see me after the demonstration." I did not fully emerge from my immersion in past memories until the audience was starting to leave at the end of the demonstration and before Trixie could exit, I pushed aside my embarrassment and approached her. I was not sure I wanted to be trained as a psychic but to hear two people in different circumstances say the same thing made it difficult to ignore.

Trixie was a short, cheery, outgoing person who greeted me warmly. She explained that she ran a "development circle" and invited me to attend, free of charge, the following evening—with no obligation. I took the information as to where it would be held and left. After thinking things through, I found myself feeling more curious than repelled so I decided to go and at least observe what a "training" of this kind entailed. Alice also encouraged me to explore the development circle.

The following evening I duly arrived at the appointed hour and was warmly welcomed into a meeting room that I found oppressive, with its thick atmosphere accentuated by Oriental rugs, dark wallpaper, heavy curtains and furniture. I felt out of place and uneasy. Others were arriving at the same time, and eventually a group of seven plus Trixie assembled in a circle. There was almost no social interaction between us as we sat waiting for the "training" to start.

Trixie introduced me to the others and asked me to sit next to her on her left in the circle of chairs. She announced that our focus that evening would be psychometry, or reading the "impressions" people and events left on objects. She asked us each to choose a small, personal article and place it in a box she provided without letting anyone else see our contribution. Then she handed an object from the box to each member of the group, ensuring that everyone received one that was not theirs. She further instructed us to close our eyes and relax while holding the article up to our face or cupped in our hands on our lap. We were told not to try too hard but just to note whatever thoughts and images appeared.

Suddenly, the whole idea of this activity struck me as absurd and I considered getting up and walking out. I felt foolish, yet the achiever in me did not want to look like a loser—I was there and somehow I had to meet the challenge so, for the moment, staying put seemed like the less embarrassing option.

Then I realized I would have to do something with the set of keys I had been given. At first I tried to guess who owned them. With a quick glance around the group, I decided, based on what I thought was a good deduction, that they belonged to a man two seats down from my left, so I stared at him for a moment while I tried to figure out what he did and what he was like, though nothing came to mind. I was left with a set of keys and nowhere to go, so to speak.

Still uncomfortable about where I was and with nothing else to do, I decided to close my eyes and try to follow the instructions. But, with my eyes shut, all I saw at first was empty blackness. The thought occurred to me that I might as well accept that I was going to look incompetent but just as I resigned myself to the inevitable embarrassment, a clear "scene" in color suddenly filled my mind's eye. The vision, as I experienced it, engendered a feeling that I was both participating in it and witnessing it at the same time.

In the scene I was seated at a large wooden table staring down at its surface, which was coated with aging, yellow lacquer through which the wood grain was visible. It reminded me of the big tables I had sat at in libraries many times over the years. Spread out over its surface were sheets of old paper covered with symbols that I recognized as Egyptian hieroglyphs. From the point of view I occupied in my inner picture I had the sensation that I was sitting at the table studying these documents.

"How ridiculous," I thought, returning to my usual critical, analytic point of view. "Now I am filling in this nonsensical activity with mystical symbols from ancient Egypt." I sat there conjecturing about the power of suggestion and associative memory and how the picture that had formed in my mind was likely the result of the quasi religio-mystical atmosphere associated with the College.

I opened my eyes to see what the other members of the "circle" were doing. All of them were quietly busy at the assigned task. As my objective, critical mind observed the situation, I felt even more like an interloper. The thought of leaving reoccurred, but I quickly decided against it because of the stir it would cause. Once again I closed my eyes and attempted to relax into the darkness of my inner visual field, hoping the whole thing would be over soon.

Abruptly, a new and vividly clear image appeared on my inner screen. This time I found myself looking at a scene from a point of view as if I was standing in a doorway, staring into the living room of what appeared to be a London flat—a place typical of the privately owned apartments found in middle-class areas such as Maida Vale. As I looked around, I could see that the room contained no furniture or curtains, but what most caught my attention was the bare floor. There was no carpet covering the wooden planks, although the presence of tack strips along the baseboards showed it had once been carpeted. The feelings I had as I surveyed the room were surprise and displeasure. If the picture had not been so vivid and clear, accompanied by the sensation that I was actually standing in the scene, it would have seemed not very noteworthy.

At this point Trixie told us to open our eyes and then she asked for a volunteer to report on their psychometry, with each person to follow in turn around the circle. When it came to me, even though the first scene seemed to have been a product of suggestion and the second did not seem particularly noteworthy, I decided not to hold back but to just describe what I had seen. I had nothing else to offer, and besides, I did not want to seem like a hopeless case. When I held up the set of keys, I learned that they belonged not to the man I had thought, but to another in the circle. Already things were not looking good, I decided, but I forged ahead nevertheless.

Surprisingly, as soon as I described the scenes I had witnessed, the owner of the keys became very excited. He told the group that he was an Egyptologist and had just returned from a study tour at the Cairo Museum, where he had been translating hieroglyphs written on ancient papyrus sheets spread out on a table much as I had described. However, he was even more agitated by the second scene I reported, because on his return to London, he discovered that his wife had left him and taken all the furniture and curtains from their flat. What irked him most of all, he said, was that she had ripped up all the carpets from the floor and taken those as well.

I was dumbfounded. I had never met or talked to this man before saying "hello" to him and hearing him speak his name when he entered the room. There had been no time for chit chat—no communication, direct or indirect, about who he was or what had happened in his life recently.

Trixie was positively ebullient about my performance and invited me to become a regular member of her group. In addition, the young woman who had psychometrized my object had seen a rainbow in her vision. Trixie excitedly told the group that one of her late husband's pet names for her had been "Rainbow," and, therefore, this was a sign that I was linked to her and should train with her.

I left that evening feeling curious about what had happened but I did not return to Trixie's group. The fact is, I have never been a joiner of organizations. Also, having been through psychoanalysis during the 1960s with an analyst from the William Alanson White Institute in New York City, I had a suspicion that she might have been projecting her relationship with her late husband onto me. In retrospect, I doubt that such a process was at work. In her book, published a year after I met her, it is clear that Trixie tended to see symbols such as the rainbow as signs of what she should pay attention to in her work as a medium and psychic trainer.[1]

The episode at Trixie's development circle marked a turning point, calling my attention to the craziness of continuing to deny what was happening to me—one event after another signaling me to stop rejecting the data being offered. It was like a final bit of evidence I could not ignore and the first crack in the wall of denial I had been living behind for years. It was clear that I would have to come to grips with what was in front of me. This event definitely caught my attention.

After that episode, tentatively, I started to explore living with the notion that a *seer* might be a part of who I was. This meant that I had to stop trying to explain away events and start paying attention to an

---

[1]T. Allingham, *The Reluctant Medium* (London: Regency Press, 1970).

information stream that I had spent most of my life trying to ignore—
what I would later call my *second stream of attention*. Not only that; I
had to act as if that stream was pointing to a reality that I had been
strenuously attempting to deny.

Nevertheless, I continued to struggle, either still trying to explain
events away or attempting to make sense of them with a kind of
scientific analysis, for example, by mapping some of the quirky ideas of
the micro-world of quantum mechanics, such as non-locality and time-
reversed negentropy, onto explanations of the strange phenomena I was
witnessing. Needless to say, this did not offer anything useful. I was
stuck, yet liberated at the same time.

Eventually, all my explanations shriveled into insignificance in the
face of my lived experience. The evidence for my capacity for *seeing*
grew faster than my success at knocking it down. My life had not in any
way prepared me for the happenings of those weeks in the late spring of
1969 as a new and amazing world opened before me. It was only after
about three years of attempting to rationalize it away that I started to
accept that the explanatory framework of science, being a reductive,
ontologically materialist system, could not deal with the nature of time
and causality suggested by the reality I was encountering.

***

I spent the summer of 1969 with Alice, filling my days by exploring
Hampstead and its surrounds while she was at work. Naturally, I
continued to question her as to what this whole thing was about and
why it was happening to me. However, Alice did not engage in
theoretical and abstract discussions like I did, nor did she respond to the
science-based arguments I offered in my attempts to reductively
rationalize what was occurring. She always listened patiently, then
either said nothing or told me a story. This was often frustrating, and my
confusion and anxiety went on unabated—yet I also felt strongly that I
should not just walk away from this strange encounter.

All of her mentoring was done utilizing the events of daily life and
what we encounter there. Typically, she would call my attention to
happenings and people around me while making me aware of the
content of my *second stream* as it related to what I experienced. In this
way, I was constantly reminded that the information that flowed

through my awareness always came from two streams—ordinary sensory data and non-ordinary perceptions.

When Alice called my attention to the perceptions of my *second stream*, which had always been in the background, she helped me to bring them front and center, making it impossible for me to just dismiss them as meaningless or see them as the product of illness or brain malfunction. Eventually, I learned to value both streams of attention and use them in combination to experience the world around me in a new and fuller way—through the dual awareness of a *seer*.

7. THE REST OF THE STORY

Over the following years, Alice and I traveled together to Denmark, the USA, and Australia, living for periods together in the latter two countries. By 1971 we had married. Although we shared a deep connection, our very different lifestyles and desires were soon at odds, and remaining a couple with a shared focus and goals became unworkable. We parted as a couple in mid-1976 but remained friends. When we communicate on occasion, it is not about *seeing* however, but about events in the world and what is happening in contexts larger than ourselves, though always from a *seer's* perspective, which is both broad and ironical.

Up until this point, I have mainly talked about my personal story and what led me to discover the world of the *seer*, but now it is time to leave that story in order to explore more deeply the nature of *seeing*—how it comes about, what it can tell us and finally, what its significance is for us today. What follows is what I have gleaned from over 40 years of research and teaching on the phenomenology and the technology of *seeing*. So, in the next chapters, the narrative changes from a story of two people coming together in a highly unusual way to an exposition of the making of a *seer*.

In the process of delineating my world, I share many of my non-ordinary experiences as examples of what is possible. No attempt is made to fit these events into an orderly timeline because their sequence in my personal story is, for the most part, unimportant. All the magic is to be found in understanding the workings of attention and the worlds of knowing available to anyone willing to deploy his or her awareness in the unique ways used by *seers*.

So, on to the heart of the matter.

III. Living as a *Seer*

Where roads are made I lose my way.
In the wide water, in the blue sky there is no line of a track.
The pathway is hidden by the birds' wings, by the star-fires,
by the flowers of the wayfaring seasons.
And I ask my heart if its blood carries the wisdom of the unseen
way.

– Rabindranath Tagore
Fruit-Gathering

8. WHAT ARE *SEERS*?

Despite the traumatic nature of my early encounter with non-ordinary perception as an eight-year-old, I now consider *seeing* to be the most exciting and magnificent development of human awareness possible. In using the term *seeing*, I am not talking about some sort of physical, visual perception or imaging, but a unique way of perceiving that gives rise to a direct, experientially based knowledge of the world, not mediated through language and requiring almost no interpretation. This *second stream of knowing*—which sometimes I also call the *transpersonal stream*—is infused with an immediate, veridical presence that conveys information derived not through the physical senses but through what I call *second attention*. Non-ordinary data is, in a sense, "given," in the same way that normal sensory data appears to be presented to our awareness, and the two are integrated into a totality of ongoing, direct knowing.

Such a totality results when we experience a balanced combination of being cognitively, emotionally, and transpersonally aware. In other words, *seeing* occurs when cognitive, emotional, and transpersonal intelligence are functionally integrated and operational.[1] Thus, *seeing* refers to a broad range of awarenesses that integrate ordinary and non-ordinary perception. Although ordinary awareness is physically sensory,

---

[1]Cognitive intelligence refers to the collection of verbal, logical, and performance skills generally measured by standard IQ tests. H. Gardner, *Frames of Mind: The Theory of Multiple Intelligences,* 2nd ed. (New York: Basic Books, 1993).

Emotional intelligence, on the other hand, is what Daniel Goleman has described as the combination of emotional awareness and balanced emotional responding necessary for a productive and satisfying life. D. Goleman, *Emotional Intelligence* (New York: Bantam Books, 1995).

Transpersonal intelligence is our capacity for accurately perceiving and experiencing beyond what is presented to our senses and includes our capacity for spiritual awareness and knowing as well. T. Hart, P. L. Nelson, and K. Puhakka, eds., *Transpersonal Knowing: Exploring the Horizon of Consciousness* (Albany, NY: State University of New York Press, 2000).

non-ordinary perception can be experienced as analogues of sight, sound, touch, and affect, but unlike the ordinary, they transcend the usual boundaries of person as well as the constraints of physical space and time. In my world, it is about looking into the *field* (see Chapter 15) that connects us to each other and across space and time.

A *seer*, then, is someone who lives in the perceptual stream given by ordinary attention while simultaneously engaging the stream of non-ordinary information using his *second attention*. To do this, *seers* deploy their total attention in a fluid manner that allows them to have a continuous, direct experience of a multi-level, multi-perspective reality.

In addition, *seers* are masters of *intentionality*—a special way of deploying attention that is capable of changing the perception and knowing of those who find themselves in its *field*. This focused use of *second attention* can also create specific outcomes that directly affect physical action. Think of this as a bit like throwing a knife blindfolded and hitting a target. Needless to say, *intentionality* is a large, complex, and subtle topic that I hope will become clearer as I explore the varieties of *seeing* in Part IV. At this point however, it should be noted that being aware of the *field* and influencing it, and thus affecting the awareness of others, occurs through the conscious use of *intentionality*.

Although *seers,* like everybody else, depend heavily on the sensate, ordinary world of perception in their engagement with life, they insist that *seeing* is where the real action is, especially when attempting to understand the world of human beings. Yet in its ability to transcend the socially defined boundaries of reality, *seeing* not only illuminates and deepens the *seer*'s understanding of the ordinary world, it can also take him into some amazing realms of non-ordinary reality unavailable to others.

***

While normal perceptions of the world are bound to the time and locality of the perceiver, remote perceptions, also called "telepathy," "clairvoyance," "precognition," and "remote viewing," can take place across time and space. In this way *seers* and others who cultivate non-ordinary perception, such as psychics, mediums, clairvoyants and shamans, are related, though not completely the same "species."

Shamans are traditional healers and psychopomps who use trance-induced non-ordinary perception combined with ritual and theater to mediate between their tribal world and the realm of spirits and deities. While a number of popular shamanic cults have proliferated in the West in recent decades, strictly speaking a member of a shamanistic society must be trained in traditional ways by other practitioners who have carried the knowledge as a cultural and epistemic system down through the ages. It is therefore improper, in my opinion, for Westerners to call themselves "shamans" at all.

Some of what *seers* do may be shamanistic, but for those living in the developed world it is well nigh impossible to fully enter the traditional shaman's realm. In my own case, having been raised to be a member of the "species," *Homo scientificus,* I was not enculturated into a shamanistic worldview and never will be. Furthermore, I am not a shaman because I do not mediate between ontological domains (for example, the "upper world" and human life) nor do I work with any kind of traditional mythology. I only cultivate *seeing* as a way of perceiving and work at articulating my knowing for those who show interest in what I have to say.

Genuine shamans, psychics, mediums, and clairvoyants share a great deal with *seers* in terms of the range and veracity of their non-ordinary perceiving and knowing, but *seeing* represents a unique tradition in which the *seer* learns to purposively live, work, and socialize while concurrently balancing two worlds of experience: the ordinary and non-ordinary. There are some other key markers that also distinguish *seers* from other non-ordinary perceivers.

First, a *seer* is continuously engaged, all day, every day, in the "felt" awareness level of *seeing* as an act of intentional, focused knowing (see Chapter 16). Whereas psychics and others use methods such as trance to perform readings and shamans enter their world of visionary experience through ritual, ceremony and altered states of consciousness, *seers* learn to cross the boundary into non-ordinary perceiving as part of daily life and then gradually acquire the know-how to live in that frame concurrently with ordinary perception. In other words, a *seer* is always "on" and engaged in *seeing*. Thus a *seer* lives in two perceptual frames at once, with attention shared between ordinary, sensate perception and the *second stream* or non-ordinary awareness. So, if someone is using non-ordinary perception part-time—whether as a psychic reader or a shaman, then he is not a *seer*.

Second, *seers* do not require the metaphysical pantheon of gods, goddesses, and other supernatural entities and beliefs that are often at the heart of many paranormal traditions. In fact, as I understand it, many *seers* feel little or no conflict with non-dogmatic scientific or religious worldviews. Personally I am not interested in issues of ultimate values, origins, the meaning of life, spirit entities, or an afterlife as psychics, mediums, and shamans often are. While some *seers* I know are interested in such issues, they are not directly relevant to learning to *see* or being a *seer*.

What *is* crucial to becoming a *seer* is developing psychological clarity about oneself and others, as well as having the balance and spiritual (not necessarily religious) perspective necessary to function well. Therefore, it is helpful if a *seer* engages in some kind of psycho-spiritual training and orientation, but not adopt a set of dogmatic religious beliefs or a cosmology in which non-ordinary events are contextualized and reduced to manifestations of some ultimate ground of being. In my own case, although my primary teacher was a highly developed *seer*, others who contributed to my entry into the world of *seeing* included a psychoanalyst, three spiritual teachers from the Hindu and Buddhist traditions, and two psychics of extraordinary ability, as well as my education in the sciences.

***

Considering my training in *seeing* and the training I have provided for others, I view my tradition to be a loose network of people who find each other through what appears to be happenstance. When *seers* meet, they quickly discover they share a unique type of perception that uses dual awareness and *intentionality* as a way of navigating through life. The network is created and maintained by mentoring relationships in which a developed *seer* puts his attention on an untrained individual who is perceived as having "potential." At times that person may be presented to a *seer* by a confluence of improbable events, the workings of which *seers* call the power of *intentionality*. This certainly happened in my case.

If the neophyte responds appropriately and with dedication, the mentoring *seer* continues to give attention and guidance to help the student develop. However, these relationships are never forced. Rather, one is invited to share perceptual worlds and given the opportunity to explore one's capacity for *seeing*. Effectively, this is an enculturation process, but unlike traditional shamanism, it takes place within and alongside mainstream culture in which the *seer* and the student are usually embedded.

For me, it is this unique training, along with my mainstream cultural orientation, continuous engagement in dual awareness, and conscious use of *intentionality* that differentiate me from other groups of non-ordinary perceivers. My primary interest is in the scientific, philosophical, and direct experiential investigation of the nature of this extended awareness I call *seeing* and to develop a pragmatic mastery of ways to live and work with this awareness in my daily life.

9. BECOMING A *SEER*

We tend to recall most clearly the first occurrence of a particular type of experience—our first sexual encounter, our first success or failure—especially when the event opens up a new vista for us. For me, one of those firsts was when I realized that my "other stream" of consciousness, my other perceptual world, was as real to someone else as it was to me.

This occurred one Saturday morning during my stay in London in 1969 when Alice and I were on our way to an antiquarian bookshop on Hampstead High Street. As we walked in silence, a woman in her forties came up the hill toward us and straight away, my "other stream" awakened, buzzing with images and descriptive words and phrases about her. At the time, such data usually appeared to emerge out of the blue without any connection to me or anything in my environment.

On this occasion, however, Alice broke the silence to say, "You're right. The woman coming toward us is spiteful and has recently been venting her rage on some hapless man."

Her words shocked me out of my reverie, as they precisely described my feelings and thoughts as well as the scene I was observing in my mind's eye. Alice then made a couple of additional comments about the woman's origins. These, too, fit the images and knowing that was spontaneously irrupting into my awareness.

That another individual could describe my inner conscious stream of awareness without hearing from me or even looking at me was a revelation, but even more startling was the affirmation that my perceptions could be shared and were as valid as any ordinary external perception that people can experience together. How Alice went about pointing this out was the essence of her way of mentoring me. She did not engage in abstract or theoretical philosophical discussions. Rather, she focused on a subject as a *seer* then called my attention to my own *seeing* experience of it, while demonstrating the similarity between her awareness and mine.

After that event I realized that, on a moment-to-moment basis, I was walking through a continuous *field* which Alice called the "psychic-emotional atmosphere." The experience was analogous to riding a motorcycle along a roadway on a summer's night. The air in places varies in terms of temperature and humidity, which generate a series of physical feelings as you ride along. In a similar way, we are surrounded by a psychic-emotional *field*, in which *seers* can perceive variations and nuances. These are generated by the activity that has occurred in the *field* as well as by the presence of other living beings in the area. These varying qualities cause an internally felt knowing—in my case, as pictures, words and scenes in my mind's eye and ear, that actually belong to the lives of the people and places associated with the *field*.

Alice and I shared many such incidents over the next five years, each one helping to call my attention to the pervasive presence of the *field* and its *contents*. A particularly important teaching moment came during our visit to the British Museum in Bloomsbury, London. I had visited the museum once on my own just before we first met. It had been on a quiet day during the week, when few visitors were present, but our visit together was on a weekend day and the Hall of Mummies was crowded with tourists. As we entered the main section of the hall, I suddenly and overwhelmingly felt sick to my stomach. Before I said a word about how I was feeling, however, Alice commented, "You're not ill. You're just picking up the feelings of that group of people over there gawking at the display containing a body of an ancient, sand-desiccated man."

About 30 feet away from us was a glass case that contained the body of a man who had been buried in the desert several millennia ago and whose remains had been preserved by desiccation in the hot sand. During my earlier visit to the museum I had been fascinated by how well preserved he was and had marveled at the opportunity to glimpse someone who had lived so long ago. However, on this occasion, as we walked toward the display case, the nausea I registered moments before intensified. Alice whispered to me that if I left the hall, it would stop. Indeed, as I exited the hall, the feeling lifted suddenly and completely. I turned, re-entered the hall, and as I approached the display, the nausea began to return.

In our subsequent discussion about this, Alice explained that part of being a *seer* is having the capacity to register the feeling state of another person, which is embedded in the *field* the person generates. Since we register others' feelings internally, they can be easily mistaken for our own.

An untrained *seer* usually finds it difficult to tell what is internally generated and what is received from the *field* of a place or from other people. Gradually, as I learned to discern the difference between my own feelings and what I was picking up through my *second stream* of attention, I was no longer affected in this way. A sense of distance developed in which I was acutely aware of the emotional and feeling states of others but was unaffected by them because I recognized they came from outside me.

Developing this kind of dispassion took a number of years and a great deal of careful attention to the non-personal source of feeling states occurring alongside personal emotions in my inner stream of awareness. I cannot emphasize enough that the clarity required to know the difference between self and not-self at this level of perception comes with a lot of reality testing and feedback over time as well as a sound understanding of one's own psychological processes.

The capacity for intimately knowing another person's state is different from what most people experience as empathy, which is akin to sympathy—a kind of mental and emotional identification and caring. The connected knowing of the *seer* is more dispassionate. In *seeing*, there is an intimate knowing of the other person's feelings but no personal connection, identification, or attachment. The *seer* experiences another's state within but knows it as other than himself. Sympathy may arise, depending on how the *seer* reacts personally to what he experiences.

***

By the end of the summer of 1969 I was living as if suspended between two worlds. On the one hand, my former ontological certainty was gone and I was forced to live in a state of ongoing, uncomfortable ambiguity. On the other, I had been awakened to the necessity of paying attention to the *seer's* stream of knowing and treating it as a source of information as valid as sensory knowing. I also felt impelled to check out (reality test) what I was receiving by comparing it, where possible, to what was known through ordinary channels.

Occasionally, I tested some of my non-ordinary perceptions with perfect strangers. An instance of this occurred in 1970 after my return to the San Francisco Bay Area. I was at the Oakland International Airport waiting for a journalist friend, Rick, to arrive. In those days there was no security screening, so one could just walk up to the arrival gate, take a seat, and wait, which is what I was doing when a lanky man sat down next to me. He appeared to be in his mid to late forties, and was casually dressed in jeans and "desert boots," a popular item of footwear in the 1960s. As I stared at his shoes, my attention underwent the unique shift that marks the activation of my *second stream* of attention.

I *saw* what looked to be an archeological dig in an arid part of the country that I could not identify but which I thought might be the Southwest. It was as if I was viewing the scene from an elevated position about 100 yards away. In it, I observed several people working, including the man sitting next to me who was walking among them directing their activity. I noticed that he was wearing the desert boots. As I studied the scene I could hear music in the background—a J. S. Bach Brandenburg Concerto. I received additional impressions about the man's personality and character and realized he would be open to me talking to him, so I turned and politely asked if he would mind me telling him some perceptions I was having about him. He seemed a bit surprised by this but he agreed. I then told him that I thought he was an archeologist and I asked him about the significance of the Brandenberg Concerto.

He looked at me quizzically and replied that indeed, he was an archeologist, and my description of the location was like a number of excavations he had been involved with. However, he said in recent times he had been shifting out of archeology in favor of cultural anthropology. He also reported that before coming to the airport, he had been at home listening to one of the Brandenburg Concertos, a favorite of his.

At that moment the plane's passengers were starting to disembark so quickly he asked how I knew these things. With my friend approaching, and realizing that an explanation would take too long, I stood up and said: "It was your shoes!" He looked a bit dumbfounded, but I had to leave before he could ask anything else.

Of course it was his shoes. I had psychometrized them. No doubt the same information would have been available if I had read his *field* directly, but I often find it easier to sense people from their personal objects. The object's *field* is less complicated and cluttered than the person's, which includes a complex mix of emotions, thoughts, and history.

By the time these sorts of events were occurring in my life, I had crossed the threshold from believing that they were impossible to regarding them as quite natural. I had started to live in an expanded reality frame where much more information was available to me, and I was starting to trust it—while endlessly questioning the conception of reality that it implied. Throughout this period my scientistic, skeptical self was alive and well, but being an empiricist, I felt I had to go with the data, which pointed toward an expanded reality that required me to modify my ideas about time and causality. Over time, however, I became less interested in the theoretical frames that could explain this expanded world and more concerned with simply developing my capacity for *seeing*.

*** *

Becoming a conscious *seer* begins with recognizing oneself as such, whether this is via self-discovery, acknowledgment by someone else, or a combination of both. Before this, however, usually when they are growing up, *seers* notice fundamental differences in the way they perceive compared to others. These differences are threefold.

First, as nascent *seers* we are acutely aware of another, causal reality that others seem to either not notice or ignore. Of course, this difference raises the sanity bogey. Anyone who claims to perceive a hidden level of reality is suspected of having delusional ideation, as seen in paranoid psychotics, for example. Unlike psychotics, however, *seers* also acknowledge ordinary consensual reality and, unlike the mentally disordered, they are not obsessed about what they perceive nor do they view people's denial of their experiences as malevolent. A *seer* might be confused and questioning at times, but he does not experience himself as a victim of others' mal-intent or "evil forces." Moreover, a *seer* can self reflect even to the extent of questioning his own sanity at times—something a psychotic person rarely does.

Developing *seers* are often struck by the contrast between the verbal reality of those around them and the felt reality they understand nonverbally through *seeing*.[1] In fact, this discrepancy is the most striking of the three factors that characterize an emerging *seer*. For us, non-ordinary knowing has an immediacy and veracity that cannot be denied and may even lead us to wonder if those around us are just pretending not to perceive it. We are aware of something else operating in social situations, and we tend to know things about people that most others seem unable to access.

A good example of this took place when I was four years old, and I was introduced to my father's new business partner. My parents were excited about this man and the opportunities he seemed to represent and they acted as if me and my brother should be pleased to know him, too. I remember the man standing in front of me smiling pleasantly, but when he reached out to shake my hand, I suddenly felt something was amiss. He was not what he seemed. I sensed a hard and untrustworthy person beneath his pleasant demeanor. Of course being so young I had no way of articulating what I saw so instead I just withdrew and yelled at him: "Get out, get out!" My parents were deeply embarrassed by my outburst and I was quickly admonished for it, but not long afterward, the new partner disappeared with thousands of dollars of my father's money. It seems I had sensed the danger in him, while my father did not.

The second factor that differentiates *seers* from others is that our dual perception tends to leave us feeling that we may never be able to fully integrate with the mainstream social world. We do not fit well in most social situations and have some difficulty connecting in standard social ways with our peers. Of course, this can be true of people with emotional or social challenges, such as those with Asperger's

---

[1] By "nonverbal" I am not referring to the usual facial and physical signs that we display as part of our physical communication, including "micro-expressions."

Syndrome, but unlike those individuals, nascent *seers* have a high degree of social awareness. Nevertheless, many struggle to find ways to respond appropriately to their surrounds as they juggle the contradictions between their dual streams of perception. Often they are left confused by the presence of what seems like too much conflicting information.

Seers perceive additional "layers" in every social situation. To them, most other people seem to be missing something in their awareness, making it difficult to develop an open, complete, and satisfying connection. By the time I was a teenager, being in social situations was like watching a play in which the characters moved inexorably toward a climax of which they appeared to be unaware because of their obliviousness to the additional layer of what was going on.

Of course, feeling different, being eccentric, or relating from an unorthodox point of view does not necessarily herald the emergence of a *seer*. It is only in the context of other signs, and with recognition by a mentor, that we can discover ourselves as such.

The third difference is that *seers* experience an ongoing stream of thoughts, words, pictures, and sensations that do not seem to directly connect to the physical and social events around them, or to their personal memories and cognitive-emotional associations. The majority of the population either do not have this extra stream moving through their consciousness or, if they do, they do not recognize it or they manage to ignore it entirely. As I mentioned, for me growing up, that additional information stream was an ongoing nuisance because, without anyone to tell me otherwise, I took it as a sign of disability.

Sometimes it is other people who make a *seer* aware of his additional internal stream of consciousness. Laurence Bendit, a British psychiatrist, wrote a book I came across during my initial stay in the UK.[2] I found it, almost hidden away, on a bottom shelf in the psychology section of the famous London bookstore, Foyles. In it he recounted his discovery of the fact that some of his psychotherapy patients had paranormal (*second stream*) perceptions, including dreams

---

[2]L. J. Bendit, *Paranormal Cognition* (London: Faber & Faber, 1945). His book is a revised version of a thesis he submitted to the University of Cambridge, which was accepted for the degree of Doctor of Psychiatric Medicine.

and fantasies that turned out to be predictive of events in his own life. Indeed, some patients regularly produced information about him, his family, and his friends that they could not have known. Since Bendit took extensive notes during his sessions, he was able to compare the patients' reports to events as they unfolded.

Such phenomena surprised him. They were not part of his own perceptual world or his training, but nonetheless he felt impelled to write about them and bring them to the attention of his colleagues. I found his book helpful and somewhat reassuring not only because of what I was going through back then but also because of my own experiences during therapy and analysis in New York City in the early 1960s.

On one occasion toward the end of my therapy, my analyst expressed surprise that some of the information I picked up about him during our sessions turned out to be true. Most of my predictions were fairly trivial. However, on one occasion I expressed to him a fear that he might die soon, a statement that he took as grist for the psychoanalytic mill and spent the rest of the session exploring my anxiety about abandonment. Then, a couple of years after that, when I was no longer seeing him as my therapist, he was diagnosed with sickle cell anemia, for which he was hospitalized, and, in November 1969, he died, aged 46, as a result of a heart attack caused by the anemia. Although he made note of my precognitive perceptions, he saw them mainly as symbols of my own psychological issues and so he ignored them as pertaining to him.

The links between a *seer's second attention* stream of consciousness and the day-to-day world are often discovered accidentally, but once they are noticed, they connect in pragmatic and realistic ways and may be calling our attention to what may emerge later. A good example is the "picture" of a beating heart I *saw* in connection with my uncle when I was eight. While it seemed to have no physical consequence at the moment, it became tragically relevant when he later dropped dead of a heart attack. It is these sorts of events occurring again and again that awaken us to the fact that we are getting information from a source other than the immediate physico-social world.

***

If our society has lost its shamans and other holders of *seer*-like traditions, where does the neophyte *seer* go for help? And when help is offered, how is it possible to know whether it is coming from an authentic source? My unusual entry into this world brought me into contact with people who could offer me useful guidance, but for others the situation may be less well defined. Initiation does not always happen as dramatically as it did for me. The majority of developing *seers* have to stumble around for some time before finding mentors who can provide realistic, pragmatic guidance. Based on my experience and that of others, the early stages of learning often feel like groping blindly in the dark. The individual may be having experiences that are paradoxical to common sense and he may feel fearful and confused.

When starting out on the path of becoming a *seer* a great deal of experimentation is required in the form of trial-and-error learning. The neophyte *seer's* primary occupation must be learning how to pay attention correctly as well as testing their non-ordinary knowings and visions against the more usual sensate-derived information. At the same time, a beginner must remain ruthlessly honest with himself by maintaining a healthy skepticism about what is experienced. This requires the application of rational thinking. Indulging in wishful imagination that goes beyond what is directly *seen* and elaborating upon it to make a more impressive story are major obstacles to becoming a clear, well-balanced *seer*. Also, indulging in self-pity ("Why am I different? Why is this happening to me?") or entertaining delusions of grandeur ("I am a psychic genius") are not appropriate.

Only through perseverance and a dedication to not deny their perceptions, combined with clear, pragmatically oriented analytic thought, can a would-be *seer* be ready to receive mentoring. There is some truth to the adage that when the student is ready, the teacher appears. However, not all teachers are going to be ideal—often *seers* do not get their fantasies met about the kind of teacher they would like but are instead confronted with challenges. *Seeing* is not necessarily a path of beauty and light leading to some angelic, purified condition in which a grand vision occurs that explains all. On occasion, it is an act of looking into an ugly pit (like the mind of a psychopathic killer—see

Chapter 20), and the teacher can turn out to be a difficult and discomforting taskmaster indeed.

As my former Buddhist teacher the Venerable Tarthang Tulku Rinpoche insisted, a life of personal development requires the application of great vigor and dedication before one is ready to be taught. Cherished fantasies about one's path and teacher usually have to be jettisoned and replaced with pragmatic learning that causes on-going confrontations with our self-image and expectations.

Unlike the structured and culturally determined training of traditional shamans, the process of moving from neophyte to trained *seer* is usually an *ad hoc* affair, depending on the attention and goodwill of others. Typically, a trained *seer* recognizes another, less developed individual struggling with the issues of *seeing* and offers a helping hand for a period of time. This kind of mentoring relationship can be fraught with the same kinds of difficulties found in psychotherapeutic relationships and does not always end successfully. As in any apprenticeship, the skill of the mentor and the quality of what is taught is as important as the potential of the learner. Although Alice did not meet what I felt were my intellectual and conceptual expectations of a teacher, in that she refused to engage in conceptual dialogues about "theory," she was a highly skilled mentor in terms of the pragmatics of *seeing* and living as a *seer* and therefore she was able to successfully guide me.

There are no schools for *seers*, nor are there academies to learn the art of mentoring *seers*. Rather, this is an informal network. Membership comes about by being recognized as a *seer* by another *seer*, which then leads to being introduced to yet other *seers*. This recognition is not necessarily heralded as dramatically and directly as it was for me, nor does it necessarily even involve the use of the term *seer*. The salient quality of such meetings is usually a recognition of the struggling *seer* by a potential mentor who, if he chooses, immediately acknowledges the usually hidden reality of neophyte's *second attention* perception by commenting on what the emerging *seer* is experiencing, apart from the usual consensus world. Thus the mentor is someone who, by giving his attention to the neophyte, gradually brings him into the world of conscious *seeing*.

Typically, the student is filled with confusion, clinging to his belief in the veracity of what he is *seeing* but still uncertain of its truth and, therefore, conflicted about what is real and even whether or not he is sane. He probably feels caught between two worlds—the one everyone acknowledges and the other that is equally real to him but largely denied in his usual social context. Using *seeing,* the mentor recognizes the neophyte's struggle to make sense of the two disconnected realities and directly comments on some aspect of his struggle that the neophyte believes is private. The teacher then attempts to call the learner's attention to how the two streams combined enable the student to grasp a more complete picture of reality.

With this, the mentor creates a bridge for the neophyte to connect both worlds in an ongoing and meaningful way. He does what most Western socialization fails to do—he normalizes the developing *seer's* perceptual world in the same way as a child's sensate world is normalized during childhood and, so, helps the learner to live in an integrated way in both epistemic frames.

Meeting a mentor who provides such a bridge often comes as a shock and a revelation, since it is in direct contrast to the neophyte's usual experience. Some shock is required, however, to convey that the mentor really does understand the inner landscape that the neophyte is experiencing. This also helps dispense with the doubt and skepticism that have built up over the years from lack of social validation and, as in my case, a highly developed scientism.

When I take on the role of mentor, I always comment on what the neophyte is experiencing, some aspect of it that I can *see* is at the center of his struggle. I speak directly to this issue, as it appears to me, as if the learner and I had already conversed about it and as if speaking about such things is commonplace. The contrast between the sheer ordinariness of the conversation and its extraordinary content usually manages to jar most students out of their self-imposed alienation so that a connection can be made and a bond formed.

Sometimes the mentoring experience is brief but more often the teacher and student enter into an ongoing partnership. The length of time spent together and the intensity of the interaction vary, but the outcome is usually the same. The mentor communicates to the neophyte a certainty about the reality of *seeing,* along with training in specific uses of attention that the mentor employs in his *seeing* as well as the attitude and practices needed for being a balanced and nondestructive *seer.*

As an example, one of my current students is a highly educated professional who, throughout her early life, was acutely aware of the split between the social consensus and her perceptions. In her younger years, this generated conflict with her peers because she appeared to them as eccentric and somewhat weird. Often, statements she made that seemed like simple descriptions of the obvious to her, were disturbing to those who did not share her awareness. Although she knew that talking about her perceptions would create problems for her, she insisted on expressing them anyway. Sure enough, she did not gain the recognition she desired and often felt like a "crazy outsider." However, this did not stop her from functioning at a high level and achieving well regarded professional standing.

I knew her for many years before I acknowledged her *seeing* ability and indicated that I was willing to mentor her. I am acutely aware of how entering into the world of *seeing* can profoundly alter someone's life. From my point of view, it is best that a person learns to deal with the vicissitudes of day-to-day living so he is fairly well-grounded before being introduced to the world of the *seer* and its challenges. Also, the neophyte *seer* needs to be looking for someone to guide him; mentoring should never be offered to anyone who does not really want it.

Currently, my student is faced with the challenge of discovering how to live with what she perceives in a non-judgmental way. She tends to experience mal-intent whenever she encounters feelings and attitudes she does not like—a consequence of the negative responses she received in her early years. Her task now is to develop a less value-laden awareness by removing her likes and dislikes from her perceptions as much as possible. This becomes an issue of the deployment of attention and recognizing the different styles of attention we bring to the creation of our knowing.

Once the certainty and veracity of being a *seer* are clearly in place—which usually takes several years—the mentoring phase of the relationship is over, and the individual either goes his separate way or the mentor and student enter into a more ordinary friendship.

***

In most cases, *seers* function as normal members of society. However, entering into the world of *seeing* can have its pitfalls, psychologically speaking. *Seers* are just as prone to mental and personality disorders as any other group of people. In fact, becoming a *seer* can exacerbate certain paranoid or narcissistic personality disorders.

In my experience, someone with a tendency towards narcissism may use his new identity as a *seer* to further inflate himself and cut off from genuine intimacy and self-awareness. The discovery that he has a capacity not possessed by others feeds his narcissistic grandiosity and convinces him that he is more important than everyone else. Indeed, I have seen some *seers* become so inflated that they turn themselves into "gurus" or "avatars." A very narcissistic *seer* may even see himself as a kind of Hegelian "world-historic individual," a savior come to rescue humanity. This can lead to the formation of a cult which can be very destructive of those who are swept up in it. Members of such groups are viewed not so much as students of *seeing* but as servants of a master— their sole purpose to facilitate whatever grand vision he is proclaiming.

Being a *seer* does not make one a teacher or leader of others. A *seer* is simply an individual with a consciously functional *second attention* that when integrated with ordinary, sensate-driven perception and knowledge, allows him to access a greater range of knowing. Recognition of oneself as a *seer* is not an indication that one is divinely sanctioned to be in a position above others. A person with a talent for tennis, such as John McEnroe, is not necessarily someone we would want to follow beyond watching tennis games. It is the same for a *seer*, who has a unique skill but might also have a temper problem that makes him inappropriate to follow in all matters.

10. ATTENTION, PERCEPTION, AND POINT OF VIEW

Meeting a mentor capable of articulating my internal imagery and the feelings I received from *fields* not only revolutionized my concepts of awareness, attention and consciousness it profoundly changed how I attended to the world from moment to moment. Alice seemed to have read my mind during our walk down Hampstead High Street. She read the emotional state of the woman coming toward us and then called my attention to the fact that I was receiving the same impressions. Although this was problematic, in that I became unsure about personal boundaries, which increased my paranoia about what was happening, it was also remarkable. In that single act she established a radically altered notion of what is real and possible in terms of shared perceptions and the objective world.

Objectivity took on a new meaning—I now experienced it as intersubjectivity, a directly shared experience of what is believed to be the objective world. What I once believed was just psychological "noise" became meaningful and part of the objective world, even though it was experienced as if it was subjective. It was through many such interactions with Alice that I realized this type of knowing requires a redeployment of attention—a shift in how and to what I paid attention to in my stream of consciousness.

I had first gained a rudimentary understanding of what it meant to redeploy attention, which I also call an epistemic frame shift, through an ordinary encounter in the mid-1960s while living in the San Francisco Bay Area. I had befriended a professor at San Francisco State University named Marv, with whom I had taken a class during a previous semester, and one evening he suggested that we go to a club in Berkeley to hear an up-and-coming electric blues guitarist, Buddy Guy. He told me that we would be joining a friend—a man he had wanted me to meet for some time. Arriving there, we soon met Jim, an

African-American man in his mid-fifties who drove a taxi for a living and also regularly worked as an orderly in a psychiatric hospital.

Jim was powerfully built with an intense communication style that seemed to be the social manifestation of an even more intense personal presence. He immediately captured my attention. When the musicians were not playing, he talked nonstop and I listened, though with some confusion for he employed what seemed to me a strange use of language. It was laden with meaning that was attention grabbing yet remained just out of reach of my understanding. The more he spoke, the more I felt as if I had to run to keep up with him—as though he was casting words over his shoulder while he verbally jogged on ahead. No matter how intently I listened, I was not sure I was really getting what he was trying to say.

Then something interesting occurred. Marv, who was also paying close attention to him and appeared to be finding meaning and even inspiration in his words, said something about poetry in relation to the conversation. I had always appreciated poetry, and, for no reason that I can remember, I started to listen to Jim as if he were doing a poetry reading. Suddenly, his words came alive and made sense. They were a commentary on what he was seeing around him and on the human condition—all expounded in a kind of free-form verse.

As I listened, he shifted from being almost unintelligible to being an inspired speaker conveying a deeply felt perspective unveiled with artistic clarity. It was marvelous—not only to hear his vision of the world but to discover how to shift my attention filter in this way. It was like switching to a different channel of knowing or to another perceptual template. Where meaning was previously out of reach, it now spoke to me clearly.

This event started to make me aware that what we pay attention to and how we do it is fundamental to what we are capable of knowing. A typical, everyday example is the way we misplace our car or house keys. How many times have you put them down for a short while only to find that they seemed to have disappeared? Most of us are on autopilot when we put our keys somewhere, giving our action little or no attention. No attention equals little or no memory of what we did, which means there is no memory of where the keys are when we want to retrieve them. We should think of attention as being like a searchlight scanning in the dark. What it does not illuminate does not seem to exist.

There is a foreground and a background to all of our perceptions, with only a small amount known in the foreground at any given time (as if looking through a small window) while a vast amount of what is happening is left in the background and, hence, in the realm of the unknown. Gestalt psychology emphasizes the need to reverse the perceptual foreground and background in order to see what was previously invisible. Not only do we tend to keep the background and foreground relationship fixed, our minds act like valves, diminishing the flow of perception to make it manageable, as observed by the author and philosopher Aldous Huxley in his now-classic book *The Doors of Perception*.[1] He argues that some psychotropic drugs, such as psychedelics, may open the valve to allow a broader and more intense flow of information as the drug makes the operating point of view more encompassing and fluid. The valve represents the focus and type of attention used. As a *seer* I have learned that these functions can be changed in a variety of ways without using a mind-altering substance, as is also evidenced in the literature of religions such as Hinduism and Buddhism and in the writings of Western mystics.

I had a direct experience of the "valve opening" capacity of psychedelic drugs in the mid-1960s while living in San Francisco's Haight-Ashbury district—ground zero for the psychedelic movement, as it was later called. The psychology department at San Francisco State University, where I was studying psychophysiology, was also the center of a range of newly emerging psychotherapies. I started to experiment with one of these when I attended a Gestalt therapy group led by Paul Goodman, one of the authors, together with Fritz Perls and Ralph Hefferline, of the seminal book on that topic.[2] Later I was to meet Perls on a number of occasions, and when I first acquired the book, I realized I already knew Hefferline.

---

[1] A. Huxley, *Doors of Perception, and Heaven and Hell* (New York: Harper and Row, 1954).
[2] F. Perls, R. Hefferline, and P. Goodman, *Gestalt Therapy: Excitement and Growth in the Human Personality* (New York: Dell, 1951).

As a high school junior I had conducted neurophysiological experiments that were publicized in a local newspaper, the *Long Island Press*. The article prompted a visit from one of Professor Hefferline's graduate students, who had been sent by him to look into what I was doing and to invite me to his laboratory at Columbia University. At the lab I was introduced to the professor's research in the use of covert neurological events to induce hallucinations in human subjects. Of course, in San Francisco in the 1960s hallucinations were a major topic of conversation in the world of the psychedelic movement. My curiosity had been piqued by all the new ideas, drugs, and psychotherapies that were appearing on my horizon at that time.

Around this time I became friends with a fellow psychology major, Linda, who introduced me to an African-American musician she had been dating named Rod. He and I quickly became friends and started hanging out together. He was often feeling down because Linda was pulling away from him and he also suffered from bouts of depression, probably because of the severe beatings he had endured growing up with his deeply frustrated and rageful father. I had gotten used to seeing him in a low mood so I was surprised one morning to find him standing at my apartment door in a calm and radiant state, looking as if all his burdens had been lifted. Amazed by the apparent transformation, I asked, "Rod, what happened to you?"

"I had my first acid trip," he replied.

"Where can I get some?" I asked a bit too eagerly. I wanted what had happened to him to transform me, too. He told me about a woman on upper Haight Street (I lived at the bottom of Haight, at Market) who was selling Owsley acid—LSD-25 manufactured by the late Owsley Stanley, who was once described as "the prodigiously gifted applied chemist to the stars."[3]

After obtaining a small capsule from her for five dollars, I made my plans for my "trip" the following week and got Rod to agree to be my guide. Shortly before the big day, my friend Tom arrived for a visit from the East Coast, where he was studying at Amherst. I asked him to join us

---

[3]*New York Times* obituary, March 14, 2011,
http://www.nytimes.com/2011/03/15/us/15stanley.html?_r=0#.

but insisted that neither he nor Rod take anything so they would be *compos mentis* in case something went wrong.

On the morning of the appointed day I took the small, blue-green capsule and we walked up Haight Street to Golden Gate Park. As we passed through the short tunnel that leads into the park from Stanyan Street, the chemical hit my central nervous system with a roar and after emerging onto the path on the other side of the tunnel, I started to experience increasing anxiety that soon reached a terrifying intensity. Convinced that I had poisoned myself and was going to die, I abruptly stopped on the path.

Although I had said nothing, my companions noticed I was not feeling well, and Rod asked, "Is something wrong?" At first I resisted saying anything because I did not want to look like I was out of control, but finally I admitted that I was feeling intense anxiety in my shins! Hilarious as that might sound, it was exactly what I was experiencing as my feelings were displacing to various parts of my body. As I stood in silence, struggling, I heard a voice in my head suggest that if I was going to die, I might as well fully participate and do so consciously. The "advice" made complete sense at that time, so I just let go of my fear and prepared to experience my death. As I did, my mood suddenly lifted, and I found the whole situation so funny I started to laugh out loud. Before long I realized that I was going to be okay with whatever happened to me and then my trip started in earnest.

Pretty soon I was in a highly elated state. I thought about my psychoanalysis in New York City a couple of years earlier and recognized a feeling I had been carrying all my life: that I was essentially bad. Therapy had never altered my fundamental point of view in this regard. However, as the old, familiar feeling arose into my awareness again, forcing me to confront it, this time I saw it through an altered epistemic frame. Suddenly, I understood it to be absurd and just like that, the belief evaporated. I could not reconstitute it, and it never returned. For the next hour or so I kept walking with my friends as similar insights came and went. It was as if everything I felt and believed was being experienced from a radically altered perspective.

Soon my friends and I found ourselves standing in front of the park's classically beautiful greenhouse, the Conservatory. Rod suggested that we go inside and look at the plants, perhaps because he was wondering what I would experience. Although I have never had an interest in plants and gardening, I agreed. I was curious, too. Entering the greenhouse, I was startled as I confronted what felt like a crowd scene, but one made up of plants. They seemed as busy and sentient as a throng of people. Awed, I wandered over to a large plant with huge leaves. It had a presence that I had never before noticed from plants, one like that of a living person. In fact, every plant in the Conservatory appeared to have a unique presence, like a personality and, like humans, some were nice to be around, while others were not. As I stood contemplating this new awareness, the crowd scene became overwhelming, so I turned and left the building.

I remember stepping through the door to the outside and suddenly there was only light—a supernal brilliance that enveloped me as though I was just a small boat in a huge ocean. We must have walked for five or more minutes while I was in this state, because when I again became aware of objects around me—grass, trees, people, and so on—we were in a different part of the park, approaching a log on the ground placed as a border between what might have been a play area and its surrounds. As I looked at the log I found myself pointing to a place in front of it, saying to my companions: "Dig there and you'll find a chain with an attached key. There is an "F" stamped on it." I had no idea why I said this, but straight away Tom got down on his knees, dug under the grass, and pulled out a chain with a key dangling from it. Upon inspection there was, indeed, an "F" stamped on it.

Throughout my trip, I became aware that the way in which I was experiencing the world had a familiar quality to it, as if the background of my day-to-day awareness had moved into the foreground. My attention had been turned to what was always just below the limen of my awareness but barely or not at all attended to in my usual state of consciousness. Presumably, the drug had altered my attention processes, allowing me to notice what was always there but unavailable in the field of awareness arising from my usual deployment of attention. At the time I wondered if it might be possible to learn how to experience the world around me in similar ways without using such extreme chemical means. Perhaps psychotherapy and meditation could be those other means, I mused.

***

During those San Francisco days, it was starting to occur to me that the dimensions of foreground and background were only one part of the picture. To my mind, reversing their polarity is primary in any attempt to redeploy attention, but I wondered if there were other epistemic frames, constituting different information and meaning realms, that might open further the range of possible attention foci—such as I later understood when I learned to attend to what I call the *second stream*. In other words, what I discovered back then was that a shift in attention from foreground to background was just a shift within a particular frame. Shifting attention to an entirely different frame would be a movement into a different realm of knowledge, and hence meaning. Many people experience this shift for the first time through the action of a psychedelic drug, just as I did during my trip.

The webs of attention in which we usually live—with their given foregrounds and resultant perceptual frames and beliefs—are what childhood conditioning and life experience have taught us are real and worthy of our attention. This is obvious to anyone who examines how he has arrived at what he now perceives and believes, but it has especially profound implications for a person becoming a conscious *seer*. Basically, how we look at the world determines to a very large degree what kind of world we perceive. When I say "how," I literally mean the psychophysiological processes of active perception that create the picture we know. These processes are driven by our attention, which has been determined primarily by learned habits. Our individual human worlds of perception are our particular slice of the reality "pie," our unique set of snapshots, and are thus constructed products arising from our perceptual activities. This slicing of the "pie" starts with the way we physically perceive the world through our senses.

For example, numerous studies have been done on the way we visually attend to the world around us. It is both what we scan with our eyes and the pattern of how we do it that determine the visual picture we construct. The experiments, reported in some introductory psychology textbooks, using mirrored contact lenses and a laser, allowed behavioral scientists to observe where a person's gaze alights when looking at, say, a painting of a nude woman. They mapped how the saccades, the quick movements that make up the eyes' scanning activity, clustered on some parts of the painting more than others. There was also a pattern in terms of where the subject looked first and where he concentrated. Parts of the painting got more concentrated attention (shown by the higher concentration of gaze dots in the graph of activity), and less interesting parts, such as the background, got little or none. With average, normal people, the patterns of scanning were fairly predictable. In contrast, some studies have demonstrated that delusional schizophrenics show radically different and less structured patterns and also report very different perceptual experiences.[4]

There appears to be a constructive process taking place in the brain, driven by how we scan the visual field, that determines how and what we know. This process, along with others, determines what we believe is out there in the objective world which, in turn, determines how we scan. The same holds true for all the sense modalities—we attend selectively and construct the data we receive into pictures and understandings of the world that fit our learned templates that create the form and meaning of what we believe to be the "real" world. In turn, this scanning and construction process confirms and reinforces how we have been taught to perceive.

The eyes constantly move in saccades when looking at an object to prevent the same spot on the retina from getting similar information over and over without a change of stimulus. This allows time for the light-sensitive chemicals in the retina to be renewed, and it prevents it from habituating, or ceasing to respond to the same type and intensity of stimulus applied continuously. Deliberately overriding the eyes' habitual movement by maintaining a fixed stare can lead to altered

---

[4] J. Fukushima, N. Morita, K. Fukushima, T. Chiba, S. Tanaka, and I. Yamashit, "Voluntary Control of Saccadic Eye Movements in Patients with Schizophrenic and Affective Disorders," *J. Psychiat. Res.,* 24 (1990), 9–24.
B. Karoumi, J. Ventre-Dominey, A. Vighetto, J. Dalery, and T. d'Amato, "Saccadic Eye Movements in Schizophrenic Patients," *Psychiatry Research,* 77 (1998), 9–19.
S. P. Liversedge and J. M. Findlay, "Saccadic Eye Movements and Cognition," *Trends in Cognitive Sciences,* 4 (2000), 6–14.

perceptions and, when radical enough, to an altered point of view and a sense of what is real.

When I teach students about the eyes' visual constructive process, I have them pick a spot on the wall or floor in front of them and stare at it without blinking or moving their eyes. It is a difficult exercise, but when done properly, practitioners become aware that there are other ways to perceive the same spot. Without the usual eye movements to allow the retina to refresh itself, the brain attempts to make sense of the input, for instance, by creating the appearance of colors, shapes, and pictures that are not present when one observes the spot in the usual manner.

When I ask the students to work with a partner, using their face as the target for their fixed staring, the visual results get even more interesting. The subject's face distorts and features appear that may change the person's visage radically. Often a succession of faces come and go, with some seeming to be present in a way that is more than just a distortion of the original face.

Some of these visual effects are merely the brain reconstituting the optical input based on a changed pattern of retinal stimulation that the fixed staring creates. However, at times a student's attention is caught by *second stream* visual information, as the usual flow of information from the retina becomes less dominant. It is as if a person's eyes become habituated to the unchanging physical stimuli so their attention can notice what is usually in the perceptual background, behind, as it were, the dominant physical vision. Of course, our habitual attention always wants to put ordinary physical perception in the foreground again and ignore the other information, which is usually taken to be an irrelevant background or just noise in the system (imagination). By returning our attention to its baseline point of view and epistemic frame, we are assuring ourselves about who we are and what is "real."

Another exercise I ask students to do is to recount what they notice as they walk into the classroom for the first time. I give them a hint: there is no correct answer. Then I ask, "Can you reconstruct what caught your attention? What were you experiencing? What feelings and thoughts emerged in response to what you were experiencing?" In other words, I ask them to track the attentional, filtering, and construction processes by which they decided what the room is and what is going on in it.

By calling attention to this process I am asking students to track how their attention works and to notice the chain of associations that emerge as part of the knowledge about where they are that seems to arise spontaneously in their awareness. What epistemic filter are they applying? How much of their perception of the room was the room they found on their arrival, and how much was it the room they brought with them? Then I ask what else they might have paid attention to. Through this process I try to make my students aware that their attention deployment and filtering are the driving forces behind the point of view they carry with them into every situation, new or old, and that this point of view is determined by learned habits of attention. A great deal can be going on in a room, but if our attention is not on it or if part of what is there is not captured by our filter, it remains invisible.

All of us have had the experience of being in a group—a business meeting or social gathering—in which an individual leaves and the quality of the group interaction changes noticeably, on occasion dramatically, even if that person apparently was doing no more than sitting quietly. For example, the group process may function much better or worse. Someone entering may have the same effect, again, even though that person apparently does nothing overt to affect the group's functioning. If other participants knew how to redeploy their attention like a *seer*, they might have perceived directly how this process works, but most of us have a culturally conditioned point of view that forbids *seeing* and acknowledging the effect of a person's *bio-field* and *intentionality* on a social group.

***

Our point of view is constructed from our beliefs, both mental (cognitive) and existential (what we do and who we are) such that it becomes the filter determining what we can know and believe, and hence what and who we are. Most of us have a highly trained and fixed attention that feeds a fixed point of view that functions to keep us within our cultural and familial norms. Such a fixed point of view can be functional or dysfunctional, depending on context and use, but it determines what we perceive, know, and believe is real and how we respond to the world around us.

The fixed point of view affects all aspects of our engagement with the world, whether it be our social or work lives, but its effect is particularly prominent in spiritual seeking. Many pursue spirituality with a highly fixed point of view, looking for "enlightenment," "God," or some other guiding force. However, I now understand the spiritual process as a "radical deconstruction" in which spiritual knowing results from a breakdown of the fixed point of view, leading to a profound revision some call mystical knowing.[5] In a later chapter in this book ("Removing the Self Point of View") I describe how this occurred for me.

Most of us have a highly fixed attention, trained from childhood, that determines our point of view. The words "pay attention!" ring in our ears from both home and school encounters with authority. Not only are we constantly taught what our attention should be focused on; we are explicitly and implicitly served up, through family values, peer pressure, and our Western education, a hierarchy of importance regarding our perceptions.

It is apparent to those who study human perception that language and the act of labeling what the child's attention is focused on are also part of the process.[6] Often I have witnessed a parent pointing at an object, telling the child what color it is, giving the object a name, and describing its function and meaning. On the other hand, I have never seen a parent calling the child's attention to the *tone* of a *field* (see Chapter 15), giving that a name, and relating to it functionally. In fact, when children express awareness of such things, most caretakers either ignore their observations or minimize their importance, often to the point of dismissal.

---

[5]P. L. Nelson, "Mystical Experience and Radical Deconstruction: Through the Ontological Looking Glass," in T. Hart, P. L. Nelson, and K. Puhakka, eds., *Transpersonal Knowing: Exploring the Horizons of Consciousness* (New York: SUNY Press, 2000), pp. 55–84; http://www.socsci.biz/resources/ME&RD-Nelson.pdf.
[6]While exploring the epistemological aspects of different languages is beyond the scope of this book, it is a topic worth examining. For an interesting introduction to some of the linguistic issues see: J. B. Carroll, ed., *Language, Thought, and Reality: Selected Writings of Benjamin Lee Whorf* (Cambridge, MA: MIT Press, 1956).

Another fundamental mechanism of maintaining a fixed point of view is self-retraining. We do the same thing over and again, whether or not it works. A good example is a person who has one failed relationship after another. Their point of view makes them believe that each new partner is different from the last one, because they do not attend to the similar characteristics among these individuals that are the primary causes of their failed relationships.

Good psychotherapy can help with such behavior, but therapy usually fails to address the attention habits underpinning this fixed point of view, keeping the person from recognizing the common thread. Since the mechanism of attention that creates an entrapping epistemic frame is never directly addressed and retrained, the basis of the dysfunction is never recognized and changed.

Still another self-training mechanism that keeps point of view fixed is the internal dialogue—the monologue in our heads that keeps our stories alive by refreshing memories and emotional responses underlying the tales of who we are from minute to minute, day to day, and so on over the years. We are dedicated to our stories, so much so that when asked to consider the opposite of what we believe and think we know, we usually refuse. Very likely all of us can remember trying to get someone else to understand an issue they refuse to even consider. This is a fixed point of view in the process of maintaining itself—something it does well.

I remember once going out to dinner with a group of people that included a criminal lawyer for whom I had worked briefly doing psychological assessments of offenders. This lawyer was an avowed believer in preserving natural ecology and, over dinner, he held forth on the importance of saving polar bears. Noting his fixed point of view, I suggested a *gedanken* (a thought experiment) in which I would invite him to consider another view. He agreed, but when I then suggested he reconsider his defense of polar bears in light of the fact that they are very dangerous to humans (for example), he exploded into a rage that appeared as if I had threatened his very existence. His point of view was so rigidly held that even being asked to loosen his grip on it as part of a thought experiment had triggered a defensive storm.

Of course, I have seen that type of rage many times over the years, when presenting a view that appears to my listener to be an attack on his ontological bottom line (the fundamental beliefs that underpin his life-story fixed point of view). Another example of this occurred in the late 1980s when I was invited by the head of the Speech Pathology Department at the University of California at Santa Barbara to give a talk on some of the problematic fundamental assumptions underpinning science, specifically, the problems inherent in making ontological ascriptions (stating what actually exists) based on a method that is purely epistemic (knowledge producing).

Although I indicated that I was not attacking the veracity or usefulness of science, halfway through my presentation one faculty member in the audience became enraged with me. He appeared to misinterpret my analysis as being an attempt to diminish science, and, presuming he was a scientist, to diminish him. What I vividly remember is his red hair as he jumped to his feet and shouted, "You're insane!" as he ran from the room, slamming the door behind him. I see this as a typical response to a perceived threat to a highly fixed point of view.

In summary, how we deploy our attention determines what we know, what we know determines what we believe is real, and what we believe determines who we are and what we can do. So, if we change how we use our attention, we change who we are and what we understand as reality. Learning to use our attention more flexibly leads to a more fluid point of view, and it is my experience that a fluid point of view is the basis of the deepened awareness and perspective that is at the heart of spirituality. By mastering the technology of attention, whose workings are at the heart of the process of consciousness, we open the doors of perception to both personal and spiritual development.[7]

---

[7]P. L. Nelson, "The Technology of the Praeternatural: An Empirically Based Model of Transpersonal Experiences," *Journal of Transpersonal Psychology,* 22 (1990), 35–50; http://www.socsci.biz/resources/PraeterTech.pdf.

11. THE TECHNOLOGY OF ATTENTION AND CONSCIOUSNESS

Around the time of my LSD trip in San Francisco, I attended a series of lectures on Eastern and Western psychology and philosophy at the Cultural Integration Fellowship on Fulton Street, along the north side of Golden Gate Park. These were given by Dr. Haridas Chaudhuri, an academic and disciple of Sri Aurobindo. A friend had introduced me to the series and encouraged me to attend. Chaudhuri talked about psychoanalysis, philosophy, and Hindu thought, attempting to integrate these different worldviews. At the end of every lecture the group meditated for about 15 minutes in the closed-eyes style. We were given instructions and then we sat, eventually finishing the evening by making a quiet exit and paying our respects to Dr. Chaudhuri by shaking his hand as we filed out of the building.

I started to practice meditation at home using a mantra that Sri Haridas (as he preferred to be called) had given me during an individual mentoring session. As I silently repeated the mantra I was often able to disconnect my attention entirely from external stimuli around me as well as silence the internal dialogue and stream of images and words that were the normal content of my conscious awareness.

At times the experience was like stepping into a quiet, open space in which everything was suspended except the inner sound of the mantra. Upon opening my eyes, everything in the room around me would seem more present, colors and dimensionality were enhanced like a mild version of the psychedelic states I experienced first during my LSD trip and later during four encounters with mescaline. However, as soon as I stood up and busied myself doing things, the expansiveness and enhanced perception would rapidly fade, and my internal dialogue and mental images would re-emerge full-tilt. The quiet centeredness would be replaced by inner chatter with its associated shifting affect and a lack of felt, physical coherence that had developed during meditation. This practice seemed to me to be a useful break from the hurly-burly of the day, but without any carryover into ordinary, daily activity.

Later in my exploration of spiritual practice I became involved in Buddhism, first with the San Francisco Zen Center under Shunryu Suzuki Roshi and then with the Tibetan Buddhist Nyingma Institute under the tutelage of Tarthang Tulku Rinpoche. During this period, when I was meditating large portions of every day, I sometimes noticed more carryover of the meditation state into everyday life, but it still tended to fade fairly rapidly. This seemed to be the case for many of the other students I encountered as well. Still, doing chores with a group of Buddhist monks was certainly quieter and it engaged a more focused attention than working with most other groups of people I have known.

My initial visit to Professor Hefferline's lab at Columbia in 1960 and my experiments with LSD-25 and mescaline were my first clues that there might be an ongoing, working technology of awareness that determines the range and content of our knowledge creation. A number of years later, I started to believe that the process of this inner technology could be mapped, and if I could construct an operational schematic that delineated its operations, I would be able to teach it to others as well as deepen my own practice and understanding.

I conjectured that such a schematic would be capable of mapping the mechanisms of attention that determine our state and contents of consciousness, how we construct our point of view and worldview, and ultimately, what we accept as real and accept as our story of "what is." As a practitioner of Hindu or Buddhist meditation, I had never received any direct instruction or heard any explicit discussion delineating the phenomenology of the inner technology of consciousness and attention. I was given general instructions on the practice of mindfulness and some vaguely poetic and metaphoric material from both Hindu and Buddhist thought that were designed to direct my attention to a particular focus for meditation, but no description of the mechanisms underlying attention and its uses. Nonetheless, I continued to practice formal meditation still noticing that shift afterward—sometimes gradual and at other times abrupt—from meditative awareness to a state that constituted attention in the usual sense.

After about twenty years of researching and thinking about this issue, as well as experimenting on myself, I wrote a Ph.D. dissertation titled "The Technology of the Præternatural: An Operational Analysis and Empirical Study of the Psycho-Phenomenology of Mystical, Visionary and Remote Perception Experiences." This was my formal attempt to operationally map the maneuvers of mind, emotions, and body—set within the dimensions of personality in which they occur—that facilitate a person's transition into a radically altered epistemic frame (story) usually understood as an experience of the non-ordinary.

I later published my research as a series of academic papers because I felt that the subject was too technical for a book intended for general readership.[1] In essence, this map of non-ordinary experiencing examines what kind of people (personality types) tend to have these experiences and how they set up their attention to allow such a shift in attention to occur—whether they are consciously aware of it or not. As I conceived it, this operational technology is the sum total of the mechanisms underlying the radical shifts that open awareness to altered experiences of what is real (a shift of epistemic frame). Later I summarized this map as a diagram (Fig. 1), a detailed description of which can be found in my paper "Consciousness as Reflexive Shadow."[2]

In summary, the diagram attempts to graphically represent how the experiential present—the moment that reveals itself as an awareness of what is understood to be currently real—is created. It is a moment's manifestation of the point of view, which is created by three forces: attention deployment, information input, and the immediate memory of

---

[1]P. L. Nelson, "The Technology of the Praeternatural: An Empirically Based Model of Transpersonal Experiences," *Journal of Transpersonal Psychology*, 22 (1990), 35–50; http://www.socsci.biz/resources/PraeterTech.pdf.
P. L. Nelson, "Personality Attributes as Discriminating Factors in Distinguishing Religio-mystical from Paranormal Experients," *Imagination, Cognition and Personality*, 11(4) (1991–92), 389–405; http://www.socsci.biz/resources/PraeterType.pdf.
P. L. Nelson, "Personality Factors in the Frequency of Reported Spontaneous Præternatural Experiences," *Journal of Transpersonal Psychology*, 21 (1989), 193–209; http://www.socsci.biz/resources/PraeterFreq.pdf.
[2]P. L. Nelson, "Consciousness as Reflexive Shadow: An Operational Psycho-phenomenological Model," *Imagination, Cognition and Personality*, 17(3) (1997–98), 215–228; http://www.socsci.biz/resources/ConscReflex.pdf.

moments just past (t_1, t_2, etc.) reflected back into the awareness that is our experiential present.

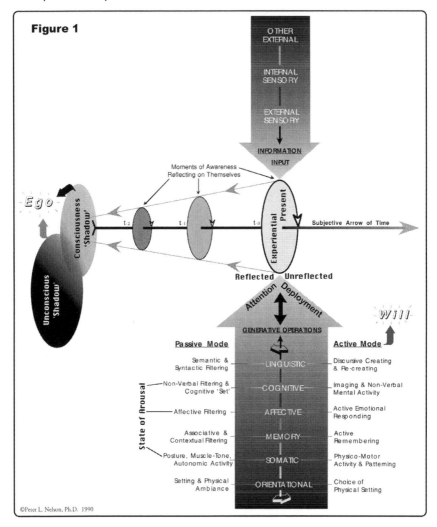

Figure 1

Attention is deployed by passive and active modes of participation, and the components comprising those and how they act are listed on either side of the upward vertical arrow, which represents attention. Consciousness is a shadow cast backward in time from our experiential present but experienced as if it is a container in which all this is happening. The technology of attention is represented by the deployment arrow. Differing states of consciousness would be represented by significant revisions of the roles and magnitudes of the different combinations of the components (inputs and deployment drivers) that determine the experiential moment in the present. The ongoing comparison we all do between our experiential present and moments not long past (t_1, t_2, etc.), enables us to reflect on whether or not our state of consciousness has changed.

Attention disorders, as they are known in the psychiatric and clinical psychology worlds, are styles of attending that do not work well for participation in the cultural frame in which we live. From my point of view, such issues are disorders in a psychiatric context only; they are not to be understood as deviations from an absolute standard of a so-called healthy brain. That standard is a fixed point of view known to work well in a particular socio-cultural context, but other attentional approaches may have uses outside of those confines.

Certainly, a *seer*'s way of paying attention—time-sharing attention between two radically different streams of knowing—is not ideal for meeting the demands of life in a Western culture, where we are expected to attend to just one stream of information, which we are taught to further filter in order to obtain opportunities for social, physical and economic gain. From a *seer*'s point of view that is a highly limited way of meeting the world and like all fixed points of view, it has even greater limitations when it comes to problem solving, especially in life and death situations. Indeed, ignoring alternative ways of knowing can be fatal in some instances (see Chapter 20).

Opening a new or modified point of view (a kind of "refreshed" knowing) results from disrupting our usual style, quality, and direction of attention. We achieve this by purposively altering the underlying drivers and maintainers (technology) of attention deployment that (consciously or unconsciously) preserve our usual point of view. In effect we do something internally that alters the parametric properties that determine what we know, hence creating a different experience of knowing.

In relation to that underlying technology of attention I have come to the conclusion that we generally employ three basic styles. These operate in most points of view in which we find ourselves, and their use often helps to fix and maintain a given point of view. For a *seer*, it is fundamentally important to understand the qualities and mechanisms of these three styles of attention and hence the tone and meaning they give to our knowing. Each determines the emotional tone and quality of the knowledge we create and our understanding of the causes and meanings of events as they unfold around us. The first of these styles I have dubbed the Watcher, or witness; the second the Judge, or evaluator; and the third the Paranoid, or reactor.

The Watcher (witness) just notices what is in awareness—not as a self-conscious act but as an open, here-now presence witnessing the goings-on in the world around it—without comment or reaction, the way an observer on a railway platform just notes the size, shape, color, and destination of the trains as they pass through. It is a present-centered awareness that does not cling to what comes into the focus of attention, but only experiences its qualities as it passes by. It is a knowing of events around us, and a knowing of that knowing, that does not hold onto the moment but relinquishes it for the next—the way a person on one of those trains views the passing landscape as a spectacle that he is in but not enmeshed with.

The Judge (evaluator) clings to what is known in order to evaluate it. The evaluator wants to know if this perception is good or bad, right or wrong, up or down, useful or useless, etc. The Judge wants to keep or discard, collect or throw away what is known. For the Judge, the contents of awareness have value and meaning and are adopted as truth or rejected as falsehood. In other words, a charge, meaning, or valence has been added to the direct, unadorned knowing of the Witness.

The Paranoid (reactor) reacts to those judgments as if they are real objects of awareness in their own right with personal meaning that can harm or help the perceiver. As part of this reaction, everything is given an intense emotional charge and is experienced as either threatening or safe, punishing or rewarding, etc. Thus the reactor (Paranoid) gives judgments a high emotional valence and reacts to the projected charge of each particular awareness as if it is a real attribute of what is perceived.

We should think of the Watcher as an open, baseline awareness, the Judge as the Watcher with something extra added, and the Paranoid as the Judge with something extra again. Remove the additions to perception and only witnessing is left. Further, the witnessing and the witness merge to become one and the same when one is not engaging as an evaluator or a reactor.

I am using the term "paranoia" here in two ways. The negative, fearful, and persecutory aspects are generally well known but to my mind the term also includes states of intense desire and obsession. This can be focused on objects (a new car), goals (a job or income level), states of being (love or enlightenment), and people. Using the term "paranoia" captures the intensity of the reactor's emotional charge and personal reactivity to his judgments. This intensity swallows the experient and leaves him obsessed with either danger and fear or desire and an obsession to possess. The intensity of this style of attention can range from mild to overwhelming and debilitating. In its most extreme form it leads to psychosis.

I certainly found myself deep in the paranoid style of knowing when Alice first presented me with those pages announcing my arrival in London written ten years before the events occurred. From within my fixed point of view such things were impossible, and anyone offering me something like that was *ipso facto* crazy or malevolent and might even represent a danger to me. Such an assessment usually initiates alarm-bells, bringing on a cascade of judgments and what-if scenarios that, subsequently, trigger an individual's hyper-charged reactions to his perceptions. Without a way to refocus attention, this can spin out of control, and in fact that was exactly what was about to happen when Alice asked me in a matter-of-fact way, "Would you like another cup of tea?"

With that she did something that I would not understand until later in my training. She used *intentionality* projected through her *field*, to push my attention onto a non-threatening subject, which had the effect of crashing my self-reinforcing, paranoid ideation loop. It wasn't the cup being thrust at me that changed everything, it was a direct use of her "will" with the cup as just a prop. As a result, I found myself rapidly calming down even before the tea was in my hand. Alice definitely knew what she was doing when she called my attention back to the present. She directly and purposively redeployed my attention and brought what had become the background into the foreground by making me aware, again, that I was there to drink tea with her.

My reaction was too intense for her words alone to work, but in combination with her *intentionality* the words forced an abrupt change of attention that terminated my Paranoid style of attending. My attention was forced to shift from an internal focus to an external one.

The Paranoid style of attention causes a kind of internal looping, where the image and feeling on which attention is fixed generate a charge that drives more fixation, which increases charge, causing renewed fixation, and so on, *ad infinitum*. Disrupt that attention cycle by shifting the awareness to something apparently in the background, and the loop is also disrupted. This gives the person a chance to notice the contrast between where he actually is and what his internal picture is telling him. Noticing the disconnect between these creates a small existential space that allows him to move more toward a return to the Witness.

Whenever my clients are in a reactive attentional style I give them a little exercise: I ask them to cast their attention on a background sound in their environment. A sound is best for this type of redeployment because it diverts a person from their usually dominant visual sense modality, a primary driver of attention. About two-thirds of the input to our brains come from the visual system, and it is therefore fundamental to maintaining the perceptual basis of our fixed point of view.

I have to add that such an exercise is only possible during moments of self-reflection that occur during non-psychotic paranoid episodes. Disrupting a subject's looping activity provides them with an opportunity to return to the Watcher or witness whose attentional position allows him to see how he is creating his current reality frame. In time, he can also learn to witness his habits of attention. Eventually, this process opens the door to being able to experiment with direct acts of redeployment of attention in more sophisticated ways than merely externalizing the attentional "gaze" to the background.

The power of a simple redeployment of attention is that it disrupts the mechanisms that maintain the old "story," allowing something new to arise in awareness. This change opens all kinds of possibilities even apart from being able to attend to the *second stream*. An inner space is opened, facilitating a refreshed perception of self and other, which has a profound effect on our ability to connect to and relate to others. It then becomes possible to see people in what I call their essence quality—a *field* presence we all manifest that reveals a person's core qualities, even when the person is attempting to hide them. The process of learning to redeploy attention at will loosens the fixedness of a point of view, making it more fluid and able to encompass a broader type of knowing—a more panoramic picture of what is there.

As attractive as an expanded, more fluid point of view may sound, the process of acquiring it often feels threatening to the new practitioner. The very ontological ground on which we believe we stand may be shaken, provoking fear. Yet as we move more deeply into this process and are able to live with the uncertainty it entails, the more panoramic view that arises will ultimately lead to greater compassion. We are recontextualized into a broader framework in which ego and a sense of self-importance remain, but at the same time we understand that, in the bigger picture, we are not important at all.

To free up our fixed point of view we first need to identify two or three of those "great truths" that we learned from our families or at school and question them. Such verities can be simple like, "Never trust a stranger," or "There is a right way and a wrong way." We need to drill down into the assumptions underlying such "fundamental truths." A common error is to believe that we must change our fixed points of view before we can question our basic assumptions. It can work that way, but attempting to disrupt dearly held beliefs to the point that it creates fear or annoyance can be an unpleasantly direct way of experiencing how we are maintaining the very fixed point of view we are attempting to alter.

Psychologist Gordon Allport did that sort of drilling down in his exploration of people's prejudices.[3] What he often found underlying these were contradictions and absurdities. For the most part, the individuals interviewed could not see or would not acknowledge these contradictions, because maintaining their fixed point of view was paramount. However, if our primary purpose is to discover these contradictions and absurdities, first we need to let ourselves simply acknowledge them.

---

[3]G. W. Allport, *The Nature of Prejudice* (Reading, MA: Addison-Wesley, 1954).

Once they are acknowledged, the entire point of view to which they give life starts to crumble and reform itself. The more we engage in this kind of activity, the more likely we are to get the essential message: a point of view is just that—a point of view, and not the absolute truth it is often taken to be. It is an assemblage of beliefs and attitudes that determine what we know, what we are, and what we can become. Once this is understood existentially, not just as an idea, it allows us to redeploy our attention at will and results in an opening in awareness that is powerfully liberating.

12. REMOVING THE SELF POINT OF VIEW

As my new and improbable life unfolded before me during my time in London, I did not at first fully register the import of those events or recognize how I was being transformed. Looking back, I realize that I was gradually discovering, without consciously understanding it, how to shift my attention and alter my epistemic frame. As I learned to deploy my attention differently, a new world of experience opened for me. Slowly, I was being shown how to attend to my other stream through a daily, living workshop where I could constantly test my awareness against another person's perceptions. As a result, my point of view was becoming more fluid and I was gaining the ability to be more flexible in the use of my attention.

Drilling down to uncover the basis of a fixed point of view requires that we examine the fundamental practices involved in its maintenance. To initiate that exploration, the first question we should ask is: "How do my thoughts and actions frame and reframe my knowing through the maintenance of my perceptions and worldview?" The next question is: "Who is maintaining that worldview? Who is the creator and driver behind the activities organizing my experiential world?"

The first question involves the machinery that maintains a fixed point of view, the second ponders who is ultimately running the show. The most fundamental driver of a fixed point of view is the self that creates a sense of one's existence. If we apply our analytic drill to our point of view regarding who and what we are, our very notion of an abiding and existent self also can be transformed.

Traditional techniques such as those described and further developed by the nineteenth century Tibetan Buddhist Lama Mi-Pham and those taught by the early twentieth century Advaita Vedanta guru Ramana Maharshi take us through the process of deconstructing our concept of self.[1] Loosening this fundamental point of view regarding who we are and what is can lead to the *sine qua non* of spiritual experiencing—called by some scholars the "introvertive mystical experience"—in which the totality of self disappears but conscious awareness remains.[2] Such a transformation happened to me as a result of my efforts to deconstruct my baseline point of view.

During one of my stays at Alice's flat in Hampstead, I noticed, sitting on a table, a drawing she had made. It appeared to be a stylized image of a human body being released from a pod-like structure and rising upward into an open space. When I asked her what had prompted her to draw such a picture, she said it came to her in a dream. As I was wont to do in those days, I immediately started to analyze her drawing as a symbolic dream about her and offered what I thought was a dazzling psychological interpretation. She listened politely until I paused to get her reaction, which I imagined would be to say how clever my interpretation was. Instead, in her usual matter-of-fact way she said, "It's not about me, it's about you." That stopped me in my tracks so I quickly dropped my attempt to guide her into an understanding of her unconscious, thinking she was perhaps not ready to face her inner self. The drawing was left behind—or so I thought.

About a year later I was living in Denmark, having become a graduate student again, this time at the University of Copenhagen. I was there as the result of a short tourist trip to Denmark during the summer of 1969. I had made contact with some students in Copenhagen who introduced me to a program at the Psychological Institute, where I applied and was accepted in 1970—subsequently dividing my time between there and London.

My first experience of a dissolution of the self point of view began as a rather ordinary evening of listening to music at a friend's apartment in the Christianshavn district of Copenhagen.[3] The building in which the

---

[1]Lama Mi-Pham, "The Wheel of Analytic Meditation," in *Calm and Clear*, ed. Tharthang Tulku (Emeryville, CA: Dharma Publishing, 1970), pp. 29–92.
Ramana Maharshi, *Who Am I?* (T. M. P. Mahadevan, Trans.) (S. India, Sri Ramanasramam: Tiruvannamalai, 1982).
[2]W. T. Stace, *Mysticism and Philosophy* (Philadelphia: Lippincott, 1960).
[3]This is an edited account that was originally published in: P. L. Nelson, "Mystical Experience and Radical Deconstruction: Through the Ontological Looking Glass," in

apartment was housed had been condemned, but as was common in Europe of the early 1970s, squatters, mainly students, often reclaimed such buildings because of the severe housing shortages at the time.

My friend's apartment was on the top story of a five-floor walk-up, and I arrived at about eight one weekday evening, somewhat out of breath from lugging my guitar up all those flights of stairs. I was a graduate student in psychophysiology and my friend, Jorgen, was in biology. Every Friday night we played music together in a local club to supplement our meager student incomes. This evening was supposed to be our rehearsal night, but as I entered, I found him preparing to leave. An emergency meeting of the squatters' committee had been called and he had to attend. Jorgen explained how to use his tape recorder and gave me a tape of blues music to listen to as he rushed out the door. His idea for our rehearsal evening was to take some tunes from the tape to add to our usual repertoire.

After he left I spooled the tape onto the machine and sat down to listen, but for some reason I was unable to focus my attention on the music. Each time I attempted to "get into" the song playing and map out the guitar lines, I found myself staring, in my mind's eye, at a very vivid and stylized visual image of myself. This image was an exaggerated caricature of a role that had long been part of my self-concept—"Peter the brilliant graduate student." In my mind's eye I could see me talking and gesturing with an exaggerated self-importance and conceit that I usually managed to disguise from myself in those days. However, seen in such direct bold relief and painful clarity, this internal picture made me mentally flinch. In my mind I scrambled to find something else on which to focus my attention and thus rid myself of this unwanted, absurd specter. Yet, each time I tried to focus my attention back to the task at hand—the music—I seemed unable to sustain any real concentration, with my focus continually drawn back, as if by a magnetic force, to my inner, caricatured self-portrait.

I cycled through this round of confrontation and avoidance several times, and as I struggled with it for the third or fourth time I was startled

---

Transpersonal Knowing: Exploring the Horizons of Consciousness, ed. T. Hart, P. L. Nelson and K. Puhakka (New York: SUNY, 2000), pp. 55–84.
http://www.socsci.biz/resources/ME&RD-Nelson.pdf.

by a voice talking to me—apparently from my left side. It seemed to come from outside like any other veridical aural perception, but no one was there and the quality of the voice was unlike my own internal discursive commentator.

It was, in a sense, both inside and outside of my head at the same time. I paused, looked around, and thought: "a hallucinatory projection." Again I attempted to return to normal thoughts and to the music, but as I did, I heard the voice again, very clearly this time, and it said, "You are what you are, and no matter what you think you are, you will remain what you are. It's all you've got, so you might as well look at it." I was startled by the suddenness and clarity of this second intrusion. My heart began to pound, but, like a man whistling in the dark, I nervously attempted once again to return to what I believed should have been my normal world. However, as I endeavored to reconnect to the music, which now seemed to be playing somewhere on the distant periphery of my awareness, the caricatured self-picture again returned. This time, for no apparent reason, other than a feeling of "why not?," I decided to heed the advice of the voice and look more closely at this image I was struggling to reject.

I now turned my full attention to that inner picture. My examination of my persona's behavior and qualities proved to be an exceedingly uncomfortable task, and my impulse was to drop the whole process and escape into some other, less confronting activity. However, as I persisted the fear abated and my interest grew in who this person actually was. A sense of curiosity and a somewhat detached interest took over. I found that as I persisted in attending to the image, my fear and revulsion lessened, and as that happened the demand that I look at it diminished. This led to an abatement of my avoidance behavior, followed eventually by the caricatured self-representation's fading from consciousness. In other words, the less I fought it, the less insistent it became. As it finally disappeared I thought that I had been released and at last was done with the whole business—not for long, however.

After this first image finally vanished, it quickly was replaced by another—"Peter the world traveler." Again I was confronted by the same feelings of discomfort and an impulse to reject, but this time I decided from the start not to resist, so instead of struggling against it, I continued the process of inner observation I had started with the first appearance. If not very pleasant, it was at least edifying in that it seemed to be a view of myself through a mirror not usually available to me.

During this process I made an important discovery—the negative power of these self-representations seemed to be directly proportional to the harshness of my judgment of them. The more I suspended the judgmental process and became an impartial observer, the more I could see and accept them, with the subsequent diminishment of their power to offend. Again, as in the first instance, the new image eventually faded but soon was replaced by yet another—"Peter the lover." This self-representation was more fraught with difficulty for me, and I found myself back in the previous, nervous struggle as I harshly judged what I saw. However, as I again gradually relinquished my stance as judge and reentered my newly discovered attitude of impartial witness, the voice spoke again. It asked, "Who is doing all this judging?" My mind raced as I attempted to find the "person" who had been evaluating all these personae.

I can only describe my next response in metaphorical terms. In an attempt to discover the knower who was observing the scenes I had been witnessing, it was as if I somehow rotated my eyes 180 degrees around to look inward to the "place" where I felt "he" resided inside my head. However, this type of total redeployment of my attention inward had an immediate and dramatic effect of its own.

To begin with, the room disappeared from my view, and then I heard a very loud rushing sound like a roaring waterfall that was accompanied by intense waves, somewhat like convulsive shivers, that ascended repeatedly upward through my body. It was like being cold, yet I was not chilled. Next, the experience rapidly increased in intensity, culminating with the sound roaring in my ears. Suddenly, I found myself standing in a great cathedral-like marble hall—much like a Byzantine mosque or church but without any evident religious symbolism or icons observable.

When I say "found myself," I mean that there was some kind of discontinuity in my awareness such that one moment I was sitting on a make-shift couch in a semi-derelict apartment and the next I was in a great stone hall without having instigated any physical change of which I was aware. The experience was fully veridical in the sense that, to my awareness, it had all the properties of me being physically in that place. It was nothing like any locale I had ever been in or seen previously, which added to its strangeness and the overpowering awe I was experiencing.

As I stood staring in amazement at this strange and impossible scene around me, I noticed that the ceiling was comprised of an enormous translucent glass dome with a large hole at its apex through which an intense, blue-white light was streaming. The light was almost like a spotlight that shone down on me where I stood, bathed in this supernal luminosity, mystified, dumbstruck. Looking down, I was shocked to discover that I was fastened to the floor in my upright position by a series of leather straps circumscribing where I stood—like spokes on a wheel—that at one end were connected by brass fittings to a heavy leather belt around my waist and at the other end to the floor by brass hooks. As I looked at my bonds they had a presence that seemed to speak to me as a symbol in a painting might convey meaning beyond form.

In this state I implicitly understood that these straps were the images or ego-trips that I had been inspecting in the theater of my mind only minutes before. At the very moment that I understood their symbolic import, the straps spontaneously unhooked from my belt one after another in rapid succession—the action circumscribing my waist like the motion of a wave. As I watched them unhook I had another thought: "It's me who always holds me down by living in my false selves." Now, no longer fastened to the floor, as it were, I seemed to become weightless and I began to float upward. My ascent was rapid, and I was soon passing through the hole at the top of the dome and into the brilliance of that supernal, white light.

As I advanced through the apex of the dome, the sound of rushing water that had continued throughout the episode abruptly stopped and, looking down (more as an act of attention than physical movement), I discovered that my body had vanished. All that remained of "me" was an undifferentiated awareness and a total conscious absorption of that awareness into the light that seemed to bathe me in total peace. I felt free—freer and lighter of being than I had ever felt in my life before or could have ever imagined feeling. My overall state was one of total and unqualified bliss and peace. There was no longer a "me," but somehow awareness was still there, although it was not really clear exactly who was having the awareness. I was conscious but did not exist in the usual sense that I had always understood as being in the world. I was one with everything.

I do not know how long I remained in this state—it might have been only minutes, but it could have been hours. There was no reference point for time, so, effectively, it did not exist. However long I remained in that blissful light does not matter. Having arrived there and being there was all that counted, but that was not a thought I had at the time. Later, when first attempting a post hoc interpretation of this episode, I came to identify my experience as a direct merger with the void—the "ultimate ground of being." No matter how one interprets this encounter of my merger into the light, what remains with me to this day is a wordless, core knowing of who I am beyond role or form—a transcendent sense of awareness-identity.

There were no thoughts while I was there, so it came as a shock when the voice abruptly returned and asked, "What are you going to hold on to now?" The impact of hearing this question intruding into my bliss caused me to become self-conscious. With that question came the thought that, indeed, I had given up everything I usually held on to, and suddenly I felt very vulnerable—like a cripple without his crutches—and I started to feel that I might go into a free fall or possibly even die if I did not grab hold of something solid and stable immediately. In retrospect, it was at that moment that I existentially understood Rudolf Otto's experience of the "creature feeling" when he confronted the "Mysterium Tremendum."[4]

At the core of my fear was an intense dread of not being able to return to my life as I had known it. This thought process generated a powerful anxiety, and with the emergence of emotional agitation the sound of rushing water returned with increasing intensity, rapidly followed by a feeling that I was plunging downward and out of the light. I was like Icarus falling away from the sun. The descent was short,

---

[4]R. Otto, *The Idea of the Holy* (Oxford: Oxford University Press, 1958).

intense, and felt like free-falling in space accompanied by a whooshing sound that grew in volume with the accelerating speed of my fall and ended with a loud, jarring but partially muffled thud as I re-entered my previous reality frame. Once again, I found myself sitting on the couch in my friend's Christianshavn apartment.

The sound of rushing water was still quite loud, and the waves of convulsive-like shivers continued as before my "exit" from the couch. I felt confused and torn. I desperately wanted to go back to that blissful state, but the requirement to let go of everything and feel like I was in a free fall with nothing to hold on to for safety kept me back. I sat and struggled between the two impulses for over an hour, and gradually the sound subsided and I knew that the window of opportunity for re-entry had passed. I tried to speak to an American friend who had come there with me that night, but for once in my life words failed me.

Later, when I told Alice what had happened, she said, "I know. That drawing of my dream was a representation of my *seeing* the event of your emergence." Not only had my self-understanding been radically altered by my self-deconstruction, I was stunned to realize that she had known this encounter was coming.

I was forced again to witness a seemingly impossible world unfold in front of me in real time. These events demanded that I become aware that I was part of something much greater than myself. The notion of a world in which people, places, and things were separate was crumbling, in spite of efforts to maintain my ideas regarding time, space and objects.

For the next three years I swung in and out of confusion and paranoia punctuated by moments of intense clarity. No matter how hard I tried to rationalize away what was happening, it continued to unfold in front of me. As many before me have discovered, denial is a tricky river to navigate without falling overboard.

13. REALITY TESTING

An important aspect of learning to live as a *seer* is engaging in the process of on-going reality testing. This is especially important during the first few years of training. Reality testing consists of matching our perceptions against ordinary sources of information to confirm or disconfirm what we believe we are *seeing*. Given my science background, I attempted to go about this process in a fairly rigorous manner and to err on the side of skepticism. For example, if I had received a particularly strong impression from a stranger in public, I would make an effort to approach him to verify or not my *second stream* perceptions. An example is the episode at the Oakland Airport reported in Chapter 9.

Sometimes this turned into a bit of a game, but I was continually surprised at the high level of accuracy of the results even as I was vigilant for signs of self-deception or misinterpretation. I continued to search for ordinary causes and sources to explain my apparent non-ordinary perceptions. Only when I was sure that what I had "picked up" was unavailable to me in any other way did I trust it as *seeing*.

For a novice *seer* self deception can arise from the influence of his own unconscious projections. During my existential psychoanalysis in the early 1960s I learned how to recognize the influence of my unconscious processes on my perceptions and later to use that awareness to identify possible sources of confabulation and projection. Through dream interpretation and the unraveling of defense mechanisms, I became proficient in tracing projections back to their source in my life and in my beliefs that may have been operating in the background. Although I had gone into analysis to deal with emotional and familial problems, the skills I acquired turned out to be of great use in learning to be a *seer*.

In my early years of training I was also learning that I did not make episodes of *seeing* happen; rather I opened to them—like turning one's head to look at something and just observing what is there. Opening to these perceptions required relaxing my usual focus and allowing my attention to redeploy to input other than my physical senses. This was not like learning the directed control required in a physical skill, such as shooting hoops in basketball. It was more like an internal act of letting go and allowing my attention to disengage from the usual ordinary perceptual stream and land on the *second stream* of information flow. The only directed or intentional aspect was the act of letting go and getting out of my own way, so to speak, which required giving up trying to make something happen, even though making something happen is precisely what I am doing when attempting to *see*.

When reality testing with people, there is the question of the trustworthiness of their responses when confronted with perceptions about themselves that may be denied or simply unwelcome. When I decided to speak to the anthropologist at the airport about my perceptions, I was aware of his openness to new and novel experiences. If he was not so inclined, he might well have become disturbed and possibly even angry at my intrusion, or he could have been a highly compliant person who likes to please others and so acquiesced to the "demand characteristics" (social pressure) to respond.[1] Maybe he was someone who was falsely compliant and manipulative and would go along with anything I said for some kind of personal gain. Again, knowing that he was an educated professional helped in my decision to talk to him, because such a person is not very likely to be compliant and is more prone to want accuracy of description.

Since I have engaged in many such testing situations over the years, the possibility that I selected for and got responses only from compliant individuals is highly unlikely. Of course, if one is really cynical, it could be argued that my unique perception was for finding compliant, passive-aggressive manipulators who would always feed me what I

---

[1] M. T. Orne, "On the Social Psychology of the Psychological Experiment with Particular Reference to Demand Characteristics and Their Implications," *American Psychologist,* 17 (1962), 776–83.

wanted to hear. Though that, too, would require a degree of *seeing* capacity.

Although successful reality-testing encounters became commonplace over the first three years of my mentoring, it still took a long time before I felt able to trust these perceptions without immediate, external verification. The knowledge I was accessing also continued to challenge my ideas about the nature of reality derived from my background in neuroscience and my philosophical training in reductive, logical-positivism. After about five years, however, I came to trust this *second stream* data. Of course, *seeing* is open to misconstrual, as is ordinary perception, but, in spite of my initial misgivings, it appeared to provide information as pragmatically reliable as ordinary sensory experiences, allowing me to make equally meaningful, consistent, and useful responses to the world.

Typical of the grounded and useful knowledge that arose out of my capacity to *see* was an incident that occurred when I was working for an internet start-up company in San Francisco in 2000. At the time I was designing performance and psychological testing instruments for an online management training website about to be launched by the company. Not long after arriving at its headquarters I was asked to attend a meeting with the senior vice president, Dave, who was in a particularly ebullient mood that day because the company had just found a new chief technology officer to replace one who had resigned. With some enthusiasm Dave described the new CTO's background, qualifications, and achievements and then asked if I had time to meet him. Of course I said yes.

Within minutes the new CTO appeared and we were introduced but as I shook his hand, a wave of unease came over me, and as he started to describe what he had been doing previously, I realized that his story was a lie—I could *see* the confabulatory process taking place as he smugly fed me what he thought would impress me. I also perceived that his *intentionality* was directed at creating deception and gaining power over those around him. After about five minutes I broke off our meeting without indicating anything of what I had *seen*.

Later I sought out Dave and told him that he must get the CEO to fire this new employee immediately. I insisted that the man was a fraud and dangerous to the company—to me it was as plain as if he was wearing a sign announcing his intention. Dave became annoyed and defended the new man, recounting his supposed achievements, which apparently included involvement in the development of the computer language XML, another of the new employee's lies. Our exchange consisted of several volleys of accusations and counters, ending with him telling me I was wrong and not to worry. Case dismissed.

Over the next couple of months the new CTO's behavior became increasingly erratic and bizarre. Then, on the last day before Christmas break, the company's CEO called me into his office. He was agonizing over what to do about a recent sexual harassment complaint against the CTO. I do not know whether Dave had spoken to him about my earlier concerns or if the boss had called me into his office just to be a sounding board because of my background in psychology. After telling me of the complaint, however, he confessed that it had been difficult to find a senior technology officer in the highly competitive Bay Area environment and I became aware that, as a "people person," he hated to fire anyone.

Nevertheless, when he asked my advice, without hesitating I said, "Get rid of him." Despite this, my boss decided on a wait-and-see approach, which turned out to be fatal for the company. Seven months later, on Friday, July 13, 2001, I received a call from the CEO at my home office as I was working on the computerization of a team-building assessment instrument. Out of the blue he said: "We're broke and the company is finished. We're closing our doors this afternoon."

I had known nothing about funding problems, so his announcement came as a shock. I said, "What the hell happened?"

It turned out that the venture capitalist who was backing the company had arrived to write another two million dollar check, but before he did, somehow he received information that our new CTO was a known felon who was on parole awaiting sentencing for defrauding a high-tech company and had been forbidden by the court to work for any other company. With this discovery, the venture capitalist lost faith in the management and withdrew his support.

My boss then told me there was just enough money to give employees their last paychecks and he was putting mine in the mail that afternoon. He was true to his word, but my interesting, cutting-edge job combining social science and high-end technology was gone. And regarding my initial *seeing* of the fraudster CTO, the evidence was in.

Later I was annoyed that neither the VP nor the CEO had taken my comments about the new employee seriously. In fact the VP never even acknowledged that I had warned him. It turned out that no one had run a proper background check either. I could have done it, but I assumed that the people who did the hiring had taken care of it and anyway my efforts might have been seen as interference by upper management. Of course, I did not say anything about being a *seer,* as I rarely shared this information with colleagues and I knew that making claims that my knowledge came through *seeing* probably would have caused me to be fired too.

These days I usually warn my students not to broadcast their capacity for *seeing* in a work environment. There can be a distinct downside to doing so, as one student of mine discovered. In the early 1980s, while living in the Northern Beaches area of Sydney, Australia, I offered a series of workshops on how to develop *seeing* capacity. The classes were publicly advertised and both sessions filled quickly. One of the workshops was attended by a man and woman, both in their thirties. She was particularly good at a number of the exercises and was quite enthusiastic, but he seemed to be not so involved and was probably only there to support her. At the end of the day, they approached me and she announced that they were detectives, although they were not attending in an official capacity—she simply had a personal interest. She told me her family were Coptic Christians from Egypt and that, where she came from, claims of *seeing* were quite normal.

A few weeks later she phoned me, all excited, to tell me that she had solved a case using one of the techniques I had taught her. The case involved a woman in her late 60s who had been brutally assaulted and raped. Afterward, lying in the hospital, the victim was semi-conscious and unable to speak, so the detective decided to do psychometry on her to see if she could perceive anything about the attack.

For a few minutes she held the woman's hand and redeployed her attention in the way I had taught her. To her surprise, she suddenly *saw* a picture in her mind's eye of a 15-year-old boy who was known to police over a series of petty crimes, mostly bicycle thefts. She thought it strange that she was seeing him in this context, but he was big for his age and, in her words, "slightly retarded" so she went to her senior officer and told him of her suspicions but did not say why she thought he might be involved.

The officer told her to pick up the boy and bring him in for questioning, which she did, but as she and her partner led the teenager into the station, suddenly he became agitated and spontaneously blurted out a confession to the assault and rape. Later my student could not resist telling her senior officer how she had settled on the boy as the main suspect but she was not prepared for the tirade that ensued when he threatened to fire her if ever again she used what he called "magic tricks" to solve a case. Her jubilation dashed, she told me that she had learned an important lesson—not to announce that she used her *seeing* ability in police work, or, at the very least, to ascertain first whether talking about her capacity for non-ordinary perception would be acceptable.

Despite the importance of reality testing our perceptions as *seers*, we are not always in a position to do so, especially in the early stages of training. Moreover, there is rarely a perfect match between *seen* perceptions and events of the ordinary, sensate world. However, with time we learn to recognize internally the unique phenomenological "signature" of a *seeing* perception that marks it as different from ordinary perception, cognitive interpretations, memories, or projected fantasies. Ruthless self assessment is imperative in not allowing ourselves to blur differences or too easily crediting ourselves with successfully *seeing*, when what we think we know may be the result of a deduction made from subtle cues or unconscious projections.

14. FEAR AND COMPASSION—HOLDING ON AND LETTING GO

Returning to the US in 1976 after two years in Australia, where I had gone to take up a teaching job, I was struck by a new fad that popped up in almost every social situation I encountered. I was asked constantly if I was "comfortable" with this or that. Being comfortable seemed to have become the highest priority in life, given the frequency with which the subject was raised.

The underlying message appeared to be that conflicts, problems, and other difficulties would pale into insignificance if only the glow of all-embracing comfort could be maintained. Now, everyone likes to be comfortable, but this is not one of the goals in becoming a *seer*. Neither my original "leap" into *seeing* nor any of my experiences thereafter have been accompanied by soft, New Age music, and supportive friends and lovers in a fear-free context. "Fine," someone might say, "I'll get to the next step in my developmental path as a *seer* when I am "ready" (read: comfortable with change), when my fate or karma lists it on the upcoming agenda. It has been my experience that even when "fate" swept me relentlessly into dramatic life changes, it was not necessarily when I thought I was ready.

A striking example of such a confrontation between opening to a new reality through *seeing* and my sense of being ready or "comfortable" about it occurred during the summer of 1976, when I was staying in a beautiful old Victorian flat on Commonwealth Avenue in the Back Bay section of Boston. The flat was the home of two brothers, Mark and Richard, cousins of a friend of mine. Immediately after returning to the USA, I had gone to Boston to visit my older brother. There being very little room at his flat, I called my friend, who introduced me to her cousins, who agreed to house me for a couple of weeks until I found work and my own accommodation. I first stayed in

Mark's room while he was away and then in Richard's larger, more private room when he went out of town.

It was during my weekend in Richard's room that I decided to resume practicing a particular attention exercise I had used regularly during my time as a graduate student in Copenhagen. As part of it I would place a burning candle on the coffee table and then sit on the couch, cross-legged, staring at the flame. There needed to be no draft in the room so the flame would remain as steady as possible. I would take a deep breath, relax, and then begin to gaze at the flame. This was not a fixed, hard stare but a relaxed melding of my attention with the flame. After a few minutes—provided I relaxed well enough—some visual change typically would occur. The light of the flame would usually alter, and then something unusual might appear. This activity was much like traditional scrying, although I did not know it at the time, nor did I have the requisite crystal ball.

That evening in Richard's room, the first change I noticed after settling into my session with the candle was to see a face briefly appear and then disappear in the broadest part of the flame. While not completely differentiated from the form of the flame, the face was distinct nonetheless.

When something unexpected emerges and then quickly vanishes in front of our eyes, the natural tendency is either to do something to avoid it occurring again or to pursue it. In this instance I chose the chase, but as was often the case, the effort was unsuccessful. Even though I still hoped to see the face return, experience had taught me that what emerges in the moment is a perception connected to a particular state of consciousness at a particular time and, unlike a video game, cannot be turned on and off. In fact, if we can manipulate it, it is probably only being generated by our imagination. So, once again I relaxed my gaze into the flame, trying to expect nothing.

After several minutes my relaxed state abruptly ended when suddenly the entire room seemed to rotate 360 degrees on its vertical axis with me at its center. The experience was accompanied by a loud whooshing sound that stopped abruptly at the end of what felt like a single rotation. I looked up and in front of me, on the other side of the coffee table, stood two life-sized, human-like beings, both staring at me.

They appeared as solid and real as any veridical object I had ever seen. One was slightly taller than the other, and both were cloaked in metallic-gray hooded robes, shaped like those worn by medieval monks. Their oval, human-like faces were pale and they had dark eyes. For some reason I thought of the taller one as male and the shorter one as female. They were looking intently but impassively at me with no discernable emotion revealed through their faces.

I was shocked. I had locked the door to the room before starting the exercise to be certain no one would disturb me. My mind raced: "How did they get in here? Who are they? What do they want? WHAT THE HELL IS GOING ON HERE?" My mind leapt from one attempted explanation to another at "warp" speed, trying to make sense of the impossible.

As I struggled, I heard a voice say, "You called us, what do you want?" I was certain that it came from the taller of the two beings.

"Called you?" I thought. "I didn't call you."

Then there occurred what can only be described as a perturbation in the *field* around me, engendering a feeling that they were annoyed or impatient with me. The voice returned: "You called us, what do you want?" it insisted.

I was in a profound internal struggle at this point, a debate raging in my mind as to whether these apparently disincarnate beings were real or unreal, good or bad, or what. They certainly did not generate any feelings of comfort.

For several moments they remained standing still on the other side of the coffee table, apparently waiting for me to say why I had called them. No matter what I came up with as I raced through possible scenarios, I could not decide whether the situation was safe enough to accept them and respond. I certainly had no recollection of having called them. Try as I might, I was unable to form a response, or even find the desire to do so, because my cognitive process was drowning in panic about who they were and whether or not I was in danger.

Another wave of impatience emanated from them as I remained in my stalled condition. My mind began looping through attempts to normalize the situation like a computer subroutine without an exit condition. I was caught in a vicious infinite regress, each conclusion about what was happening taking me deeper into the impossible situation I was attempting to rationalize away. My fear started to spin out of control but then, as my internal process made a screeching turn into panic, the room did another rapid, horizontal spin, accompanied by a rushing sound similar to the earlier one, and they were gone.

I was still on the couch, the candle burning, the door closed and locked, but now the room, except for me, was empty. I looked at the flame again, half hoping, half fearing to see the face that had preceded the appearance of the two entities, though I knew that, in all likelihood, nothing would be there. By this stage, my levels of fear and adrenalin were too intense to allow any focused attention or engagement. Afterward, however, when I replayed the event in my mind, I could see clearly that the *fields* of the two beings had been like calm and open pools, emanating no discernable threat at all. The real source of my fear was myself. It came from the loss of my sense of control. Later I regretted reacting this way but realized that I would have to just live with the lost opportunity as any attempt to chase down and recapture that non-ordinary moment would be futile.

***

Fear is a highly significant issue for *seers*. First, there is the fear we encounter when we enter a world of experience that is unexpected or disturbing, especially in relation to our beliefs about reality. Second, there is the fear others have about the existence of non-ordinary knowing and therefore about us as *seers*. The former is an inner obstacle to the range of experience possible for us as *seers*, while the latter can create roadblocks to our development, including whether or not we choose to engage the world openly as a *seer*, because it engenders in us doubts about who we are (a delusional crazy, perhaps?). Both types of fear are disturbing, and the desire to not feel disturbed can facilitate denial that inhibits our development. On the other hand, if we choose to rebel against social forces such as scientism, we may find ourselves adopting a whole range of mutually supportive beliefs based more on fantasy than the direct, pragmatic experience emphasized by *seers*.

Regarding the first type of fear, becoming a *seer* can engender the loss of our sense of who we are and what being normal is, as happened in my case. The perceived risk of being considered a social outcast can exacerbate anxiety. Yet once the neophyte *seer* has commenced this path of development, no return is possible; the only way forward is acceptance of what is unfolding. We are not required to, nor can we, erase our personal history in order to deal with this transformation, as the character don Juan suggests Carlos Castaneda do in his famous books.[1] Rather, we have to accept that from now on relationships are going to be made on a different basis and some people who have been close in the past will become more distant. For me, during the early phase of my transformation, I always tried to remember what I had learned from my LSD experience—that when fear arises and threatens to overwhelm me, I should embrace it.

Regarding the second type of fear, those who maintain that *seeing* is impossible often react with rage and condemnation to the suggestion that non-ordinary perception can occur, as the Sydney detective's senior officer did. I have often observed the resistance of many "fair-minded" people when they are asked to depart even slightly from what they hold to be true. I also remember how threatened I felt when being introduced to the world of *seeing*. The loss of ontological ground, our basic sense of what is real, is like a death, and we usually try to avoid it at all cost.

I now believe that it is fear that prevents us from changing our perspectives, whether as a *seer* or as someone merely entertaining the possibility of the reality of *seeing*. Ultimately, this is a fear of death, whether that be the "little death" of beliefs and values or the "big death" of one's physical self.

I once read an article about fire-walking in which the author described his experience of walking over burning coals as a confrontation with fear. In that case, we can agree, I think, that there was something to be frightened of—burnt feet. Beneath such corporeal fear, however, is the fear of any change in what and who we are. This confrontation is like waking up to a world where nothing is the same as it was before, forcing one to ask, "Who am I? How should I behave? What am I now supposed to think and feel? What can I believe and

---

[1] For example: C. Castaneda, *Journey to Ixtlan: The Lessons of Don Juan* (New York: Simon & Schuster, 1972).

what are the rules in this new place? Will I still be okay, if I let go and move with the changing tide?"

It has been my experience, while going through my evolution as a *seer* and watching others do the same, that no matter how open to change we think we are, in the face of transformation we try to hold fast to the familiar. It's safe. We know who and where we are, which gives us the illusion that we can control our situations. Ironically, we seek the new but want to accept it from the security of the old frame. No one actually likes the arrival of the radically new any more than they enjoy the shock of icy water on their warm body first thing in the morning. The recoil is instant, and the number one task becomes re-establishing the previous state of comfort.

The first step in dealing with ontological disruption is to acknowledge fear. The second is to accept fear as the inevitable partner of growth of awareness as a *seer*. Fear is a messenger sent by us to ourselves. It tells us that we are nearing the perimeter of our comfort zone and no longer feel in control of where we are going. Yet fear only becomes a hazard when we allow it to run wild and turn into panic. In fact, since it often heralds the approach of something new and unfamiliar, it signals that it is a time to become a Watcher.

Our only chance at successful navigation of the waters of fear is to let go of trying to control the situation and, instead, accept it as it appears. I failed to do that when I encountered the two beings in Boston. On that occasion I experienced my confrontation with the non-ordinary as too far beyond my comfort zone. The more tightly I clung to my notions of what was reasonable, the more I panicked, until I succeeded in disrupting my attention sufficiently to make it stop. There are sound reasons for controlling panic. Sometimes an extreme level of panicked, internal struggle can precipitate a psychotic state, if the subject becomes decentered enough and does not have the capacity or skill to reground himself.

During my transformation into a conscious *seer* I often wondered why a change in belief was so painful and difficult. Clearly, it was because I was struggling to explain my experiences in terms I already understood and accepted and could not see them as "real" until I did so. Since I could not really achieve this, my life became a paradox that for several years required me to live in an uncertain world. During that time, I discovered another important quality needed when entering into the world of *seeing*—perseverance in the face of ambiguity. I had to give up demanding that the events fit into a rational and coherent picture and just stay with the open-endedness of the direct experience of the process.

There are two types of perseverance to consider. The first is the capacity to keep our attention on whatever is happening without rationalizing it away or running from it. We must remain steadfast, in spite of fear but without panicking. If we do run away we should not consider it a failure if it leads to a learning opportunity that helps us in future encounters. In short, perseverance means patience and focused attention, which together allow for non-judgmental, trial-and-error learning through the eyes of a Watcher.

The second type of perseverance is the faith needed to continue practicing the steps necessary for *seeing* over long periods without a payoff or even the promise of an explanation—an end to the movie where all is revealed. I found that attempts to artificially force *seeing* situations to occur were doomed to failure. Instead, there is something natural and spontaneous about the developmental steps into *seeing*. I learned that I had to just set the stage, as it were, and then go on living my life, to become a seeker without *trying* to seek. This is the same paradox that surrounds personal or spiritual growth—effort without effort, trying not to try until we even give that up, only to find that the door was open all the time.

Having said this, I recognize that trying to make events occur is a universal response, as I discovered when I became a teacher of *seeing*.

The fundamental error lies in thinking that we can adopt a belief system and then set rules and perform rituals that will do the trick by bringing on visions and enlightenment, for example. In my own case, I was so uncertain about the outcome and even whether or not my efforts paid off that I held on to my old beliefs and practices just in case. The result was that I was torn by indecision yet it was through this internal struggle that I eventually learned about the most important act we can engage in—letting go.

An Australian Buddhist monk once told me that holding on is like witnessing a tree that is starting to break down and die.[2] If the tree is in a forest, then we witness its transformation as just part of the wondrous cycle of nature—and that's okay. If it is in a neighbor's garden, then it is his problem and not a tragedy either—still okay. But if it is in our own backyard, then the change becomes serious, indeed. We try to save the tree and worry a great deal about its condition. It is not okay and we hold on to keeping the tree as we always knew it. In all three cases, however, it is just a tree and the process is the same. Letting go allows us to become a witness, no matter what our relationship is to the tree. This is how we must learn to view our fear and discomfort when pushing our boundaries and, as I have said, learning to live as a *seer* does push boundaries in profound and fundamental ways.

***

Fear is probably the most basic force determining how we behave. It underpins our fundamental orientation, determining what we pay attention to and how we evaluate what comes into our awareness. Fear is not always conscious like that experienced by a character in a horror movie. Most fear is primarily unconscious, shaping what we allow ourselves to do and know, and it prevents us from really communicating with each other.

Our fear is a filter that determines whether a situation is "safe" by imbuing encounters with a charge—a valence that provides a read out of either "good" or "bad," "us" or "them." While becoming a *seer* I had many opportunities to experience my fear in action, which led me to evolve a different way of meeting people. These days, generally, I pay minimal attention to what people say or how they present themselves in dress or manner. Instead, I experience all encounters as if the person and I are suspended in a common existential pool—a shared *field*. Each wave or perturbation transmitted by one is felt by the other as it spreads through the *field*. Yet, unlike visual and verbal communications, I experience these signals not as external signs moving through objective time/space but as belonging to both sender and receiver, even as the source of the wave of activity remains clear. In other words, both otherness and selfness are perceived as taking place within the all-

---

[2]Thanks, Malcolm Huxter.

encompassing connectedness of the *field*. However, when fear underlies our interactions with others, this kind of meeting through a consciously shared *field* is not possible.

As a *seer*, I believe you have not actually met another person until there has been this kind of conscious *field* interaction. All else is an abstract, interpreted, imagined knowing of oneself, not the other. From this perspective, the notion of any real social connection via the internet in chat rooms and through email and social media is absurd. A developed *seer* can reach out across space and time and connect to the *field* of another person, to know them in a profound way, but for the average person this is mostly not possible. Many people do glimpse a direct knowing of another when they fall in love, for example. However, this kind of *field* connection takes place in a storm of accompanying fantasy projected by both individuals, based on their pasts and their desires for specific outcomes.

A clear, *field*-connected knowing of another person is also muddied by our prejudices, for example, when we only interact with people who we consider "good" or of our own kind. Whether or not we are *seers*, becoming aware of our evaluations (not necessarily throwing them away) allows us to remove an obstacle to perception. As a *seer*, I am always aware of the action of my filtering system—my point of view—in its role as perception sorter. Whenever I notice that I am in the Judge mode of attention—when people, things, and situations become good, bad, worthy, unworthy, and so on—I open out and connect with my *field* in order to know them in a less mediated way. This not only allows a deeper appreciation of whatever I am witnessing; it gives greater access to the *second stream* of knowing and thus a broader picture of what is in the *bio-field* of the other.

From my understanding, this way of meeting and knowing another person—a direct *field* connection without fear—is the basis of compassion. It might surprise you when I say that I am not compassionate by nature or on principle. Compassion as a principle does not work because, in my experience, it is often applied in a judgmental and contrived manner, as if the supposed compassionate person is playing a part in a drama called "being good." *Seeing* makes me aware of the very real difference between the *intentionality* in a person's *field* compared to their behavior. The latter may be designed to look like compassion, while the former shows the "hook" of an *intent* to create the impression that the subject is compassionate. At the heart of real compassion is dispassion—the act of open witnessing that I call "no-me, here-nowness."

The failure to establish and maintain connections of dispassionate, empathic knowing within a shared *field* leaves us in a self-encapsulated, self-focused state of *radical disconnectedness*. It is like living in a bubble and wherever you look, you see only your mirrored, projected self. At the heart of this disconnect lies fear of truly encountering another in a highly connected manner without judgment. From my perspective, many people are, in effect, interpersonally and intrapersonally stunted, attempting to do high-level people-centric tasks by relating to a fantasized other while staring at their own reflections. In contrast, the direct knowing of another is characterized by lack of a desired outcome and the wish only to know the other in his essence and as he knows himself.

***

As we can see, fear presents the novice *seer* with problems on multiple levels and, as we have also discovered, the only cure for it is to let go or, as I am wont to tell my students, "get out of your own way". But what exactly does this mean?

There are two stages to letting go. The first stage starts long before you find yourself in a situation of *seeing*. It entails a fundamental change in perspective, that begins with relinquishing "one cause fits all" beliefs and the absolutist thinking that maintains such beliefs. An unfortunate habit of many people is their attempt to find a single, final cause that explains everything in the universe. In most religions that cause is the Divine. In science it is the notion of a fundamental particle or form of energy. For people engaged in psychodynamic psychotherapy, everything that happens is due to the influence of unconscious psychological complexes. For the health conscious, what they eat appears to determine their physical, psychological, and spiritual wellbeing. Similarly, when one discovers the world of *seers*, "energy" and *seeing* are often reified as the ultimate explanation.

In my view, the best position to adopt is that there is no single cause or ultimate explanation for anything we experience (even this statement is at risk of being a one-method approach to understanding). In fact, experience is a mystery best summarized in the words of the Soto Zen Buddhist patriarch Dogen-Zenji: "There is no body and no mind... Everything is just a flashing into the vast phenomenal world."[3] In other words, phenomena appear and disappear, and the sources and meanings we ascribe to them are just that—our own ascriptions.[4] So, when we experience the phenomena of *seeing,* we must have planted in our minds that we probably will not know from where and how these phenomena ultimately arise, and their "goodness" or "badness" is most likely our own projected interpretation.

When we take as our fundamental position that there is no fundamental position and recognize the paradox that this implies for our existential world, the only choice is to let go and accept the experience of what is present to our awareness in the moment. Through this act of relinquishment, the inner cognitive-emotional struggle that often interferes with *seeing* can be released. If we are prepared in this way and sufficiently disciplined, then at the critical moment of confronting a highly ambiguous non-ordinary situation we will avoid entering into an internal battle as I did during my encounter in Boston. Instead, we will make ourselves wholly available to the experience.

By recommending that you adopt this fundamental philosophical position I am not suggesting that at the moment of *seeing* you undertake a deconstructive intellectual analysis of the ontological reality of the situation (though I have undertaken such analysis elsewhere).[5] Fear does not function at the level of intellect. When a *seeing* experience

---

[3]S. Suzuki, *Zen Mind, Beginner's Mind* (New York: Weatherhill, 1970), pp. 101, 103.
[4]I have written in more technical detail about "ontological neutralism" in relation to science and research in P. L. Nelson and J. D. Howell, "A Psycho-social Phenomenological Methodology for Conducting Operational, Ontologically Neutral Research into Religious and Altered State Experiences," *Journal for the Psychology of Religion,* 2–3 (1993–94), 1–48; http://www.socsci.biz/resources/Methodology.pdf.
[5]P. L. Nelson, "Mystical Experience and Radical Deconstruction: Through the Ontological Looking Glass," in *Transpersonal Knowing: Exploring the Horizons of Consciousness,* ed. T. Hart, P. L. Nelson and K. Puhakka (New York: SUNY, 2000), pp. 55-84; http://www.socsci.biz/resources/ME&RD-Nelson.pdf.

emerges, apparently *ex nihilo,* fear strikes as a kind of shock to our systems that is certainly not amenable to any kind of analytic discourse.

The second stage of letting go is to relinquish the process of panic and just remain present with the experience and any attendant fear. Panic is the desire to run or fight that often accompanies fear. The more intense the fear, the more urgent is the desire to counteract it by either attacking its source or fleeing. Another technique we have is to disguise fear by rationalizing what happened, which is nothing more than a symbolic mental "fight or flight" response.

The key to this and all other acts of letting go is to remember that no matter what is happening, there *is* someone "minding the shop"—the Watcher. The style of the Watcher is to witness what is going on—the setting and the actors in the drama. This "observing self" in a "receptive mode," as Deikman described it,[6] is the witness, while the constant commentary in your head is you telling yourself what you are observing: "Now you're feeling panicky, now you're trying to push for what you want, now you want this, now that." It observes, it knows, and if you know how to listen for it, it tells you what is going on in a straightforward, unadorned way.

What is actually required at the moment of a *seeing* encounter is to consolidate oneself into one's center while relinquishing the desire to engage in "fight or flight." The only way we can do this is by centering ourselves through long-term, regular meditation or similar contemplative exercises (non-macho martial arts, for example, or non-supplicatory prayer). If some kind of self-defense is really required, it will only become apparent after relinquishing the fight or flight response. In other words, the only truly self-preserving act is, again, to let go and get out of your own way by being present as a witness—the dispassion at the heart of compassion.

---

[6]A. J. Deikman, *The Observing Self: Mysticism and Psychotherapy* (Boston: Beacon Press, 1982).

IV. The Varieties of *Seeing* Experience

This is the mystery. When you understand one thing through and through, you understand everything. When you try to understand everything, you will not understand anything. The best way is to understand yourself, and then you will understand everything.

– Shunryu Suzuki Roshi
Zen Mind, Beginner's Mind

15. The *Field, Content,* and *Tone*

Now it is time to discuss some of the technical aspects of *seeing*, to talk about how *seers* deploy their attention, what they do in this process, and to uncover the various types of *seeing* that are practiced by me. This exploration of the styles and mechanisms of non-ordinary attention deployment begins with a description of the primary ground of all *seeing:* that which I call the *field.*

The *field* is an energetic emanation associated with all living beings as well as most objects and places. It exists in varying density both within and around individuals and is affected by human activity and presence, just as it affects human beings in turn. Embedded in the *field* are types of information about people and places not available to our ordinary senses but which can be perceived by *seers.* Perhaps the best way to describe the *field* is that it carries the psychic-emotional *tone* associated with an organism or a place. Although it is analogous to a condensed physical energy field, having both charge (psycho-emotional) and intensity (presence), it is not, strictly speaking, a physical effect and cannot be directly measured using detectors such as those employed to show, for example, electro-magnetic activity.

I refer to the type of *field* emanating directly from any living organism as its *bio-field*, although throughout this book I also tend to use the term *field* on its own when talking about living things. While I coined the term *bio-field* in the 1970s, without knowing about parapsychologist Bill Roll's earlier use of the term, I discovered, in discussions with him in 1995 at his home in Villa Rica, Georgia, that we were generally in agreement as to what it denotes. It is my observation that the more complex the organism, the more specific and intense is its immediate, personal *field* and it takes a higher-order system, such as another organism, to detect it. That is, it takes one to know one.

As a *seer*, when perceiving someone's *bio-field,* I can articulate a description of the subject's emotional and psychological state, recount events from that person's history as well as directly perceive the connection of those events to aspects of the person's present psycho-emotional functioning. I refer to this as the *content* of the *field*. There is additional *content* that is transpersonal as well and may connect individuals to other places, people and entities.

What I call the *tone* of the field is generated by a combination of its informational state and *intentionality*. (I say more about *intentionality* in Chapter 17.) The *field's tone* is analogous to the frequency of a sound wave, which is usually understood as pitch, although the information conveyed by the *tone* of the *field* (and its *content)* is far more complex and detailed than a simple measure of frequency.

The *tone* can be thought of as equivalent to an intricate complex modulation of both frequency and amplitude of a physical signal and the *seer* perceiving the *field tone* acts as a "demodulating receiver" of the embedded information. The *tone* of a person's *bio-field* always has an overriding unique quality, as though each of us has a musical theme that defines us, much like those used to identify the characters in Sergei Prokofiev's orchestral work *Peter and the Wolf.*

The *fields* of places and objects are affected by the *bio-fields* of living things, and the more intense the *bio-field,* the more it affects the quality of the *tone* of other *fields*. Intense human activity associated with strong emotion tends to have the greatest impact. A good example is what I encountered in 1970 in the *field* of a building in Edinburgh, Scotland.

I had sailed by ship from Denmark to the United Kingdom to visit the relative of a Danish friend—an aunt who was living with her Scottish husband in Edinburgh. Arriving at the address I had been given, I found it to be one of those typical gray stone Victorian buildings in which each floor houses an individual apartment, or flat. My friend's aunt lived on the fourth floor. I entered the building and looked up through the central, open stairway to the skylight above. As I did, I felt an intense emotional jolt as I *saw* a man in workman's overalls fall through the open stairwell to his death. This perception was of an imprint in the *tone* of the building's *field* left by the intense burst of emotion discharging from the man as he fell, hit bottom, and died.

When I reached my destination, and after the usual social formalities and a cup of tea, I inquired about what I had *seen*. My hosts confirmed that, two to three years earlier, a painter had fallen from a scaffold suspended above the stairwell and died. Immediately they switched the conversation to another topic, and the incident was not mentioned again. No one even asked me how I knew about the workman and I felt that they did not want to know.

This is not unusual in my experience. I have often had people confirm an event I have *seen* and then show no interest in discussing it further. This is because, for many, an act of *seeing* raises a deep but unexpressed fear. The reaction is reflexive, unconscious and self-preserving as they close the shutter on awareness, metaphorically speaking. The topic and any related thoughts and feelings simply cease to exist for them. I can understand that, when confronted with an act of *seeing*, non-*seers* sometimes do this, as simple denial works best for them. A few will show interest, but this can have negative consequences. Either they try to undermine the credibility of the *seer* or conversely they seek to attach themselves to him, as if he is a guru with access to possibly divine revelations. Neither response is realistic or useful, in my view.

What are often described as hauntings or ghosts are usually intense imprints left in a place's *field*, giving its *tone* a certain quality that can influence what people report as the "feel" of the place. Unless they are *seers*, they will not necessarily know what is causing this feeling, but it will not stop them from registering a presence.

In my view, emotions are not only sensations that one feels in one's body as the result of various associated physiological functions, they also emanate as energetic forces that affect people and places around them, leaving their marks on *fields* and altering *tones*. Conversely, the *tone* of a place affects the people who enter it, and places, in turn, are affected by human activity occurring in them. Hence, a place with a particular *tonal* quality will attract people who like to be in such a presence.

Whether we believe it or not, the *bio-field* plays a major role in the maintenance or dissolution of behaviors and beliefs as well as one's physical and psychological well-being. A great many problems result from failing to give sufficient weight to the role of the *field* and its *contents* as the cause of what happens to us. Those consequences range from mental and physical health problems to the difficulties inevitably encountered when we stumble through life, blindly attempting to think our way to an understanding of what we perceive rather than directly knowing it.

The structure and quality of a *bio-field* are partially determined by stored information embedded in it. Each individual's field is comprised of a number of *tonal* layers with *content* embedded in them. This has its origins in our physiological functioning, life experiences, habits and beliefs, as well as in *content* picked up from the *fields* of animals, places and other people. These habits, beliefs and other *field* components, which directly influence the form and quality of the *bio-field,* are implanted consciously and unconsciously by parents, friends and society in general, starting in pregnancy, when there is a direct transfer from mother to child, as well as the other way around, and continuing throughout life.

When we interact with one another socially, our *bio-fields* interact too, and some *content* of the *bio-field* of one individual can, and often does, transfer to another. This activity usually occurs outside the awareness of the individuals involved, unless at least one of them is a *seer*. In addition, the intensity of the *bio-field* varies from person to person and within an individual over short and long terms.

The *bio-field* influences and in turn is influenced by the organism it is associated with–our bodies. This ebb and flow between the *bio-field* and our psycho-physical organism is fundamental to maintaining a sense of identity and a continuity of perception and awareness. The cycle of self-creation and maintenance is subject to change through internal actions and outside influences.

Through an act of *intentionality* one person's *field* can also be made to influence another's. By focusing his own *bio-field* using *intentionality*, a person can consciously and directly affect another's *field* and therefore his emotional and mental state and, in some cases, his physical state as well.

The plasticity of the *bio-field* has important consequences for a person's appearance. Unlike the physical body, whose physiognomy and morphology change slowly over time and in fairly predictable ways, the *bio-field* can change shape and intensity rapidly and with much greater variation. We often comment how different someone looks as a result of a changed emotional state, for example. The difference often seems greater than what physical markers, such as dress and facial expression, can account for. We occasionally even witness our friends' appearance changing from minute to minute as they go through mood shifts—with their mental and emotional changes showing in their *bio-fields*. Also, many of us have had the experience of walking down a street and seeing someone who seems quite large at a distance but close up appears smaller than we initially thought. In such cases, we are combining our conscious knowledge of physical size with an unconscious perception of the person's proportionately much larger *bio-field*.

The *bio-field* usually extends a distance ranging from inches to several feet from the person's physical body and in shape is generally congruent with it, though more ovoid. In some cases, however, the *field* is so diminished that it does not extend past the body's boundary. This situation may be indicative of a number of problems, ranging from severe psychological disorders, such as a dissociative state, to ill health and even impending death. In addition, the size and shape of the *bio-field* as well as its content may vary from a person's front to his back. Psychologically related *content* that he wants to hide from himself or others tends to appear in the back of the *field*. Thus, for a *seer*, the *bio-field* offers a unique window that allows direct access to many qualities indicative of a person's state of being.

When people speak of seeing auras around others, the colors perceived are actually picture analogues of the energetic qualities of the *bio-field*. Attempts to interpret the meaning of these colors and so-called "thought forms"—such as those described by occultists like Annie

Besant[1]—are fraught, as are all attempts to understand a person or a landscape with predefined interpretive maps. From this *seer*'s perspective, any perception of the *field* that has to be interpreted against some standard set of values and meanings is of little use. In fact, a directly felt and uninterpreted phenomenological description of the *field's tone* and *contents* yields much clearer and more useful information than can be gleaned through any interpretative scheme. Of course, it is fun to see colors and differently sized and shaped fields around people, but I urge caution to anyone who wants to make a decision about another person based on perceived visual form and color.

All *bio-fields* appear to have what can best be described as a membrane, or *field* edge, surrounding them. While it is not a physical membrane, it can be felt as one moves into another's *bio-field* as if popping through the outer edge of a bubble. The membrane is usually the outermost layer in a series of concentric "shells" that surround an individual. The size and number of shells depend on the person's physical, emotional, and existential state. Most people who are aware of these layers as they walk into them notice that the force required to penetrate each successive membrane as they move closer to someone's body varies depending on the subject's emotional openness as well as the degree and quality of *intentionality* he has directed into his surrounding *field*.

***

Many people attempt to practice empathic behavior by the unconscious merging of their *bio-field* with that of another, however this can give rise to two problems. Firstly, when a person merges his *field* with another, he may pick up *content* from the other person that may not be good for his emotional, psychological, or physical well-being. Just as you might avoid touching a person who has a cold to avoid getting a virus, so you should act with caution to prevent undesirable *content* from another to cross into your *field*. Secondly, the practice of merging tends to cause confusion about personal boundaries and identity. In order to *see* another person you should not mix yourself with them because in doing so, you are projecting your feelings and

---

[1] A. Besant, *Thought Forms* (Bel Air, CA: BiblioLife, 2008).

state of mind onto them and therefore, in effect, you are primarily seeing yourself. *Seers* understand that to perceive another's *field*, to know it directly, one must not be merged with it at the time.

Some highly pathological individuals, psychologically speaking, attempt to merge with many people during their lives. Especially prone to this behavior are those suffering from borderline personality disorder (BPD). These people are often psychically "starved" and therefore seek to "feed" wherever they can. The psychological processes that BPDs engage in are well documented in academic writing,[2] but what is less well known about them is that they also operate through *bio-field* merger and, in doing so, cause havoc for those who allow it. Although the disturbance caused is at the *field* level, the victim rarely understands this, making it difficult for him to comprehend what is occurring and even more challenging to extricate himself.

BPDs are not the only psychologically disordered people who operate this way, but they are the most extreme cases I have witnessed. Having said this, merging with another should not always be avoided. For instance, it is one of the beautiful experiences people can have when they are in love. It is also what takes place between a mother and child. However, merging with an ill-chosen person certainly can be disastrous.

A related problem is the case of those with highly narcissistic personalities. These individuals attempt to dominate others by overwhelming them with their *field*-presence, in effect taking over the *fields* of those around them. The recipients of such attempted control may experience this as an expanding pressure wave or an all pervasive enveloping of others that leaves no psychic space for anyone else to be noticed, and it is often, but not always, accompanied by verbal and physical acts of dominance. This is related to the topic of the person who "pushes the room" and I will explore that in more detail in Chapter 17 on *Intentionality*.

Another type of problem arises with those whom I call "open receivers" who believe that the way to be "kind" to others and be seen as "nice" is to offer a *field* merger to anyone who engages with them.

---

[2]T. Millon, S. Grossman, C. Millon, S. Meagher, and R. Ramnath, *Personality Disorders in Modern Life,* 2nd ed. (Hoboken, NJ: John Wiley & Sons, 2004).

Even though these "open receivers" appear warm and friendly, in reality they can be frightened and defended individuals who are using their "receiver" stance for self-protection. In effect they are manifesting hyper-vigilance, monitoring everyone for signs of danger, and attempting to disarm any potential threat through a type of "no-resistance" availability. It is the *intentionality* of the act that determines whether this is so. The danger in such behavior is that it rarely works and may leave those who do it feeling strange and unwell and open to the psychopathology of others.

Yet another source of problems related to the *bio-field* is unwanted openings, or "leaks," in the *field* edge. These can be caused by interactions with others, previous psychic or physical wounds or illness, and/or failure to engage in exercises designed to consolidate the personal *field* and keep it whole. For consolidating the *field,* sitting meditation is helpful, as well as breathing exercises designed to quiet the emotions and create a sense of well-being. These methods can be supplemented with direct, focused work on one's *field* or engaging the services of an energy healer who knows how to repair it. An additional method I have found helpful is to identify an energetically outflowing *field* source in nature—often found around streams or in forest groves—which, when you are in it, increases your sense of peace and wellbeing. Visiting such sites is something I have done throughout my life in order to recharge.

Often, experiences early in life condition people to suspend the filtering function of their *field* membrane, and as a result, the membrane allows just about anything to pass inside, resulting in physical or psychological illness and an unclear sense of self. In particular, lack of emotional nurturing in childhood, which has been identified as a cause of some personality disorders, is a primary source of developmental *field* problems, the borderline personality being a classic case of poor *field* formation. Such malformations are immediately apparent to a *seer.* The *bio-field* is irregular, ill-formed, and often swirling restlessly, attaching itself to any strong *field* source, in the hope that it will be nourished by it.

On the other hand, people with certain types of psychological disorders sometimes try to unload their unwanted *content* onto others.

In some cases this has a sadistic component, but for the most part, it is unconscious and driven—an internal struggle to remove anxiety and fear or to find a target for pent up anger. A developed *seer* can detect such an attempt to off-load *content* and does not permit it to happen.

In my experience, the most useful response to anyone trying to merge, draw, or off-load *content* is to remain neutral. If one's *intentionality* sends a signal of impartial disengagement, no unwanted connection will be possible. The ability to do this depends, in large part, on a person having a highly developed capacity for meeting the world as a Watcher.

16. FELT *SEEING* AND THE PERCEPTION OF *FIELD CONTENT*

Felt *seeing*—having a feeling about some person or place—is the simplest and most common type of spontaneous *seeing,* even in untrained people. For them it is experienced as a kind of generalized perception of the quality (*tone*) of a *field* that may also include bits of information about things, people and places (*content*) associated with it. For example, non-*seers* may say things like "I have a feeling that something good (or bad) happened here (or to someone I know)" even though they have had no direct contact with the events being sensed.

Of course, many people say this sort of thing when they are merely reflecting on their own emotions or expressing likes, dislikes, anxieties, and fears that are associatively triggered by a particular situation. However, the feeling level of *seeing* really has nothing to do with liking or disliking or the triggering of personal reactions. It is not an expression of our concerns and anxieties about others either. Rather, it is the ability to use feeling awareness to pick up the quality or *tone* of people and places apart from any verbal or physical information that may be available. Space and time are not obstacles to the felt level of *seeing,* although this kind of knowing occurs most often in relation to those with whom we are emotionally connected or during face-to-face meetings.

An experience I had in 1972 is a good example of felt *seeing*. At the time, I was a guest of a friend who lived near Berkeley Square in the fashionable West End of London. I had gone out in the early afternoon and arrived back at her apartment a few hours later. I opened the door and called out but then realized no one was home. Upon stepping into the entrance hall, I was confronted with a felt awareness of intense sadness, even despair, which had nothing to do with my own mood. It seemed to be a *field* effect coming from my right, so I followed the feeling to its source in the living room, where it was most intense around the couch in a corner opposite the door.

There I perceived my friend's presence at the center of a "cloud" that hung "condensed" in the air above the couch. At that instant, I knew she had been sitting in that spot earlier in the day and had experienced a sudden dive into depression that led, momentarily, to thoughts of suicide. It should be noted that, throughout this episode, my friend's emotional crisis seemed like it was going on in the present even though it had occurred in the past. This is very typical of the felt *seeing* of a *tone* and *contents* in a *field* associated with a place. Although I had become more confident as a *seer* by this time, nonetheless I reality-tested my perceptions against my friend's own experience by asking her, when she returned home, apparently in a good mood, about what I had perceived. She confirmed that she had been sitting on the couch and had started to feel deeply sad and did indeed briefly contemplate ending her life but she decided to shake off the blues by going out and becoming active. The importance of this type of testing in the course of becoming a balanced and accurate *seer* cannot be over-emphasized. All learning has a trial-and-error component, and this is no less true for *seeing*.

What is required for felt *seeing* to happen is an open, panoramic "no-me, here-nowness" that is the non-judgmental, aware attention of the receptive Watcher. This open witnessing momentarily removes us from the usual bustle of daily life, particularly from the dominance of physical sense perception. In suspending our engagement with physical and mental activity while in a mindful state, a kind of internal space is created that allows for *seeing* awareness to open. Most of the time we are too "noisy" internally, or too busy doing activities or focusing on the immediate aspects of our social and physical environments, to notice this more subtle *second stream* knowing.

This manner of receptive witnessing does not require figuring out what is going on. Rather than trying to ascertain meaning or making a judgment, one allows the mind to go into "idle" with the intention of absorbing whatever is in the field of one's awareness. This requires abandoning direct conscious control over the focus of the physical senses, as well as relaxing. Think of it as a bit like being in a meditation state that seeks no particular outcome.

As the *seer* achieves a more relaxed, receptive mode, he notices, after a time, that his attention is automatically drawn to certain objects, places, or people. Once the inner verbal activity of evaluating, categorizing, and naming things has ceased, a sense of presence or *felt* intensity in one part of the environment will seem to "call" our attention to it. Often this is how we first notice a particular *field* before gaining cognitive access to it.

The open awareness required for *field* perception is much like witnessing the passing scenery as we sit in a train and stare out the window. As we observe the changing scenery, we tend not to remember much of it. This is because we are in a purely observational mode, in which short term memory is not being translated into the long-term kind. Permanent retention seems to require linguistic engagement, such as commenting on or discussing some aspect of the observed landscape either in our minds or with others. For our *seeing* experiences to enter memory we need to be in the witnessing mode but also we need to take note of a particular perception and articulate it.

Only in the witnessing style of awareness can a person leave the object-oriented mode of daily, sensate consciousness and enter into a *seeing* state. This receptive mode has been extensively studied in the practice of meditation and the generation of mystical states of consciousness. The inner "opening" required to register such awareness tends to be found at times of centered stillness and is not unlike the frame of mind required for creative thinking or quiet contemplation. *Seeing* requires it, too, but when properly done, it is *not* an entry into an imaginary realm. Rather, it comes about because we open our awareness to the still place within us, enough to allow our attention to be caught by the special type of knowing that arises from attending to the *second stream*.

For those not trained as *seers,* it can be tricky to discriminate between one's own joys, fears, creative imaginings, and reactions, on the one hand, and genuine felt *seeing* (i.e., the joys, fears, creative imaginings, and reactions of others), on the other. However, with practice and guidance from a good teacher, one can learn to recognize that the "place" in our awareness that registers and knows our own feelings is also registering the *tones* that permeate the *fields* around us. Once we learn the technique of directing our attention in a discriminating way, we can usually separate personal feelings from those occurring "outside" us. The separation between personal and transpersonal is not always perfect, but neither is the interpretation of events known through ordinary perception.

For it to work well, it is essential that *seers* have a reasonable level of intrapersonal intelligence and a working knowledge of their own psychological processes.[1] By this I mean that they should have a non-resistive relationship with themselves, so they can know who they are in a non-defensive way. They must be deeply in touch with their personal feelings, have an understanding of how their unconscious desires and fantasies manifest in daily life, and be unafraid of acknowledging their own psychological issues.

By this I am not suggesting that a *seer* needs to be psychologically "fixed" by some therapist before he can practice *seeing*. The notion of "psychological health," so often touted in our culture, is actually an absurd idea. It grafts the pathogenic disease model of medicine onto psychic and emotional processes, as if there could be a trouble-free psychological condition. The real question is: does the *seer* understand his own processes well enough to differentiate what constitutes his inner, personal world from what he is receiving from the world around him? In other words, is he capable of knowing when his attention is folded in on itself (self-involved), and does he have the practical understanding of how to redeploy attention in order to perceive beyond himself?

Seeing awareness often is experienced as if it is coming through one of the five physical senses, even though *seeing* experiences are not physical perceptions of sight, sound, touch and so forth. Alice talked as if she felt the *field* and many of its qualities on her skin as a kind of somatic sensation, even though she could draw more information from it than was normally available through ordinary physical touch. My

---

[1] H. Gardner, *Frames of Mind: The Theory of Multiple Intelligences,* 2nd ed. (New York: Basic Books, 1993).

own *seeing* often produces emotions as well as pictures, words and sentences that appear in my mind's eye and ear, as if I am looking at an internal "scene" and/or hearing someone "speak" to me. In this way, information gleaned through an act of *seeing* the *field* can be understood as any combination of visual, auditory, and/or somatic awareness. The way it translates into the knowing of a *seer* depends on his perceptual style. In effect, each *seer* has a unique phenomenological approach.

***

When attention is deployed on the felt perception of the *field* of a particular location, what emerges into awareness is specific and localized information that can be about the place, people who have been there, and a variety of less common energetic constellations that have origins outside human activity. All of this *content* has a presence and life of its own and is connected to and resonant with the *tone* of the *field*. When I was first becoming aware of *fields,* I would walk around with my attention focused on the immediate *field* and, noting the *tonal* qualities or a specific place, I would move on to observe and compare my first perception with the attributes of subsequent places. Walking down a street was like moving through a variety of *tonal* pools that not only had very different qualities but had stored in them specific *content* and information that varied from place to place. Such information would cue me as to what was going on at a particular location, including what had happened recently—if it had been significant enough to leave more than a passing imprint on the *field*.

In those early explorations of *field tones* and *contents*, I used extensive reality checking to work out whether my perceptions were accurate or not. If something stood out in the *field's tone* or *contents*, I would start asking questions of people in the area, if possible. While some *tonal* and *content* formations bear no resemblance to and have no connection with physical events, most do. My constant checking proved a useful tool for refining my *field* perception to be able to discriminate the finer details of content.

Sensing the *field* while walking can be like moving through "soup." Some areas are "warmer" than others, and each place, besides having a particular tonal quality, contains a unique cluster of *content*. Sometimes these are intense and dramatic, as in the case of the building in Edinburgh, but mostly they are quite ordinary. The result of living consciously in the "liquid" that surrounds us is being aware of moving in and out of other people's *fields* all day long. This can be pleasant or not, as is true also in the world of ordinary perception. If someone is full of repressed rage, duplicitous intention, or is ill, I have to interact with those *field* emanations and *tonal* qualities along with dealing with the person on physical and verbal levels. I also have to keep this *felt* knowing separate from myself and prevent external *content* from resonating in me, causing an inadvertent merger and possibly adversely affecting me. It sounds complicated, but no more so than driving a car, once these processes become automatic.

Occasionally, I test situations before I arrive at a location. I can extend my felt *seeing* awareness over a distance and "touch" a person or situation so I have a direct line to the *field* and its *tone*, not unlike an amoeba extending one of its pseudopods as it tests the environment for the presence of food or danger. This approach is illustrated by an event I experienced some years ago.

A good friend called and said her little dog had been attacked by a larger one. Afterward, her pet seemed to be fine. That night it played and went to sleep but, in the early hours of the next morning, it jumped off the bed, ran out of the house, and was missing for the next two days. My friend wondered if I could *see* where her dog had gone. I extended my awareness but could not find the presence of this animal, which I knew well, so I decided, unhappily, that he was probably dead. What I had *seen* would have been different if the dog was alive and just in someone else's car or a long distance away. Because I was already connected to the animal and knew its *field*, noticing its absence (i.e., the absence of the *field*) was all I needed to know.

A problem I often face is what to tell someone about what I *see*. Going around *seeing* and quietly registering what I *see* in my own thoughts is one thing, having to communicate unwanted news to someone with an emotional attachment to the result is quite another. In this case, I knew the owner well and understood that she could handle it, so I simply said, "I'm sorry, he's dead. I'll come over and help you find him." After two days of summer heat since her pet had disappeared, it was not hard to do that just by using my nose.

Seers who specialize in some form of the healing arts do their work by first extending their awareness into the *bio-field* of a patient in order to examine its *contents*. Just as I look for psychological constellations, those *seers* tend to notice unusual markers left in the *field* by dysfunctional organ systems or physiological processes. A young medical practitioner who attended one of my development workshops in Sydney, Australia, in the 1980s was particularly gifted at doing this, even though, when he arrived for the training session, he did not mention that he was a doctor or that he used his *seeing* capacity with his patients.

In the course of the workshop I assigned people to work in pairs for an exercise involving body "scans." This required one student to extend his personal *field* to examine his partner's body and to report any prominent or unusual perceptions. The person being scanned was then required to provide feedback about the accuracy of the scanner's perceptions. The physician surprised us with the accuracy and depth of his observations. Not only did he correctly report every medical condition known to his subject (and there were several), he was also able to name, without physically seeing them, the locations of scars on her body from prior surgeries. Later he revealed to us that he did this as part of his medical practice but kept it quiet. In line with proper procedure, he called for all the standard tests to be done, but allowed himself to be guided in part by his *seeing* ability.

Another example of perceiving the *tone* and *contents* of the *field* occurred when I visited a farmhouse outside the town of Keswick in the north of England. The original building was four centuries old and looked like it had been continuously occupied since it was first built. The long period of human presence left a strong *tone*—varied, dense, and disjointed—in the *field* in and around the building. As I stood in the downstairs section, I was aware of a mix of activities from the past and a heaviness that hung in the air like a suffocating pall. I wanted to leave, but my friends, with whom I was staying, wanted me to see more of the house, so I suppressed my desire to get out of there and acquiesced.

The second floor was like a partially finished attic, consisting of a large, open space under the roof where the rafters could be seen. I stood in the middle of the attic and slowly turned as I scanned the room, examining both its physical construction and its *field*. As I turned to face the only window—a small, rectangular portal framed by a gable—my attention was caught by a spot on the floor six to eight feet from the window. There I could clearly perceive a "glow" in the *field*. Visually, it appeared like a luminous pool on the floor not caused by any light from the window. This vision, like many similar ones, appeared in my mind's eye while also conveying to me the distinct impression that I was looking at something outside myself.

Next came an image of a woman, in what appeared to be late nineteenth century garb, sitting in a chair in the very same spot as the glowing presence. The felt quality of the *tone* was peaceful and expansive and similar to how I experience my own state of mind when in meditation or deep contemplation. As I continued to take in the quiet beauty of that glowing place near the window, words appeared in my mind telling me that the woman often came to sit in that spot to escape the grinding hardships of her daily life. I understood that she came to it the way someone might enter a private chapel in a church to engage in solitary prayer. I felt that I was witness to a small island of beauty in an otherwise oppressive, harsh environment.

***

Another type of *seeing* awareness associated with felt attention to the *field* is the direct and sudden appearance of specific knowledge for no apparent reason. Often it just shows up in awareness immediately following a felt perception of the *field*, adding more depth of information to what already has been gleaned. This knowing can appear as a generalized understanding or as a completely formed verbal thought that pops into awareness. The unsought thought about the woman in the attic that came into my awareness after I scanned the house had this latter quality.

As with other forms of *seeing*, a clear and well-developed self-knowledge is essential for mastering this form of *seeing*. All of us constantly free associate through our chains of internally connected thoughts, memories, and feelings that tend to dominate our stream of consciousness. A sudden uninvited thought is not necessarily an experience of *seeing,* unless it is independent of the personal associative chain of thoughts and possesses a detached, "directed" quality. By "detached" I mean clearly not belonging to me personally so I feel no emotional push or pull in relation to what appears in my awareness. In addition, the information seems to come from a place outside myself, even though my perception of it is as if it is internal.

In the earlier case of me picking up on my friend's emotional state in London, the felt *seeing* impacted me like a separate, outside force as I entered the room. I immediately knew that it was not my feeling, it was hers, and simultaneously I felt its quality of despair. After the initial impact of the *tone,* I stood there in the *field* and allowed the information associated with it to enter from my *second stream* awareness—the picture of her sitting and ruminating, followed by the words "thinking of suicide."

A common form of this type of non-ordinary knowing is when people report someone's name popping into their mind shortly before the person calls or turns up suddenly without notice. These events may be examples of *seeing,* but often they are not because people are simply making a backward (retrospective) connection. They might think of their friend several times a year, but each thought quickly slips out of their mind and is forgotten. Then if, after one of these regular associative thoughts, the friend suddenly calls or pays a visit, it can look like a psychic event or an instance of *seeing.* Again, only with practice is the distinction between personal and transpersonal knowing clarified. Like any skill, it takes considerable time and attention to master.

Unambiguous examples of *seeing* in this context have the quality of genuinely emerging "out of the blue," and when we check in with our inner associative chain, the irrupting knowledge appears to be a non sequitur with respect to our usual stream of thought. We realize that it matches real-world situations we could not otherwise have known about. This is well illustrated in the example of my friend in London. I first registered the feeling *tone* coming from the living room, and after I connected to it, the words "thinking of suicide" just popped into my awareness. There was nothing in the physical surroundings or from her to indicate such dire thoughts. Indeed, her flat was tidy and tastefully appointed, and normally she was humorous and upbeat and I had no reason to associate her or her flat with a potential suicide. However, as I subsequently learned, she had a "dark" side that she kept hidden and allowed out only in private.

To reiterate, many of our encounters with *seeing content* are perception-like in that they seem to come from outside, yet they are also experienced as being internal. As in all types of *seeing*, these sorts of inner/outer perceptions can only be distinguished from personal material through the application of self-knowledge and the trial-and-error learning of ongoing reality testing. In time, however, a neophyte *seer* begins to discern the difference in quality of these internal perceptions compared to ordinary, personal material.

For example, the pictures that form from inner perceptions cannot be manipulated or altered like imagined thoughts and images. *Seen* images appear like a picture hung on a wall in front of me and have a vivid and insistent presence, as if I am being shown something. Then, after a time, they fade away. When I recall them later, they take on the quality of a memory rather than the here-now presence of their initial presentation. This allows the presence to be "replayed" allowing me to spend more time with the material and sometimes gain additional information.

An experience I had in 1975 while living in Melbourne, Australia exemplifies this perception-like type of *seeing* and also illustrates how it works together with felt *seeing*. I had been living in a flat on the north side of the city for about six months while teaching at the Preston Institute of Technology (now absorbed into LaTrobe University). At about three a.m. one night I abruptly awoke from a deep sleep with my heart pounding. My felt *seeing* was registering a powerful sensation of despair, fear, and suffering coming toward me from somewhere to the southwest. It was like a beam of light, but without any luminosity. In my mind's eye, I could *see* a picture of the upward extended arms of numerous people who seemed to be reaching out in desperation as waves of intense fear pulsed from them. I could hear voices moaning and begging for mercy. These perceptions went on for what seemed like half an hour, and then they subsided. I fell asleep again, hoping that whatever I was *seeing* was over.

The following night I awoke at about the same time, with similar feelings and images appearing in my mind's eye and they seemed to radiate from the same southwesterly direction. The next day I asked a friend to drive me to where I sensed the source of these phenomena. He worked as a part-time cab driver, knew the city well, and was able to weave through the streets in the direction I was pointing, even though it was at an odd angle to the grid work of the roads. When we came to a large, Victorian-era structure surrounded by a high stone wall, I knew at once that it was the source of my perceptions. My friend informed me that we were looking at Pentridge Prison and that for many years it had been the place of execution for condemned prisoners in the state of Victoria.

With further investigation, I learned that at the same time I awoke that first night, an inmate of this prison had committed suicide. More research revealed that, in addition to executions, the area near the prison had been the scene of a slaughter of Aboriginal people by British authorities during the nineteenth century. Later it occurred to me that the death of the inmate activated the *content* and *tone* generated by those earlier deaths which were stored in the *field* surrounding the prison. In all likelihood the hands and arms I *saw* reaching up were those of Aborigines at the moment they were being killed. The reactivation of the *field* was strong enough to radiate a "signal" over several kilometers and awaken me from sleep.

It is interesting and somewhat amusing to note that years after I had that experience, Pentridge Prison was closed and, surprisingly, the prison and grounds were renovated and turned into up-market condominiums. From a *seer's* point of view, it would have been one of the worst places to live—a literal nightmare-in-waiting foisted on unsuspecting buyers by cynical developers.

***

So far, many of my instances of *seeing* seem to involve death, disaster, and despair. Why would one want to be able to *see* that, you might ask? The fact is I use such examples because they are very clear and because, like most people, I tend to remember dramatic events, especially those that resemble what psychologists call "flashbulb memories." These are what people remember of where they were and what they were doing when a major event took place, for example, President Kennedy's assassination or the explosion of the space shuttle *Challenger*. I have had thousands of *seeing* perceptions over the years, but, like ordinary perceptions, most of these have been lost to memory over time due to the never ending stream of events that impinge on my daily awareness.

Sometimes, however, grim experiences, like the one in Melbourne, place me in exalted company. George Fox, the seventeenth century mystic and founder of the Quakers, once recorded a similar vision of mass murder. William James, in *The Varieties of Religious Experience*, quotes Fox's account of this seminal episode that deeply influenced his religious life.

> As I was walking with several friends, I lifted up my head, and saw three steeple-house spires, and they struck at my life. I asked them what place that was? They said, Lichfield. Immediately the word of the Lord came to me, that I must go there. Being come to the house we were going to, I wished the friends to walk into the house, saying nothing to them of whither I was to go. As soon as they were gone I stepped away, and went by my eye over hedge and ditch till I came within a mile of Lichfield; where, in a great field, shepherds were keeping their sheep. Then was I commanded by the Lord to pull off my shoes. I stood still, for it was winter: but the word of the Lord was like a fire in me. So I put off my shoes and left them with the shepherds; and the poor shepherds trembled, and were astonished. Then I walked on about a mile, and as soon as I was got within the city, the word of the Lord came to me again, saying: Cry 'Wo to the bloody city of Lichfield!' So I went up and down the streets, crying with a loud voice, 'Wo to the bloody city of Lichfield!' It being market day, I went into the market-place and to and fro in the several parts of it, and made stands, crying as before, 'Wo to the bloody city of Lichfield!' And no one laid hands on me. As I went thus crying through the streets, there seemed to me to be a channel of blood running down the streets, and the market-place appeared like a pool of blood. When I had declared what was upon me, and felt myself clear, I went out of the town in peace; and returning to the shepherds gave them some money, and took my shoes of them again. But the fire of the Lord was so on my feet, and all over me, that I did not matter to put on my shoes again, and was at a stand whether I should or no, till I felt freedom from the Lord so to do: then, after I had washed my feet, I put on my shoes again.

> After this a deep consideration came upon me, for what reason I should be sent to cry against that city, and call it the bloody city! For though the parliament had the minister one while, and the king another, and much blood had been shed in the town during the wars between them, yet there was no more than had befallen many other places. But afterwards I came to understand, that in the Emperor Docletian's time a thousand Christians were martyred in Lichfield. So I was to go, without my shoes, through the channel of their blood, and into the pool of their blood in the market-place, that I might raise up the memorial of the blood of those martyrs, which had been shed above a thousand years before, and lay cold in their streets. So the sense of this blood was upon me, and I obeyed the word of the Lord.[2]

It appears that when Fox spied the steeple towers, his attention was radically redeployed so that *content* in the *field* was precipitously available to him, giving him the feeling that God had called him to this new awareness. Undoubtedly, the slaughter of a thousand people in the market square would have profoundly affected the *tone* of the *field* around Lichfield.

Given his Christian beliefs and intense religiosity, Fox would have reacted strongly to the awareness of these murders of his fellow believers and the preacher in him would have wanted to call the attention of other Christians to the enormity of what had transpired. Walking barefoot into Lichfield was consistent with the practice of a Christian pilgrim when approaching a holy site and his statements about the "fire" he felt was probably due to his overwhelming emotional response to the intensity of the *field tone*.

Fox experienced his "call" to go to Lichfield as coming from the church spires. From my perspective, I would say he sensed an activated *field* and then followed the direction set by its *tone*. Upon arriving at the marketplace, with its crowds of people, he then had a vision of the streets running with blood and was instructed by an inner "voice" (his *second stream* knowing of *content*) to decry the town, which he did loudly as he paced up and down the market square. Later, at home, trying to make sense of his experience perhaps, he did some background research on Lichfield—his form of reality testing—and

---

[2]W. James, *The Varieties of Religious Experience* (New York: Modern Library, 1936), pp. 9–10.

discovered that in Roman times, under the rule of Emperor Docletian, the marketplace was the scene of the martyrdom of a thousand Christians by Roman troops. The streets literally ran with blood. His vision was validated.

While I *saw* a similar vision involving slaughter of many people, unlike Fox, I did not start a religion afterward, however. For me, as a *seer* without any religious orientation, it was just another event on the endless *field* horizon, and no matter how momentous it seemed I remained just a witness.

***

Seers are continuously aware of *second stream* perceptions, but, as with everything we observe, we tend to contextualize our observations in terms that make sense to us. I am a psychologist and social scientist, so, naturally, when talking about what I *see* in people, I first discuss their psychological-emotional constellations and then focus on what appears to need resolution in their life. In other words, I contextualize my *seeing* by looking for what is meaningful to me in the same way that I do with ordinary knowing.

Occasionally I *see* pictures of places or events without understanding what they mean, though often the person to whom I reveal the information recognizes their significance immediately. I remember describing for a client a scene that took place at a dinner table that meant nothing to me, though straight away she knew what I was talking about. It turned out that what I *saw* was the enactment of a scene that regularly took place in her family home and involved the idiosyncratic behavior of her grandfather toward a maid. From these kinds of experiences I have learned the importance of first just describing what I *see* and only then contextualizing it into my preferred form, the psychological profile. To be a *seer*, one has to become a good phenomenological reporter, interpreting as little as possible.

After a great deal of trial-and-error learning and working on being a good reporter, I have come to trust my felt *seeing* perceptions of the *field* to the same degree that I trust sensate perceptions. As a result, I am confident about the truth of my *seeing* even in the face of pressure from others to take a different view. Indeed, I have been known to stand in front of a room full of people who are all disagreeing with me and insist on the veracity of my *seeing* perception.

17. Pushing the *Field*—*Intentionality*

During my time as a graduate student at the University of Copenhagen in the early 1970s, I used to engage in twice-daily meditation, as I had been doing since the mid-1960s. My style of sitting, whether with eyes open or shut, was formal, in that I sat with legs in a half-lotus position and my spine straight. In the eyes-open style, I often used a feature of the room or a candle as a point of focus. With a candle, the flame would move and flicker if the air in the room was not perfectly still, which could prove a distraction. However, my small student apartment at Amagerkollegiet south of Copenhagen's city center was ideal for candle meditation because when the window was shut, the air was perfectly still.

One evening, with the window shut against the Danish chill, I decided that the room was sufficiently still for a candle meditation. I found a candle and placed it in a small ceramic holder, but immediately realized that it would be inadequate for catching all the wax that was likely to drip. Placing the candle and holder on a ceramic plate, I sat the whole assemblage on a low table in front of my couch, which doubled as my bed. With my legs crossed, I straightened my back and relaxed to each out-breath as I gazed at the quietly glowing flame.

After about ten minutes I became aware that my *field* was like a large, translucent, softly glowing bubble surrounding my body and extending in front of me to where it intersected with the candle. Realizing this, I wondered if it was possible to directly affect the candle through my *field*. I was not certain what was required, so I started to generate a pressure toward it from a vertical line extending from my abdomen to the middle of my chest. This took a lot of concentration and was difficult to maintain, but in persevering, I generated a pressured "push."

Suddenly, during one of these focused "pushes," I saw the candle and its ceramic holder jiggle slightly, accompanied by a rattling sound as the holder vibrated against the plate. After a few more tries, I noticed the effect only occurred when the pressure in the vertical line connecting my abdomen to my chest reached what felt like a critical threshold.

Each time the candle vibrated and the flame flickered, I tried to evaluate what was occurring but such effort altered my attention, which in turn halted the movement of the candle and holder. Attention had to be deployed to the task with such a high degree of focus and intensity that any sharing of my attention with my internal evaluator seemed to disrupt it. In retrospect, I wished I had filmed the exercise to capture what happened so I could evaluate it afterward. Before long, the effort left me fatigued and I had to stop. This was my first encounter with consciously directing *intentionality* through the *field*.

***

By *intentionality* I mean the ability to create meaningful force directed through the *bio-field*, although this description is not wholly adequate to convey what I mean to describe. I coined the term *intentionality* (called *intent* by some of my former students) for this fundamental aspect of being a *seer*, but later learned that the nineteenth century philosopher Brentano had resurrected it from a medieval scholastic philosophical term used to distinguish mental from physical phenomena.[1]

This is probably the most difficult chapter of this book for me to write and for you, as reader, to grasp, for even though *intentionality* is everywhere present in the activities of human life, it cannot be seen from the linguistically driven cultural frame of reference (read: fixed point of view) in which we are taught to live. If this chapter frustrates you, come back to it again, because it offers an opportunity to give birth to an expanded view of oneself as an intentional awareness-being.

Allowing this transformation to happen is not under your direct control the way you can control the speed and direction of your car. A person does not just choose to *see* and engage *intentionality*; he must

---

[1]F. Brentano, *Psychology from an Empirical Standpoint* (Leipzig: Verlag von Duncker & Humblot, 1874).

open to it and let it move through him. Here I am not referring, directly or indirectly, to some notion of fate or divine intervention. *Intentionality* can be thought of as a force that is present everywhere, like gravity, to which it is in some ways analogous. It wants to carry you in the direction it dictates. Because of gravity you cannot roll uphill without some other force acting on you. Similarly, without mastery of *intentionality* one is unable to understand or change the "direction" of human awareness and behavior in anything other than a superficial way.

Conceptually, *intentionality* can be confused with the notion of "intention" as used in New Age literature and belief. Writers and teachers of this ilk often talk about "setting an intention" to gain a particular outcome—material goods, a new partner, career advancement, and so forth—which is quite different from acting with focused *intentionality* through the *field*. "Intention," as used by New Age practitioners seems to be more about wishing for imagined outcomes that confer benefits, rather than about the focused force of *intentionality* that is always present as part of the *field* and embedded in the larger *intentionality* of society and culture.

Here is the secret: The control required to gain mastery of *intentionality* is the act of relinquishing control—you have to get out of your own way to let something happen. If you do, and then remain an open Watcher, you will be able to see *intentionality* operating in your life. Of course, once you see it in yourself, you will start to notice it working through others, which opens the possibility of engaging it directly. If you give up attempting to create movement in the *field* through ordinary, forced action, you are then in the position to allow yourself to act from an emergent psychic-emotional "force" not otherwise available. To really understand this, however, it has to be experienced.

My journey to England exemplifies the workings of *intentionality*. There seemed to be some kind of force driving my experience and leading to my choice to go there, but it was not related to causation as understood in physics. In a sense, *intentionality* carried me to England, and once I started to accept what was happening, this force driving my transition became apparent to me in both the macrosphere of my life overall as well as the microsphere of my daily gestures and actions. One of my most important jobs in becoming a *seer* was learning how to pay attention in such a manner that I could perceive *intentionality*. Then I could learn to work with it—a process in which I am still engaged.

To undergo this transition required the attention of another *seer* who was capable of directly and consciously using *intentionality* directed at me. The action of Alice's awareness was part of the process of my fixed point of view being disrupted enough to allow me to perceive and act differently—to do what I never thought I wanted to do: pick up and leave the USA to follow the line of *intent* to England. With my usual point of view disrupted, my awareness became sufficiently fluid to countenance such a radical shift. In effect, I had to permit a larger *intentionality* to work through me and not resist it. In a sense, my dream of the rolling English hills and the events that followed were about my moving with that larger *intent*—aligning myself with it and acting accordingly.

It is difficult to understand the notion of *intentionality* from a standard fixed point of view because the metaphoric descriptions of it are too easily taken literally. A metaphor is like a finger pointing at the moon. It indicates something other than itself but in a standard fixed point of view, the signpost (finger) becomes more the object of attention than what is being pointed at—the moon. *Intentionality* is what drives the working of consciousness and action for human beings, but this goes largely unrecognized because our attention is usually fixated on the signpost. Until one experiences the workings of *intentionality* directly, the understanding of human will and behavior remains purely metaphoric and therefore subject to speculation. *Intentionality* does not need interpretation; it speaks for itself through direction, felt quality in the *field*, information *content*, and result.

When the line of a person's life is viewed from the fluid point of view of one who can perceive *intentionality*, where that person lands is as obvious as where a stone will end up when released from the top of a hill. One can say that behavior and awareness follow the "lines" of *intentionality* set by the doer, in combination with the *field* of the particular time and place, which also includes the *intentionality* of other participants. Again, "line" is a metaphor for a non-physical, directed force of action. The language used to discuss *intentionality* is meaningless unless we share a common ground of experience in directly perceiving it. This direct perception of *intentionality* is what ultimately defines the perceptual frame of a *seer*, and that perception requires the development of a more fluid attention and a non-fixed point of view. It all comes back to the issue of attention.

***

In spite of my admonition about metaphoric language I will say that we are *intentionality* beings suspended in an oceanic *field*. Just as fish are probably not conscious that they spend their lives in water, so most of us remain unaware of ourselves as immersed in a *field*-ocean. In fact, we are connected to the universe and each other through this medium, which allows for a kind of simultaneity and action at a distance manifested in moments of knowing that we call clairvoyance and precognition. To complete this analogy of the *field* as an ocean, the fish (ourselves) are more concentrated instantiations of the *field*, created and driven by the same *intentionality* that is forming the *content* of the *field*. Conceptually, this is not unlike the idea of matter being intensely folded time/space, as in some interpretations of the general theory of relativity.

As water is the defining medium for the ocean, so the *field* is the medium where focused *intentionality* and the physical world intersect and interact. A wave in the ocean changes relationships between objects or creatures floating in it. In a similar way, *intentionality* acts as the direction, force, and quality of activity generated in the *field* in which we are all embedded. When I was conducting my concentration exercise in Denmark, I was creating a "wave" in my *field* that was capable of interacting with the candle. What "capable" means here and what the physics of this process is, I do not know. I only know that I had to stop my usual methods of paying attention and making things happen by some kind of internal effort so that a "force" could flow through my *field*. However, this example is one of the simplest and perhaps least interesting examples of *intentionality*.

Thoughts and particularly emotions generate *intent* in a person's *bio-field*, and it is this "wave" moving through the *field* that determines what someone really means when he speaks or takes action. Good storytellers have a rudimentary understanding of *intentionality* and, in a sense, demonstrate for us how worlds are created by its direct action. Stories have presence and create a scene for us because of the projection of *intentionality* by the storyteller. When a story is told without *intentionality*, it seems hollow or flat and when *intentionality* is sufficiently intense, the *field* moves the listener's awareness to a level where events are given a life of their own.

In fact, all the arts rise or fall on the presence or absence of the artist's mastery of *intentionality*. Listening to Maxim Vengerov, the Russian violinist and violist, when he is playing Henryk Wieniawski's *Variations on an Original Theme* (Opus 15), leads one to realize that musicality and technical virtuosity are only part of what makes his performance great. It is when those qualities are focused as *intentionality* through his *field* and into the audience's that we are left profoundly altered by his playing.

In the case of a brilliant performance, a musician uses *intentionality* much the same way *seers* do, but for a different purpose. Because of his conscious use of *intentionality*, a *seer* can extend his *bio-field* outward at will, which is how *seers* often "reach" into the *fields* of other people or objects to perceive things about them. A great musical performance, on the other hand, is a much broader reaching out into the collective *bio-fields* of the audience. When playing, the musician is "pushing" the *field* in a way that alters its *tone* and thus creates a changing *field-resonance* in the audience.

If a musician fails to achieve this act of *intentionality*—even if he has superb technical mastery of his instrument—the performance comes across as mediocre. I remember attending a flute recital in Santa Barbara given by Jean-Pierre Rampal, considered at that time to be one of the greatest living flautists. His performance was technically flawless, but his playing almost completely lacked *intentionality*, and so this *seer* was left feeling that Rampal was merely practicing scales. Of course, I cannot say that all his performances lacked *intent*, but that one certainly did.

One of the most important examples of *intentionality* in action is the person who "pushes" the room as alluded to in Chapter 10. By that I mean he uses *intentionality* (consciously or unconsciously) to change the *field* thereby setting the *tone* for the room's occupants. As I have said previously, a meeting can be made to work or disabled by the presence of such a person. Physical participation does not determine the impact of an individual who "pushes" the room, whether his impact dampens forward motion of the group or facilitates it. Whenever I run a group training these days, I utilize my scenario of a business meeting that seems to be helped or hindered by one person who on the surface appears to do little. Without exception, the majority of my workshop participants report having witnessed a similar scene.

In most people, including the majority of psychics, *intentionality* is mostly unconscious and does not manifest as a directed action, so its effect on social interactions at home and at work go largely unnoticed. In *seers,* however, *intentionality* is a consciously engaged and directed action. For us it creates an alignment of belief, desire and will that allows for acts of *seeing* perception or the manifestation of particular outcomes in the *field* directly.

The effects of *intentionality* manifest when a *seer's* attentional resources are consciously and directly focused with a "push" into the *fields* of other persons. This focus differs from mere attending in that it is directed with a "force," which projects *tone* and *content* into the targeted *field,* thereby directly conveying a felt quality and meaning to those receiving it. This projection is the actual intention or meaning designed to achieve a specific outcome, rather than that which is conveyed by the words spoken or actions done. Even when the projected *intent* apparently contradicts verbal or physical nonverbal messages (which it often does), it can be more potent and have greater effect. In the case reported earlier of the con-man who swindled my father, my reaction to him was because of his projected *intent.* Although his words and facial gestures were friendly and reassuring, the *intentionality* manifest in his *field* revealed someone who was manipulative and deceptive and who had ill will toward others.

The *field* is always responsive to the *intentionality* of living beings—particularly humans. It is molded by acts of *intentionality,* conscious or unconscious. They organize *fields* into the direction of their intended actions and determine what information is projected into objects or given to people's minds. *Content* (information) in *fields* is generated or altered by *intentionality* and it is the force of *intentionality* that generates the activity that captures our attention, thereby generating belief and knowing.

Such shaping and imprinting of the *field* is what *seers* directly perceive and from which they often are able to "read" the history of a person (or place) and know who the key players were at a particular time. The more intense the human activity, physically and particularly emotionally, the more likely the *field* of an individual or place carries a "message" of that activity. The degree of imprinting of *content* and *tone* often is enhanced by the intensity of the physical actions alone but not always.

A Japanese student of mine has told me that there is a location near her home, in Sojya-city, Okayama prefecture, where she always senses an intense local *field*. She sent me the following email describing her experience of it:

> I was driving on a road from east to west in Sojya-city to take my son to a doctor. When I switched to a feeling mode while driving my car, I felt the energy and heard in my mind's ear the shouts of soldiers and saw thousands of horses running and people's cries like "owaooooo!" (a battle-cry).
>
> But the actual scene in front of me was a rice field. There were large rice fields spreading on both sides of the road and I also saw a temple with a five-story-pagoda on the right. I also saw people visiting the temple for sightseeing and it was sunny.
>
> I switched (my attention) back to the feeling mode, and again, I heard the sounds of horses running in the paddy fields and, also, the sound of metal swords hitting each other. Words, "a battle field," popped up in my mind.
>
> There was a place where I felt the energy of the dead people or graves. That place was on the slope of a hill on the right side of the road (I could not find whether or not this place was where the soldiers were buried in the history I read). I saw in my mind's eye the wounded or dead soldiers' bodies lying with their bellies on the earth, their hands reaching forward and their faces to their sides. I saw the blood running from their bodies. To me, it was the smell of death. The energy there was cold, sad, and I felt misery. I felt a chill. The place (in the present) was in the shade and there were stair-like small rice fields and old Japanese farm houses.
>
> After I drove up over the hill, I did not feel the energy of the battle any more on the other side. On the way back from the doctor's office...I still could feel the energy of excitement, heard

> so many people shouting "owaooooo—!" and the sound of so
> many horses running, and the sounds of the many metal swords.
> I saw dust, swords, houses and people on horses, but I could not
> see what they wore.

After reading this I asked my student to do a reality check in the form of research into the history of the area. She discovered that in the year 1336, a massive battle had taken place in the area of those rice fields. The emperor Godaigo had assumed control after the collapse of the former government (Kamakura) in 1333, but the Samurai class was opposed to the emperor, so they formed an army and fought the loyalists. Reports of the size of the Samurai forces vary, depending on the source, but it is believed to have been between 200,000 and 300,000 men against 15,000 to 20,000 loyalists. The slaughter that resulted must have had an intensity capable of permanently "marking" the *field* of the battle site for it to last almost 700 years. Through the *intentionality* generated by the intense activity and emotions of battle the *field* at the scene became deeply imprinted, as Samurai and loyalists fought, were wounded, and died.

***

The source of personal *intentionality* is the totality of our psycho-physical being and its use by us is both conscious and unconscious, with far more of it manifesting in our actions unconsciously. The connection of *intent* to our individual *fields* is so direct and powerful that our *field* can be marked by almost anything we think, feel, or imagine that has emotional force behind it. The range of our imagination is limited, of course, by our beliefs and the culture and times in which we live. Perhaps this is why the forms of the *field* known through *seeing* in different places and historical epochs can appear so different. Just a cursory examination of Aztec iconography, for example, highlights how far removed their expression of belief and action was from ours today.

The condition that most dilutes the force and direction of *intentionality* in humans is the fragmentation and defocusing of will and attention caused by fear, ambiguity, inhibition, and habitual beliefs and behavior as well as attentional patterns. We carry these as ingrained unconscious habits. For a developing *seer,* it is essential to seek alignment of *intentionality* with consciously focused choices through the practice of attention deployment (meditation, for example), as well as to develop a greater awareness of the manifestations one's unconscious.

If this is not achieved, a neophyte *seer* may think that he is unified in his *intentionality*, but instead his fragmented attention will be undermining the alignment of *intent* and action required for *seeing*. It is for this reason that I recommend an apprentice *seer* engage in a progressive deepening of his understanding of his unconscious mind through some kind of psychological training. Anyone who does not develop this understanding of himself can run the risk of his *seeing* being dominated by his psychopathology and imagination.

Intentionality is not only a product of our psycho-emotional selves and existential direction, it also acts to set our life's direction and focus. As a result, a closed loop can be created which becomes self-fulfilling, trapping us in our own belief systems and behaviors. In fact, this mechanism is a fundamental part of how a fixed point of view is maintained in each of us. The circular reinforcing mechanism can be a major drawback to *seeing* and other non-ordinary practices and traditions, since these are built upon generations of prior *seeing* done within specific cultures and worldviews maintained through a self-reinforcing process.

As biologist Rupert Sheldrake has suggested,[2] certain habit patterns in nature and society tend to dominate, but ingrained habits of perception create limitations for *seers* so a teaching system that requires skeptical self-examination, with a dedication to empiricism rather than theory, is essential in the process of becoming a good *seer* or a good scientist. In fact, a fundamental skeptical stance has been my companion throughout my life as both a *seer* and a social scientist.

It is a sad fact that probably the first and most important aspect of *seeing* to be obliterated in our social enculturation process is the awareness of *intentionality*. In many people it remains in vestigial form as "gut feelings," but in most of us it is partially or wholly replaced by a belief in what is apparently intended through language and gesture alone. There is little doubt in my mind that those who have met an

---

[2]R. Sheldrake, *A New Science of Life: The Hypothesis of Formative Causation* (Los Angeles: J. P. Tarcher, 1981).

awful end by unwittingly stepping into danger have done so because the words and physical signals used to seduce them provided a false message that disguised the true *intent* of their killers. The ordinary physical message became the victim's primary focus of attention because it was all they had been trained to attend to. If they had been educated to notice true *intent,* maybe they could have averted disaster.

In summary, *intentionality* is the directed force that guides human attention and activity toward an end—physical, emotional, mental, and existential—through its effect on the individual *bio-field* and the greater *field* surrounding us all. A person's *intent* indicates where they are going behaviorally, no matter what they claim. It also predicts the end result of their actions. It is up to the neophyte *seer* to break through the bounds of his fixed attention to directly *see* the *field*-direction created by *intentionality*.

In my own case, I had to learn to stop attempting to analyze and define the nature of *intentionality*. It cannot be understood by trying to logically "work it out"; it must be experienced. Think of this chapter, then, as a finger pointing to *intentionality*.

18. Psychometry—*Seeing* with Objects

One of the more common methods *seers* use to perceive across time—particularly to past events—is called psychometry. Utilizing it, the *seer* detects and attends to the psychic-emotional imprint left by people in the *field* associated with an object or place, and then describes human activity associated with this imprint, or "afterimage," contained in the *field*. I have never felt that "psychometry" is the best name for this practice, since the term implies some kind of psychometric measurement, such as those obtained through personality or IQ tests. *Seeing* through psychometry is not any kind of measurement, rather, it is the detection of the *tone* and *contents* of a *field* associated with an object or place.

My first taste of using this method occurred in Trixie Allingham's training group during my trip to London in 1969. At that time I did not know exactly what I was doing—my knowledge of temporally and geographically remote events just seemed to pop into my mind when I held a man's keys and quietly redeployed my attention. I understood later that objects often become imbued with aspects of a *field* in which they are embedded over time. They develop a mini-*field* that includes *tone* and *content* related to the people who used or handled them. When a *seer* is in the presence of an object, he can experience aspects of the human beings who most contributed to the *tone* and *contents* of its *field*.

Typically, events *seen* through psychometry are experienced as sudden flashes of visual or auditory material and/or feelings that appear in a "space" that is neither an inner, subjective vision nor an externalized, objective event but something in between. These perceptions are not experienced as truly veridical in the present, yet because of their persistence and apparent immunity to cognitive manipulation, they stand apart from normal internal imaginary productions, which can be cognitively influenced. They seem to come to the *seer* from the outside world, yet they have qualities of both objective experience and internally generated, subjective knowing.

On occasion I have done remote viewing for clients using techniques based on psychometry. The "address" of the remote target can be obtained by reading the *field* of an object associated with it, followed by extending one's awareness to the original source of the *field*. For example, in Santa Barbara in the 1980s, a woman I knew had engaged in a vehicle trade with a man—swapping her car for his van. Within days, my client discovered that he had lied to her about the van and there was a major problem with it. She needed to resolve the situation urgently before he left the area so she asked me to locate him, but all she had was his signature on the registration release document.

I held the piece of paper for a moment, then put it up to my face and silenced my mind. A picture opened in my mind's eye. I was looking at a trailer park at the north end of town, and as I peered down the driveway from the street in my vision, I saw her car and knew the man was there. After I described where he was, my client left immediately. A few days later I ran into her, and she was quite pleased with herself. She had found him where I had said he would be, and she had forced him to give her back her car.

Another example from the 1980s in Santa Barbara involved using psychometry to *see* the past through an object. I was introduced by an art restorer friend to a so-called "collector," who, in reality, turned out to be a professional grave robber. He specialized in pre-Colombian sites in Mexico, and worked with a particular village whose inhabitants helped him to locate graves and excavate them. Then he would smuggle the artifacts into the United States, where he sold them on the art market, splitting the profits with the village. He justified his activity by claiming that it was a financially good arrangement for both parties.

Shortly after one of his trips to Mexico the "collector" turned up in Santa Barbara, whereupon I was invited to the restorer's studio to perform a psychometry on some of the artifacts he had with him. These included a few terracotta figurines of pairs of figures, one seated behind the other, such as the one I am holding in the picture (next page). I found them not very interesting as sources of *field* presence. At first I thought they might have been in the ground too long, so that whatever *field* they had once possessed had diminished to a level not detectable by me. Later I realized that they had been made specifically for burial and had not been used for any significant time in anyone's life, so they were not imbued with much of a *field*. Rather, they were placed in the grave to represent and keep alive the *intent* of the ceremony that I eventually *saw*.

Also among the artifacts was a small, unadorned clay cup containing a black, resinous substance that had been cooked or burnt in it. My initial impression was that the cup had been used as part of the burial ceremony, and as I held it near my face and redeployed my attention, a vivid picture formed in my mind's eye.

I found myself standing at the edge of a clearing with my back to a forest, looking at some huts, made entirely of plant matter, grouped on one side of the clearing. In my mind's ear I could *hear* the sound of chanting coming from one of the larger huts, and as I focused on the sound, I found myself standing inside the hut. Most of the village's population were seated on the ground, facing the body of a dead man stretched out in front of someone I assumed to be a shaman (he was wearing feathers and regalia that made him look like one). He was chanting over the body and behind him sat a woman with her hands on his back or shoulders, her head slightly bowed. The air in the hut was very warm and humid, and the shaman's black hair hung limply over his face as he chanted and rocked back and forth next to the corpse.

At that moment I realized that the figurine I had been holding earlier was a symbolic representation of this ceremony and that it was designed to carry the power of the ritual into the grave. Then, as I watched the shaman sway back and forth, intoning a pulsing, guttural sound, the intensity of the activity over the dead man increased. Suddenly I understood that the woman was the dead man's wife and the shaman was using a chant to drive the spirit of the deceased out of the village into whatever constituted an afterlife for these people.

The wife seemed to be fearful, but the shaman's efforts appeared to reassure her as well as the others present in the hut, convincing them that the dead man's presence would go away. As the chanting reached a crescendo, I caught a glimpse of something moving up and away from the corpse at about a 45 degree angle. It moved off into the distance and into the brightly lit sky, where it disappeared. When the chanting abruptly ceased, my attention was again drawn to the exterior of the hut. As I took another look around the village, it became clear to me that this was a slash-and-burn agricultural society and the settlement I was viewing was only temporary.

Among those who witnessed the psychometry in the restorer's studio that day was an anthropologist, though neither he nor anyone else could tell me anything about the ceremony I had apparently witnessed. All the anthropologist and collector could confirm was that the people of that time did indeed practice slash-and-burn cultivation.

As is often the case with such experiences, I found it difficult to convey to the group in the studio the intensity of the ceremony I had witnessed. It was hard to forget the power of the shaman and his vocally pulsed, driving *field*-force. The presence at that moment was so strong that, for weeks afterward, I felt as though I had returned from a journey to another world, back to an ordinary, humdrum life.

***

It is my view that the imprinting of a *field* on an object usually takes place gradually over time. In most situations, the longer an object is used by a person or the longer the space is occupied, the more deeply imprinted is its *field*, so that more is available for a *seer* to "read" from it. However, other factors also come into play. First, the emotional intensity generated by the individual imprinting an object will determine how strong its *field* presence is. Second, any emotional shock around the object will especially increase the intensity of the *field*. A particularly violent emotional outburst occurs with the sudden death of an individual, especially if the person is conscious of what is going on in those last seconds. In the case of the pre-Colombian artifact, its use in such an important and emotionally charged ceremony would have strongly imprinted it in a very short time, or it might have been used in a number of similar ceremonies over a long period.

Places, too, can carry a *field* that allows *seeing* into past events. In 1984, I had occasion to visit a fourteenth century castle, Schlöss Weissenstein, at Lauterstein, Germany where I was asked to enter the chapel, one of the oldest parts of the castle.[1] I had been invited by the owner and was told nothing about what I might find.

When I first enter a location to perform a psychometry, after giving the place a cursory visual inspection, I focus my attention on my *second attention* awareness. I deploy my attention to the *tone* and *contents* of the *field* by sensing them through an area immediately in front of my body that extends as a vertical line from a point between my eyes to a place at the center of my solar plexus. When doing this, I am actually creating a specialized opening, like a slit, in the part of my *bio-field* through which I can sense various qualities of the *field*. Different places along this *field*-sensor resonate to qualities of the *field*. The opening allows me to directly experience the *tone* and *contents* around me without letting them enter and remain in my personal *bio-field*.

---

[1] This entire visit was recorded by North German Television as part of a film about my work as a *seer*. Part of it is viewable online: http://www.youtube.com/watch?v=q_RwvD7kPPY.

In the chapel I moved my *field*-sensor around the space, focusing mainly on its walls because of their capacity to hold *contents* and *tone* from the past. While engaging in this way, I came to a small statue embedded in the wall to the left of the altar. With my attention on the *second stream*, suddenly, in my mind's eye, I *saw* a set of images, accompanied by feelings and verbal descriptions. Prior to this, all I had experienced in the chapel was what I call a "crowd scene"—a conglomerate of hundreds of years of human emotion and activity layered into it by the many people who had entered and contributed to its *field*-presence. Over time, the totality of these human presences had become implanted and layered in such a way that differentiating specific "voices" was difficult.

But when it came to "reading" the *contents* of the little statue's *field*, I saw a clear image of a man I thought was a knight, kneeling in front of the figure. Holding a small scarf, he kissed it, touched it to the statue and then kissed the scarf again. The feeling around him was one of supplication and desire for protection. I became aware that the figurine was considered good luck, and in touching it, men believed they would be helped when going to war. The owner of the castle confirmed all this, telling me the story of a duke who survived a battle and how the statue was associated with bringing good luck to him and others.

***

The scenes, feelings and thoughts one experiences when using *seeing* to look across space and time can be confusing at times. Often, with my *second attention,* I have found myself "staring" at a scene that is not intelligible at first. In such circumstances, I have found that I can shift my point of view in order to better *see*. For example, I can change position in the scene and alter my viewing angle to gain a different perspective, like one would while attempting to get a better view in a physical situation.

I learned to make this shift in perspective early in my life as a *seer* when I was given a letter to psychometrize. As the scene opened in my mind's eye, all that was in my visual field was a gray, rough-surfaced mass. For a moment I was stumped. "This is very strange," I thought. "What am I looking at?" Then I had another thought suggesting that I take a few steps back, as it were. Until then, I had assumed that whatever image came to me in an act of *seeing* was all there was and sometimes this is true. However, in this case, I took my own advice and found that, indeed, I could "step back," perceptually speaking. It was then that I realized I had been standing in front of a large tree whose bark was rough and gray. From my new perspective I could see the whole tree as well as a scene that included the person whose letter I was holding.

Often when engaged in *seeing*, we are unaware of all the impressions being conveyed to us from the *field* because they come so quickly and tend to carry more information than we can take in at one viewing. However, any act of *seeing* can be mentally "replayed" afterward. In fact, an important part of learning to *see* is finding out how to replay events, in order to take in as much as possible of what is available to be perceived. By asking questions like "What did I miss?" the *seer* can return to the ground of his perception and pay attention to what is usually relegated to the background. Switching from foreground to background is a useful skill similar to that used in Gestalt therapy exercises.

Having said this, any replays of *second stream* attention are less intense than the original experience but, like the original, they are not able to be altered by mental manipulation. Additionally, there will be some loss of clarity and detail with increasing time between event and replay. However, like "flashbulb" memories, the replays retain much of the vivid presence of the most salient features. Revisiting this recalled material allows for a more thorough examination of the scene than when it first appeared. This is particularly true if, during the original *seeing* event, people were wanting explanations, there and then, of what was being *seen,* which would have interfered with the concentration required during the process of observation. I find that when I revisit the scene, at a time of my own choosing, I can savor its *tone* and *content* more fully and examine it from different angles, gaining a more complete perspective. In a sense, since I already have the "address," I can revisit the scene like a remote viewer might.

It should also be noted that what is presented to us in the first few seconds of a psychometry is often the most accurate and significant. However, our neurological wiring, shaped by our education and cultural training, can make us automatically dismiss part of what we first perceive, particularly if it contradicts one of our standard processing "templates"—the neuropsychological filters that maintain our picture of the world.[2] Anything that opposes what we have been taught about reality and how it works, tends to be rejected as irrelevant. In fact, if we do have this tendency to filter out aspects of what we first perceive when it runs counter to our "expected picture," replaying *seen* events is important because it gives us the opportunity to re-experience those first few seconds of the original event.

As I learned to be more fluid in my use of attention, I became increasingly capable of noticing what is habitually filtered out of my awareness, both during acts of *seeing* and in my ordinary perception as well. Nevertheless, replaying still remains a central part of any psychometry I perform because of its capacity to deepen and broaden the picture I *see*.

---

[2] Templates include our "top-down processing," the conscious cognitive model we hold and apply to construct our picture of the world, and our "bottom-up processing," which refers to the unconscious, emotional, and perceptual filtering processes that allow into awareness what we expect without any use of thought.

19. PRECOGNITIONS AND VISIONS

How is it possible to experience scenes from the lives of people about whom we have been given no information through our usual, perceptual channels—our five physical senses? How can we know specific events from the future? In the language of science, such experiences involve no discernable transfer of momenta (information), and knowing future events violates the arrow of time of thermodynamics, which is considered one of physics' most fundamental pillars. In spite of the revolution created by relativity theory and quantum mechanics, thermodynamics is still believed to provide the truest and most accurate picture of information flow over time.

Among non-ordinary perceivers, accurate descriptions of the future are less common than observations about the past or distant events. Precognitive perceptions, as *seeing* the future has been labeled, can be tricky and often are not terribly accurate, yet there are psychics and *seers* who specialize in it and whose results are very good.

Stanley Poulton, who dictated the notes to Irené that predicted my arrival in London, 10 years before I got there, and gave accurate descriptions of me and my life, was clearly exceptional at precognition. He employed psychometry as his primary method of *viewing* forward in time. When I visited him during my first London sojourn he provided me with information about future events that also proved very accurate, and were too improbable to occur by chance alone (i.e., as a normal statistical variation). For example, he predicted that in about two years, I would have a legal problem for which I would employ a lawyer whose initials were "J.J." However, he assured me that this lawyer would write just one letter that would resolve the situation quickly and easily.

Sure enough, two years later, while I was living in Keswick, Cumbria, in the northwest of England, I had my first-ever legal dispute with a former landlord, a wealthy, retired RAF wing commander and former World War II Spitfire pilot on whose estate I had been living. After I left the estate, I received from him a legal demand for a large sum of money for electricity and supposed "damage" to the rundown trailer home I had been renting from him as temporary accommodation. I could not pay it, so I asked a friend to refer me to a lawyer. Since there were only two in town and the letter of demand came from one of these lawyers, I was advised to see the other one, whose name was John Jones.

John was a tall, lanky man with a quiet, thoughtful manner, and he was familiar with the former wing commander. He told me: "Knowing how he operates, I advise you to write a check for a small amount (much smaller than the demand). I'll put it in with a letter I will write, and I'll wager he'll take it." He then told me that if my former landlord cashed the check, I would be absolved of any further obligation. I duly wrote it and, as predicted, the wing commander cashed it, so for a total of £30, including the lawyer's fee, the matter was settled, just as Stanley had predicted.

While the episode is fairly trivial, the accuracy of the prediction, including the specifics of the lawyer's initials and how the issue would be resolved, were startling and gave credence to the fact that Stanley was in touch with a non-ordinary source of information. And of course, his description of me in the notes Alice wanted me to see—what I was doing, my first name, names of my closest friends, and the roles Alice and I would play in each other's lives—offered further evidence of this skill. A theoretical physicist friend of mine described those notes as the best evidence for precognition he had ever come across.

I have had precognitive perceptions many times over the years, although I am not sure of their value, since in my experience, people often do not use the information well. A typical example is a woman who came for a session with me in Santa Barbara. As I connected to her *field*, I found myself, in my vision, standing in the lobby of a public building, a bit like a hospital. It was as if I was seeing the world through my client's eyes and what I was witnessing I understood was going to occur in the near future.

In front of me was a tall man in a light-colored summer suit. He was handsome and powerful, and I could sense my client's immediate attraction as her attention was riveted on him. But as I observed him further I realized that he had a way of consuming people, like a basking shark that never stops eating. It seemed as if he was always on the lookout for someone to fulfill him, yet never satisfied with what he found. He did not appear to know that this came from a yawning need inside him that he could never fulfill, and instead, he seemed to believe that if he just kept "sampling" he would eventually find what he was looking for. I sensed that he had swept up a lot of women into his life but then dropped them.

After a few minutes of reading his *field* and *intentionality*, I redeployed my attention back to my client and told her what I had *seen*. Then I warned her: "Do not get involved with this man. It will be a very negative experience for you, perhaps disastrous. Do you understand?" She acknowledged that she did, and I let it drop, ending our session shortly after that.

Two years later when I returned to Santa Barbara, I ran into the woman on State Street. She greeted me warmly, and after we had exchanged a few pleasantries, she said she had met the man I *saw* during our session and he had been exactly as I described. When I asked if she had avoided getting involved with him, she said, a bit sheepishly, "No." In fact she admitted that she got very involved with him and the relationship had ended only days before our chance meeting.

"How did it work out?" I asked.

"A disaster, like you said," she replied.

When I asked her why she went ahead after I specifically warned her not to, she said she was curious to find out if I had been right! Perhaps the attraction was so strong that she used whatever excuse she could muster to give herself permission to pursue him. She certainly did find out that my description was correct, but at great emotional cost.

***

What are generally labeled apparitions and ghosts are another class of externalized vision. For a *seer*, these presences are known as a "felt awareness" long before they are visually *seen*, and usually more information about them can be gleaned through felt *seeing* and direct knowing than from what is observed visually. The sudden arrival of something totally unexpected can be shocking as I discovered with my experience of an apparition that appeared after my uncle's death. When shocked, we tend to try to stop these experiences by normalizing the situation as quickly as possible. We turn on lights, close doors, close our eyes, or as William James so marvelously put it, we ascribe our altered experiences to ordinary physical causes, such as food that "disagreed" with us—anything to avoid accepting an experience that is clearly non-ordinary.[1]

Another incident of this type happened to me in 1970, soon after my first visit to London, while I was sharing a house with my friend Andrew in rural, western Massachusetts. Andrew was a brilliant and original contributor to the early development of the computer industry, but in 1970 he was unhappy about how some of his work in information retrieval was being used for government surveillance and military purposes, so he decided to take time out. The property he rented had once been a sawmill, most of it hand-built by the original owner, including two houses and much of the machinery. A fire had gutted the mill but left the houses intact, and the owner had died suddenly in his house soon afterward. The property was then sold to an individual who chose not to reactivate the mill but to rent out the houses.

Soon after I arrived to join Andrew he mentioned that he had observed some strange occurrences in and around the house, the latest being when he awakened in the middle of the night to find his Danish rocking chair quietly tilting backward and forward for no reason. He pointed out that if he pushed the chair, it would rock on its own just three or four times before stopping but on the night in question he saw it rocking away, apparently unaided, for about a minute. We discussed possible causes but drew no conclusion and the subject was dropped.

A couple of months later, I was awakened at about three a.m. and, glancing at the closed window to my right, I saw a large, glowing ovoid shape about three feet tall float through it and then hover between the window and the bed. The form consisted of a bluish-white light emanating from a translucent core that appeared to have currents swirling through it. The felt presence was one of restlessness and

---

[1]W. James, *The Varieties of Religious Experience* (New York: Modern Library, 1936).

unease, but because of its sudden appearance and my inexperience at that time I failed to properly take note of its *tone* and *contents*.

The next day I mentioned what I had seen to Andrew, who admitted that he had caught sight of something like that at night behind the house, on the same side as my bedroom window. We concluded that it might have been some kind of *field*-remains of the original owner who had died suddenly in the house but that was a guess. I had not picked up any direct information from the presence. In such cases I leave it up to others to speculate about the "meaning" of such events.

***

Another type of *seeing* experience that transcends the constraints of space and time occurs through shared dreams and memories. I have often noticed that being in the presence of certain individuals facilitates a mutual *seeing* experience. It is as if our *fields* blend and the combination causes an alignment of *intentionality* that is more powerfully directed than either of us can create separately. One such event happened when I was visiting my brother and his girlfriend in Cambridge, Massachusetts, many years ago. They were sharing a house with a young woman, Patti. As soon as I was introduced, I was drawn to her on account of her dark, striking physical beauty and the intensity of her *field*-presence. I was surprised that she seemed drawn to me, too, since I was by no means a match in physical looks.

The attraction turned out to be mutual and quite magnetic. The day after my arrival, we began an affair, and during the two weeks I was there, we were almost always together talking about psychology (she had recently graduated as a psych major), our personal history, philosophy and feminism. One evening after making love, as we were lying next to each other enjoying the afterglow, a vision opened in my mind's eye. As usual, this *seeing* event was both an internal and an external perception. I was witnessing a girl, aged about eight or nine standing with a boy a year or two older than her. Straight away I knew they were brother and sister. The place in which they stood seemed grim: a muddy ground surrounded by a high, multi-layered barbwire fence against a dark, overcast sky.

Looking at the scene I felt sadness and despair but also joy at seeing the young girl. Suddenly I blurted out: "I thought I'd never see you again" just as Patti exclaimed the same to me. There was a rush of recognition combined with confusion as we hugged and shared our joy at "finding" each other. It was a strange moment—we were simultaneously in the present as lovers and in some unspecified past moment as brother and sister. The encounter left us both deeply moved.

I am certain that none of our prior conversations contained anything connected to that *seeing* event, and so I believe they did not precipitate the shared vision, nor did I tell Patti straight away what I had *seen*. Yet when we eventually shared the experience of our mutual vision, it was clear that we were looking through the same window into a dismal past whose *field tone* was filled with death and despair. Although we did not *see* what happened to those two children, we were certain they had died—they appeared to have no way out. Again I report this event only in terms of what I directly *saw* and what apparently physically transpired, leaving any interpretations to others.

***

For me, the rarest, weirdest, most startling, yet apparently objective *seeing* encounters are those that I have when entering into a radically different reality frame. These appear to be discontinuous with the normal, day-to-day world and are related to what some people call shamanic encounters. My experience of the two entities in Boston is a striking example of this form of *seeing*. My entry into it was heralded by the experience of the room rotating and casting me into another world, which appeared similar to the one I knew, except my sense of reality had been radically altered both in its felt quality and by the appearance of beings who could not possibly have been there under "normal" circumstances.

In 2007, while living in Alstonville, Australia, I had another of these fascinating and bizarre "other reality" encounters. For several weeks I had been experiencing headaches and a gnawing sensation in my chest, like the beginning of angina, but never developing into the full-blown thing. One morning, after getting to bed late the night before and sleeping fitfully, I awoke early with another headache and began to toss and turn—dozing briefly and then reawakening with pain still in my head. As I roused myself I could feel the sensation in my chest starting up again, too. After tossing and turning for almost an hour, I lay on my back with my eyes closed but fully conscious of my surroundings.

All at once I was aware of someone sitting down on the bed next to me, to my left. I sensed that this person was female, although I had not yet looked at her face. I was aware that she was sitting cross-legged on the bed next to me and I could *see* that her *field* formed a pyramid shape around her. Her *field* glowed, but I could still perceive her body clearly through it.

I became aware that she was asking me (with words that were not spoken out loud but heard in my mind's ear) if I would permit her to remove something from my body. I do not remember whether she actually said "remove something from" or "fix," but I am sure that I did not hear the word "heal." I agreed to let her do it.

Straight away, she bent over and put her mouth to my chest at my sternum whereupon her face penetrated below my skin as if she was immersing it in a dish of shallow water. I was aware that she was sucking something out of me, and when she lifted her face, I could *see* she had in her mouth a bright green worm that squirmed as it was held captive by her shockingly pointed teeth. It had a head with two little pincer claws and I saw that it realized it was about to be eaten but, as it writhed in a frantic attempt to escape back into my chest, the woman simply chewed it up and swallowed it. Although I understood what was going on I maintained a strangely detached demeanor and felt more like a passive observer than the subject of such a bizarre procedure.

Next I became aware that she had noticed more of these creatures inside me so this time she thrust her hand into my chest as if my thorax was merely a bubble. As she maneuvered behind my right lung, I could *see* another of the "worms" trying to get away but she reached in further, her arm up to her elbow, grabbed the second worm and popped it into her mouth too. I thought I heard the creature crying in fear as she calmly chomped it up and swallowed. At this point I could *see* the inside of my thoracic cavity and perceive hollow, empty trails where the worm-creatures had been living and eating. As I observed the damage, however, the "worm holes" were already being reclaimed by surrounding tissue. I lay there a while longer wondering what would happen next, but then I realized the mysterious helper had left and I no longer felt unwell.

All the experiences I have related here were carefully observed and written down and described to various people numerous times over the years. Although such occurrences have been fairly commonplace in the course of my life, I still feel their strangeness as I try to reconcile them with the empirical, positivist world of scientific materialism. In a way, I live in two worlds: that of the scientist and the *seer*. Even though the work of the *seer* does not easily yield the inter-subjective verification essential to the creation of reliable, scientific knowledge, as laid down by philosophers like Karl Popper,[2] nevertheless I try to take as much of an empirical approach to it as I do to my work as a social scientist.

---

[2] K. Popper, *The Logic of Scientific Discovery* (New York: Routledge, 1959).

20. *SEER* AS DETECTIVE AND MESSENGER

In December 1976, while I was living in Santa Barabara, I received a telephone call from my friend, Susan. The sister of her boyfriend had disappeared and the family was worried, she said, adding that it was not like this woman, whose name was Jackie, to go off and not stay in touch with her family. Susan knew I had the ability to do psychometry on an object and from that, provide information about its owner, including her whereabouts, so she asked me if I could help.

If I was asked the same thing today, knowing what I do now about the emotional consequences of such cases, I would say "no" but back then I was prepared to try something new, so I said "yes." I agreed to meet with Susan's boyfriend, Tom, and his sister, Barbara, who were instructed to bring me a few of Jackie's personal items to psychometrize. On the appointed evening, Susan came to my small apartment, followed by Tom and Barbara soon after. The collective anxiety among the three of them was palpable. Obviously they were nervous and afraid of what I might say.

Straight away Tom announced that they had consulted a psychic who told them that Jackie was fine and would be home by Christmas. I nodded, but as I always do when hearing someone's hopes and beliefs, I attempt to put them aside in order to prevent their desires from "leaking" into my perceptions and interfering with my ability to *see* with a degree of objectivity.

Tom and Barbara had brought with them a box with some of Jackie's clothes from her college dorm room but no really personal objects, such as a ring or watch she would have worn constantly. I was concerned that the signal left on the clothes might not be clear enough for me to connect my attention to Jackie, but they assured me that she had worn the sweater, in particular, a great deal and that it had not been cleaned or worn by anyone else since her disappearance.

As I picked up the sweater and held it close to my face, immediately, in my mind's eye, I found myself in a remote location, standing in some chaparral near the side of a road heading up into the hills northwest of Santa Barbara. To my horror, in the brush, only meters from the road, lay the body of a woman, face down, partially covered by shrubbery, with only her lower half visible. As I looked at the scene before me, I had a direct knowing that she had been sexually assaulted and shot dead. It was not as if I witnessed it, nor were there any visual clues I could discern. I can only say that the scene somehow "spoke" to me.

For a minute or so I was too shocked to speak. How was I to relate what I had just *seen* to Jackie's siblings? It seemed to be an horrendous thing to have to tell a family, so I began to "waffle"—a British term meaning talking without really saying anything—while struggling to find a way to convey to these people that I *saw* their sister had been murdered. The picture in my mind's eye was very vivid and had that unique phenomenological signature that tells me that I am witnessing a real event external to me, but for the next half hour I continued to struggle with the problem of how to break such awful news.

Before long, Tom and Barbara—deciding perhaps that I had nothing useful to say—decided to leave. Only at the last minute, standing beside them at the door, did I finally blurt out what I had seen. "I'm sorry, she's dead." I said. "She's been shot and is lying near a roadside in the mountains in that direction" (I pointed to the northwest). "I can see her legs and what she was wearing—dark-colored jeans and sneakers."

The shockwave that hit the room was seismic. Tom and Barbara froze and then they fled without saying another word.

Within a few weeks, on January 21, 1977, the body of Jacqueline Anne Rook, age 21, was found by hikers in an area near the Santa Ynez Mountains to which I had pointed that evening. Although Tom had reported our meeting to the police, they did not take my information seriously, which is a common response in such cases. Most police are not interested in the utterances of psychics or *seers*.

This episode left me with a question I would spend many years trying to answer: how to be the bearer of bad news. During that half hour with Jackie's relatives, I felt a bit like a squirrel frantically racing up and down a tree, trying to avoid the "danger" of bringing a dreadful message, while feeling compelled to deliver it.

Back then, I often felt caught between telling the truth of what I had *seen* and protecting those who came to me for help. There were no rules or standards of behavior for such encounters, and nothing in my background or education had prepared me for such a role. In the Jackie Rook case, it was about eight years before Barbara would not flee at the sight of me and Tom, an accomplished professional, would not feel agitated in my presence.

But there was more to come in relation to Jackie's murder. About a week after the initial psychometry, as I was walking along upper State Street, unable to shake the dark cloud hanging around me associated with what I had *seen*, I had another vision, this time of a sneering, light-haired man driving north toward the suburb of Goleta. He appeared to be filled with rage and disdain for others, and I knew at once that I was *seeing* Jackie Rook's killer.

Later I learned that this man had taken the lives of two other women in the area as well. From police forensic evidence, I found out that he murdered his victims with a gunshot to the head before sexually assaulting them. This would account for the gruesome "feeling atmosphere" surrounding my first vision and the pain and horror I felt, which stayed with me for many weeks afterward.

During their investigation, the FBI published a profile of the possible killer, in which they mainly described him as a "drifter," but as a *seer* I knew they had this wrong. From what I *saw* of the killer he was no mere stranger passing through, but a member of a prominent, local family. This turned out to be true when later he was identified as Thor Nis Christiansen, the son of restaurateurs from Solvang. He was finally arrested in 1979 and convicted in 1980. A few years later he was murdered by one of his fellow prisoners at Folsom State Prison, California.

***

Violent death caused by another person almost always leaves a deep impression in the *field* of the place where it has occurred. Inevitably the *tone* is unpleasant, and connecting to such scenes tends to evoke intense sadness in me. On the few occasions when I have taken on such cases as a kind of psychic detective, it has been at the request of friends or interested parties. The story of Jackie Rook was one such case. Another was the incident of a child who went missing in Isla Vista, a university town north of Santa Barbara, in the late 1970s. My friend Ray, with whom I shared a house in Isla Vista at that time, wanted me to become involved. After my experience with the Rook family I did not want to work on such a case again. However, Ray, being enthusiastic about my work as a *seer*, kept at me for several days until I finally agreed to at least "scan" the area.

I soon realized that although the authorities had included in their search a northern section of undeveloped beach jutting into the ocean and much favored by surfers, called Devereux Point, they had missed the body, which I clearly *saw* lying under a large, spreading tree. Ray wanted to tell the police, but I discouraged him because they had previously showed little interest in the information someone like me could offer. However, the issue became moot when, very soon afterward, the boy's body was discovered under the tree I had *seen* by someone walking on the Point.

My primary technique for doing a search like this is similar to the one employed by remote viewers who are usually given maps or coordinates and then asked to scan designated locations and report what they perceive. I had seen the press report about the missing boy before I started a "scan" of the area, *looking* for anything that resonated with the available information. When I focused my attention on the Point—partly because the news report mentioned it—I was drawn to the tree. Then, through an act of *intentionality*-driven *seeing*, I searched the ground around it and *saw* the boy's body partially covered by debris. This was all done at a distance without me ever visiting Devereux.

Another, historically interesting example of my detective work as a *seer* occurred on a commercial tour of Great Britain that my wife organized in late 1984. We drove a small group of participants around parts of Britain to visit sites of historical interest that she had researched and decided would be interesting. The plan was that I would perform a psychometry at each location and help participants learn to do the same. My wife chose the sites for us to visit, but kept them and details surrounding their history a strict secret until after we had scanned them.

It was kind of a "magical mystery tour." The locations ranged from ancient barrow tombs and stone circles to the ruins of a manor house called Minster Lovell Hall, located west of Oxford in the Cotswolds.

It was at this last location that I had one of my best "hits" on that trip. I remember walking around the property sensing the *field*, scanning for any interesting anomalies in the *tone* or *contents*. After ascending a few steps at the rear wall of the crumbling building, a clear and dramatic image came through my *second stream* of awareness. I *saw* a rider on horseback galloping toward the manor with a sense of panic and urgency about him. Upon arrival he dismounted and delivered a message to a man whom I surmised to be the lord of the manor. The gist of this message was that some military action had been lost and the lord was in danger. Strangely, however, he seemed not as perturbed as the man bringing the message.

Next, the scene shifted to a tiny room inside the manor where I found myself looking, at a downward angle and from a distance of 50 to 75 feet, at the same man who had received the news earlier. He was sitting at a small table or desk, apparently writing by candlelight. I had the strong sense that he was trapped in the chamber somehow.

After I described my vision, my wife told us that Minster Lovell Hall was known to be haunted, possibly by Francis, first Viscount Lovell, who had sided with the Yorkists during the Wars of the Roses. According to Ferne Arfin, a writer on travel sites in Great Britain, the story goes that

> Lovell had been made a Viscount by Richard III, but within two years, Richard and the Yorkists were defeated at the Battle of Bosworth. Briefly exiled, Francis returned from France only to take up the losing side once again, in an abortive Yorkist rebellion. According to local legend, he hid in a vault at Minster Lovell Hall giving a servant the only key. The servant died shortly after and, so the story goes, his skeleton, surrounded by mouldy books and the skeleton of his little dog at his feet, was found by workmen in 1708.[1]

This was another case of an imprint being left behind in the *field* to be picked up, centuries later, as *content* by a *seer*. My *intentionality* had focused my attention sufficiently to allow me to sweep the area like a

---

[1] http://gouk.about.com/od/thingstodo/ss/Minster-Lovell-Hall-Haunted-And-Haunting-Ruins-Near-Oxford.htm

bloodhound sniffing out a scent. Once the hot spot was located, it was only a matter of stilling my mind in order to allow the *contents* of the *field* to enter my awareness—bringing what was normally background into the foreground in order to perceive what was no longer physically present.

V. *Seeing*, Reality, and Knowledge

My thesis is that if we start with the supposition that there is only one primal stuff or material in the world, a stuff of which everything is composed, and if we call that stuff "pure experience," then knowing can easily be explained as a particular sort of relation towards one another into which portions of pure experience may enter.

Just so, I maintain, does a given undivided portion of experience, taken in one context of associates, play the part of a knower, of a state of mind, of "consciousness;" while in a different context the same undivided bit of experience plays the part of a thing known, of an objective "content."

– William James
Essays in Radical Empiricism
and a Pluralistic Universe

21. A SHIFT IN PERSPECTIVE

As we move through life, we develop a life perspective—an overall "theory" about what exists and how people, things, and events interconnect and work. A perspective, in my thinking, differs from a point of view, which is the immediate field of direct knowing given to us by the filtering action of the deployment of our attention. Our beliefs are formed and driven by what we allow ourselves to know in the immediate situation, and what we know, in turn, is driven by our point of view. Consciously and unconsciously, we combine our immediate knowledge with what we already know and believe in an attempt to formulate a "theory"—a perspective—about how it all works and what the future will bring. A perspective, therefore, is an overarching conceptual summary that, in effect, condenses knowledge into beliefs and understandings drawn from the picture of reality our point of view dictates. It is a story telling us who and what we are, as well as how the world functions.

Although parts of our perspective endure throughout our lives, certain events disrupt belief and cause that perspective to alter. A shift in perspective can occur when we go through a major life event. For example, the first time someone cheats us, our perspective on the nature of people and how they behave may change. The story of who we are is elaborated and modified as previously unknown possibilities impinge on our lives.

My blind leap across the Atlantic to London in 1969 and the start of my training as a *seer* caused a major shift in my perspective. At the time, as I have said, the manner in which this happened caused me to consider whether such events might be orchestrated by forces outside my scientific understanding of time, space, and causality. Were there "intelligences" or guardian angels directing and driving this process, or some kind of "overself" as Alice suggested, I wondered?

If not, then what? Science was no longer of any help to me, or so it seemed. Certainly the act of *seeing* did not appear to be bound by the usual constraints of physical distance and time or ruled by the laws of physics, such as the requirement that there be a transfer of momenta for information to move from one place to another. According to science, physical vibrations of sound and electromagnetic vibrations, such as radio waves or light, must travel from some place to us before our senses can detect them and our brain can turn them into perceptions and knowledge. However, demonstrations of remote viewing, including those by the United States military, showed that information could be obtained across distances without any apparent physical transfer of information. Remote *viewers* engaged in these experiments clearly demonstrated a capacity for non-ordinary perception according to the data.[1] In short, many acts of *seeing* occur in a manner that appears to violate common sense and physical law and thus threatens to disrupt our usual stories of how things work.

Like the evidence of remote viewing across space, there is also evidence from psychics and *seers* to make a case for information travelling across time, from the past or the future to the present. (An alternative explanation is that the perceiver's knowing is able in some way to "reach" into the past or the future.) As impossible as this seems, my experience and that of others, as reported by reputable researchers, demonstrates that this violation of the supposed constraints of the time arrow of thermodynamics does happen in *seeing*. It was certainly a major factor in the disruption of my perspective during my initiation.

So what was I to make of all this, how was I to explain it and fit it into my perspective? In the early days of becoming a *seer* I made several attempts to create a grand, explanatory theory—in particular, of how the apparent violation of the time arrow might have happened during my "call" to England. In fact I used to get into heated arguments with colleagues because it was exceedingly important for my theory to be correct. Then one day I realized that all of the speculation and arguing was a waste of time. It was not facilitating what I cared about

---

[1] R. Targ and H. Puthoff, "Information Transmission under Conditions of Sensory Shielding," *Nature,* 251 (1974), 602–7.
J. Schnabel, *Remote Viewers: The Secret History of America's Psychic Spies* (New York: Dell, 1997).

most by then—knowing the world as a *seer*—and there was no way anyone could ascertain whose speculations were ultimately correct, in any case.

Often we believe that we are rowing the boat of life, largely directing it ourselves, down a causal stream along the path of the arrow of time, but this is nothing more than a metaphor or a perspective, one of many that are possible. Conceivably, a point of view exists somewhere "above" our life river from which we can look down and see the twists, turns and currents, and thereby perceive how we arrived at the present as well as predict where we will end up. However, I do not have access to such a meta-perspective regarding my life stream. These sorts of explanations are only metaphors, and each is one possible perspective I could adopt as a *seer*, but I am unwilling to engage in grandiose speculation about how the human scene "really" works because I do not have a tower from which to view it and report back.

Today, as a dedicated *seer* and an empirical social scientist, all I can do honestly is observe, note, and continue the journey. I report only what I encounter and know through my direct experience, rather than trying to make sense of it by theorizing about how it all works. When it comes down to it, my version of the "big picture" would probably be no better than anyone else's, anyway.

So, in spite of what I was told at the time and what I have learned in subsequent years, I still do not have an explanation that resolves the conundrum of my London experience. I walked out of a neuropsychology lab in New Mexico with a scientist's pragmatic, real-world perspective and within weeks was confronted with a series of phenomena that challenged it. I can only say that to accept and incorporate those events into my life required a major shift in my perspective about reality that led to a profound alteration in how my point of view would subsequently be formed and function.

***

There have been a number of episodes in my life where, like the London encounter, I seemed to be keeping appointments that I did not make. I would just show up somewhere to discover an important meeting for which I was expected—although this idea of an appointment is just a way of interpreting, just a perspective. These occurrences can look as though some supernatural intelligence or "overself" is directing them, but I leave that for others to speculate on. What remains salient is that such events do happen. Among my experiences have been episodes when I have heard disincarnate voices talking to me, offering help and providing the feeling that I am being protected and guided toward a solution to a pressing problem. One of the more useful of these occurred in the early 1980s.

My wife and I were sharing a condo in Montecito, California with our friend Ray, who had been diabetic from childhood and now, in his late thirties, was going blind as a result of worsening diabetic retinopathy. He often commented that he wished he had a "contrast control" for his vision, like we do for video monitors, so he could increase the clarity of his visual field. One evening, because of a headache, I went to bed early, seeking darkness and quiet. As I lay there with my eyes closed, my inner visual field was suddenly filled with a clear, panoramic picture of craggy mountains framed by a bright blue sunlit sky. The air was clear and thin, which made me think the scene must be taking place at high altitude. The quality of the light and the "otherness" of the image signaled that it was coming to me as an act of *seeing*.

While examining the "scene" I became aware of a dirt road running horizontally across my field of vision about a hundred yards in front of where I stood. As I stared toward the road, I could see a man leading a horse laden with goods, leftward, in an uphill direction. They walked slowly, and as I looked at them from where I stood, the scene shifted, and suddenly I found myself standing by the side of the road about three yards from them. I took note of the man's traditional Himalayan dress and Mongolian features. He stopped and looked at me, then he introduced himself and told me he was a healer. His face was sunbaked, leathery, and lined. He had sparkling eyes and a very kind smile and seemed to be a friendly, good-natured person. Without me asking or either of us speaking, he conveyed a message directly to my mind that he would show me how to make a poultice for my headache.

Another shift followed, and I found myself witnessing the preparation of an herbal compress as I listened to him telling me the names of herbs to be put inside it and giving me instructions on how to apply it. I had never heard of the plants he listed and was struggling to remember their names when, suddenly, it occurred to me to ask if anything could be done for Ray's diminishing vision.

As I posed the question—either out loud or in my mind, I cannot recall exactly—there appeared in front of me what I later learned was a standard acupuncturist's chart showing a picture of a stylized human body with the meridians and points drawn on it. The old man indicated a point on the heel of the figure and a couple places on the ear and head and told me to have someone put needles in those locations to help Ray's vision. At that time, although I had heard about acupuncture, I had never seen the chart, nor did I have any idea of which points could be utilized for improving Ray's vision. However, I made sure to memorize what he had shown me—unfortunately at the cost of forgetting the names of the plants for my own poultice. At that point, I became excited about the possibility for Ray, and so I bade the healer good-bye and opened my eyes. The headache was gone.

Straight away I got out of bed and went into the living room to tell Ray that I thought he should see an acupuncturist. I described my experience to him, and later, when we found a suitable practitioner, we were told that the points relevant to treating Ray's problem were the ones the healer in my vision had indicated. The treatment gave my friend some temporary relief, a degree of "contrast control" for a while. However, the inexorable progress of the blood vessel growth behind his retinas eventually left him almost totally blind.

Like so many of these sorts of encounters, this event forced an alteration in my perspective on how the world worked. It was another reminder that reality is much broader than the ontological model implied by most interpretations of science, which had been my tightly held interpretive perspective before becoming a *seer*.

For me, science definitely remains one of the most useful methods we have of obtaining a workable picture of the world, but it is arrogant to believe it is the final picture. This change in my perspective came about gradually, after the evidence for the veracity of what I was experiencing as a *seer* became so overwhelming that it was beyond denial.

22. SEEING AND WAYS OF KNOWING

If, the "stuff" that comprises our world is "pure experience," as William James suggests, this offers us a basis for connecting the worlds of science and *seeing*, for, if reality is largely experiential, then what we attend to should determine how we construct our ontological "bottom line"— our view of what *is*.

There is little doubt that the dominant worldview underpinning Western intellectual life today is that of science. Although I do not feel that *seeing* has to be explained in terms of science, it would be appropriate to raise some of the issues that connect and separate these two realms of knowing.

Although science tends to use a probabilistic, reductive, causal model of explanation, its language and conceptualizing frequently offer teleological explanations of how things have come to be as they are. In other words, the science-driven picture of reality suggests that the world is the result of an evolutionary march of progress toward higher states. A typical example can be drawn from biology, where accepted wisdom is that the brain's cerebral cortex represents the end point of an inexorable process of phylogenetic development toward higher functioning (and, of course, the human cortex is "it," from this mythologized perspective).

No doubt this idea stems from the cortex's primary role in language and rational thought as well as from the ancient Greek belief that the rational mind represented the pinnacle of human development. This helps to explain what has produced the notion of cortical evolution toward a "higher" brain.

I believe that it is a useful heuristic device to reverse standard beliefs and assumptions and then examine the implications that arise as a result. So, for a moment, let us turn this idea on its head. What if the frontal and pre-frontal cortices and related structures are just tools of the limbic system—the so-called appetitive and emotional "lower brain?"

What if the "higher" cortical system is just a means for the limbic brain to extend its efficacy? In this hypothetical model, the cortex becomes no more than a purpose-built system arising out of evolutionary pressures to extend the basic survival and pleasure functions of the "lower" brain for obtaining food, sex and comfort. It posits that cortical functions might exist solely to create particular feelings and awareness states, such as organismic well-being, rather than rational, logical thoughts.

According to this revised interpretation of brain function, language and rational thinking become "spin-off" technologies that are both useful and problematic, since they add to our strategic capacity to meet our appetitive, organismic needs but also generate a kind of chatter that dominates our awareness. Quite often we mistake this chatter for who and what we are and the extraneous noise is taken to be a signal— indeed, the signifier of what is real.

An important part of the limbic brain's function lies in its receptive power—its ability to not only know its own feeling states but to register those of other people and animals.[1] The interpretation of these feelings is done by the cortex. My hypothesis is that as the cortex grew to include the prefrontal areas, cortical capacities for conceptualization, forward thinking, planning, and analytic problem solving came to dominate the field of conscious attention (which is primarily language-driven), largely drowning out the limbic brain's transmission and reception of felt knowing as one of the primary methods of social connection and exchange. This receptive, felt method of knowing is fundamental to *seeing* perception, so as the cortical functions have become dominant, we have lost a great deal of access to our *seeing* capacity as well as our connection to other beings and the natural world.

What I am suggesting is that reality, created through linguistically driven attention and knowing, has become the experience of a world reflected through language. This language-map is a picture of what we consider to be external objects. The result is that we are driving along

---

[1] J. Decety, "A Social Cognitive Neuroscience Model of Human Empathy," in E. Harmon-Jones and P. Winkielman, eds., *Social Neuroscience: Integrating Biological and Psychological Explanations of Social Behavior* (New York: The Guilford Press, 2007), Kindle edition, Location 3381.

our life roads without looking up from our internalized, self-created "roadmaps."

I do not want diminish the power and usefulness of higher cortical functions or what they add to basic limbic drives and state-seeking. The benefits are immense. Our cortical functions help us to strategize how to get more of what we want, and with them, we can also figure out how to control the competition around us. Indeed, an examination of the contents of our consciousness reveals that our thinking is dominated by activity dedicated to making us feel more secure. However, the downside is that since the experience of our conscious processing is the most immediately available sense of who and what we are, it is easy to adopt the idea that cognitive functioning is all that being human is about. Because of this, the limbic "owner" of the cognitive apparatus is easily forgotten and may even be seen in a negative way, especially when it irrupts into a supposedly rational thought process by being "emotional."

In evoking this cognitive-emotional divide, I am harkening back to a type of self-understanding that existed long before our present picture of "higher" and "lower" brain function. I am referring to the ancient Greek metaphorical division of the human personality into Dionysian and Apollonian archetypes. The former, named after the god of nature, Dionysus, is the sensualist who lives more for feeling states (not just pleasure), while the latter, named after the heavenly lord of light, truth and prophecy, Apollo, represents the cerebrotonic personality who is emotionally restrained and tends to live in the linguistic world of conceptual thought and intellect. Of course, no person is purely one or the other, except in extreme cases. We all have elements of both types, though one tends dominate. For the minority of individuals who straddle both styles, their experiential, Dionysian side tends to feed the cognitive output of their Apollonian selves and vice versa.

For a *seer* to be properly rounded, he must have access to both. The goal is to find a method for getting in touch with emotional perception, or non-linguistic felt awareness and balance it with cognitive knowing. Both are important, and the sacrifice of one for the other can lead to an unbalanced, fantasy-prone way of meeting the world—either by too much insistence on the "truth" of an objective existent reality or by believing that what you feel is true simply because you feel it.

Today, Apollonian-style thinking seems to dominate the education of children. It becomes the primary shaper of their perception, whether it works with their emotional style or not. As the child grows and develops, most of his attention and awareness is forced to focus through the linguistic-rational lens so that the voice of direct, felt knowing is lost, except for sporadic instances when it breaks through to conscious awareness. Such instances range from what Mircea Eliade, the great scholar of religion and shamanism, described as the irruption of the sacred into the profane,[2] through mystical experience, to moments of *seeing*, such as a direct knowing about someone's past through their *field*. From my perspective, it is unfortunate that, in our current worldview, we give little attention or credence to these moments of reconnecting to our felt knowing, which lies at the heart of *seeing*.

For the most part, poets, painters, dancers, and musicians gravitate toward the Dionysian mode of knowing, while scientists, logicians, actuaries, and the like tend toward the Apollonian. Knowing this makes it easier to understand the hostility often shown by adherents of science toward people who claim to have paranormal experiences. The more Apollonian a person is, the less likely he is to accept a breakthrough of emotion and felt knowing into his consciousness or to appreciate it as reliable or trustworthy. Such events are simply too disruptive for the Apollonian mind.

The British biologist Richard Dawkins is the quintessential Apollonian who insists that the scientific way of knowing is not only correct but the *only* way one should meet the world of direct experience. He even argues that artists should draw their inspiration and activate their imaginations from the "wonders of science."[3] In this case, perhaps he thinks that Mozart might have written a better piece of music if he had just known about the fate of the dinosaurs, perhaps. Such an idea is preposterous, of course. Like all great artists, Mozart

---

[2]M. Eliade, *The Sacred and the Profane: The Nature of Religion,* trans. R. Trask (New York: HBJ, 1959).

[3]R. Dawkins, *Unweaving the Rainbow: Science, Delusion and the Appetite for Wonder* (Boston: Houghton Mifflin, 1998).

wrote music based on his felt connection to the events and issues of his time—love, death, humor, poverty (his), and religion—not a theory.

By personality, temperament, and predilection, most scientists believe that to be objective is to eschew limbic intrusion as a fault in the cognitive system rather than the voice of its "owner." Having said this, some neuroscientists believe that cortical function is at least influenced by limbic input. Without the limbic system's appetitive drives, such as curiosity and yearning for rewards, there would be no cognition and no science, they argue.[4] In other words, the very impetus for scientific activity (including the hope of getting a Nobel Prize) comes from the drive arising from the limbic emotional level of human functioning—the very same aspect of themselves scientists most often eschew in their search for objectivity.

While I believe in the scientific method as a way of addressing certain problems, I do not see it as the only way to understand every life-knot we may want to untangle. As Nobel Laureate Sir Peter Medawar argues, science is not for the "big questions" such as: "What is the meaning of life?" or "What is the ultimate ground of being?" These puzzles probably are addressed more appropriately by religion or philosophy.[5] When physicists such as Stephen Hawking apply the thinking that governs his area of expertise—the mathematics of black holes—to such questions,[6] the resultant discourse is sophomoric at best. To say that mathematics, a product of higher cognitive functioning, sits at the core of the so-called "mind of God" is not unlike saying that She probably speaks English, too.

On the other hand, when people in the humanities and social sciences use ideas and mathematically rigorous constructs such as topology, quantum mechanics and chaos theory to explain the human experiential domain, they, too, sound out of tune. Each group appears to want to deal with the fundamental issues of the other, not realizing that their methods and ideas are designed to serve different ends: the scientific way of thinking to create functional, mathematically rigorous,

---

[4]A. R. Damasio, *Descartes' Error: Emotion, Reason, and the Human Brain* (New York: G. P. Putnam's Sons, 1994).
[5]P. Medawar, *The Limits of Science* (Oxford: Oxford University Press, 1984).
[6]S. Hawking, *A Brief History of Time* (New York: Bantam Dell, 1988).

and predictive models of how things work; the humanities and social sciences to understand existential questions.

That said, both emotional knowing and cognitive knowing are important, and eschewing one comes with the risk of losing a major part of one's capacity to be aware and know.

***

As a *seer*, it is my view that the primary assertion of existence should be: "I feel, therefore I am," rather than the famous "I think, therefore I am" in which the seventeenth century philosopher Descartes wrongly equated thought with existence. I have often observed the cognitive dissonance that strikes when a logical contradiction is forced into the awareness of someone who has adopted the Cartesian myth. The disorientation that results when one thought slams at high speed head first into an opposing thought not only brings the person's cognitive mind to a screeching halt, it fundamentally disturbs his very sense of existence that is built on this cognitively based self.

Minor versions of this crash take place when someone reports that he has lost his "train of thought" and then attempts to rearrange his cognition to avoid a second crash. I have witnessed this in myself and in others many times over the years. Indeed, I have been present at some major scientific cognitive crashes as well, none more graphic than one that occurred in the summer of 1962, when I was working as a research assistant at the Woods Hole Marine Biology Laboratory (MBL) in Cape Cod, Massachusetts.

My job that summer was to assist the international team of neurochemists who were working with Professor David Nachmansohn of Columbia University Medical School in an effort to uncover the mechanism of the nerve impulse—the basic digital signal that nerve cells use to communicate with one another. At the time, a scientific race to explicate the physiochemistry of this mechanism was in its final stages and had boiled down to two positions: the acetylcholine theory of impulse generation led by Nachmansohn and the ion-gradient explanation being developed by a team in Britain consisting of Andrew Huxley, Alan Hodgkin, and Sir John Eccles.

In Nachmansohn's view, a chemical called acetylcholine, produced in each nerve cell, caused the nerve's membrane to change in a way that initiated the pulse, which was then propagated down the nerve fiber, causing a progressive change along its length. In contrast, the team of Hodgkin, Huxley, and Eccles believed that the pulse did not require acetylcholine and that ionic forces across the membrane, from outside to inside, were responsible for the generation and propagation of the pulse.

My primary task was to dissect giant axons (three-centimeter-long single nerve fibers) from freshly caught squid, place them in the research apparatus, and assist as trials and experiments were performed. (A bonus was that we got to eat the squid as well as the Maine lobsters used in our work.) The research proceeded at a feverish pace, and near the end of that summer Alan Hodgkin arrived from London to present the results of his team's work and to engage in debate with the Nachmansohn group. Whispers were going around that whichever team got it right would win the Nobel Prize. Needless to say, the atmosphere in the lab was highly charged with anticipation.

It was a sultry August day when the Woods Hole researchers and lab assistants from all the departments of MBL gathered in the main lecture theater to listen to Hodgkin. The experimental work he presented was brilliant—an ingenious and meticulous approach that covered almost all contingencies. It made an exceedingly strong case in support of his team's theory.

After his presentation, members of the Nachmansohn team invited him back to our lab to debate what they considered unresolved issues. There, Hodgkin asked for a copy of Nachmansohn's book,[7] which was duly removed from a bookcase and handed to him. He opened it to a page that detailed the theory of acetylcholine-mediated transmission and asked the scientists present if they still stood by the figures reported there. The response was an enthusiastic "yes." Specifically, Nachmanson's theory stated that a certain amount of acetylcholine was required to generate each nerve impulse, and that once the nerve cell was prevented from producing any more of this neurotransmitter there was still enough to generate approximately 100,000 additional nerve impulses without the need for more synthesis of acetylcholine.

---

[7]D. Nachmansohn, *The Physico-Chemical Mechanism of Nerve Activity*, vol. 47 (New York: New York Academy of Sciences, 1946).

At this point, Hodgkin produced his weapon—a pencil—and performed a simple multiplication: 100,000 times the amount of acetylcholine required for a nerve impulse, which equaled enough neurotransmitter to just about fill a quart jar! The volume of the fiber that supposedly held this large amount of chemical was 0.003 fluid ounces, less than 0.0001 of a quart. Clearly, short of invoking the as yet unknown "Tardis effect," this was impossible.[8]

The impact of this revelation was profound. A stunned silence descended. Apparently no one on the Nachmansohn team, not even the highly respected neurochemist himself, had thought to do this simple arithmetic, which would have immediately revealed that something was wrong with the theory. The emotional atmosphere in the lab was so tense that Hodgkin himself—in a peculiarly English way—became uncomfortable and fell silent too, after which he simply closed the book and quietly left the lab. Nothing more was said for five minutes or more as the Nachmansohn team remained almost motionless where Hodgkin had left them.

What happened next was a revelation to me that shook my devout belief in science and the integrity of its practitioners. Within half an hour of Hodgkin's departure, the team members were talking as if their work contained no fundamental logical flaw and it was just a matter of time before their results would yield the evidence needed to win the ultimate scientific prize. Indeed, the summer finished with no further discussion of the event and I returned to New York and my studies. Needless to say, the following year the Nobel Prize for Physiology or Medicine was awarded to the team of Sir John Eccles, Alan Hodgkin, and Andrew Huxley "for their discoveries concerning the ionic mechanisms involved in excitation and inhibition in the peripheral and central portions of the nerve cell membrane."[9]

Hodgkin's presentation and his defeat of the Nachmanson theory that day in August 1962 was a great moment in science that I had the privilege to witness. However, the terrible dishonesty that followed it

---

[8]The TV sci-fi character Dr. Who travels through time and space in a police phone booth called a Tardis that has a much greater internal volume than the external measurements could possibly contain.
[9]http://www.nobelprize.org/nobel_prizes/medicine/laureates/1963/.

shook my belief in science as an enterprise conducted by dispassionate and objective individuals. As a young man eager to join the scientific ranks, this was fairly confusing.

It seemed to me that the whole of Hodgkin's revelation was rationalized away. It did not fit the story of the group, so its importance was diminished to nothing more than a temporary distraction. No one denied that he had been there, nor presumably did they forget the calculation he did. However, the logical contradiction it revealed was never discussed, and the outcome of the meeting was talked about as if something much less significant and not nearly as upsetting had taken place. It was if the Nachmansohn team told themselves: "There really is no reason to abandon years of work, is there?"

In retrospect, it is clear to me that the demolition of this foundational pillar of their neurochemical theory had been too much for the minds of otherwise highly skilled and dedicated researchers. It was potentially ruinous to careers, self-concepts, and personal belief systems, and this potential loss had to be obviated by making the event that caused it to *functionally* disappear.

Put differently, reality had slammed into belief in the minds of the members of the Nachmansohn team, causing a temporary but powerful dissolution of everyone's sense of self. The only way to rescue their understanding of who they were after this cognitive train wreck was by denying its conclusion. Afterward, they reassembled the world (their cognitive beliefs) as they previously knew it, but with the addition of an inner wall designed to block awareness of critical aspects of that fatal moment of Hodgkin's revelation so they would not have to deal with its implications. This was futile, of course, for in spite of the team's dedication, the writing was on the wall.

As time passed, I came to realize that there is a schism between the idea of science and the way in which it is practiced—a split between what scientists and their supporters believe goes on and what actually occurs inside laboratories. Of course I do not wish to imply that scientists are any more prone to denial than the average person. The point is: given circumstances that threaten, upset, or derail dearly held beliefs, individuals try to restructure their world so as not to disturb their bottom-line idea of what is real. They try to stick with the picture they know by filtering out what is disruptive to their way of knowing.

Interestingly, the same can happen when some act of *seeing* irrupts into someone's conscious awareness and the ontological contradiction it causes is too disturbing to be taken on board. When this happens with the use of a psychedelic drug, such as LSD, and results in a failure to restructure awareness to exclude what is not wanted, it can create a cascading sense of panic that may lead, in some instances, to psychosis.

For me, landing in London and discovering that I was "expected" precipitated such a crisis, and, try as I might, I could not rearrange events in my mind to make what happened go away. I had to live with the facts of the situation—that I was in London talking to a person whose claims were proved by the very fact that I was there. Like the team in Woods Hole, I engaged my intellect in an effort to remove the unwanted evidence that contradicted my beliefs about how the world worked. If it had been a one-off, isolated event, I might have succeeded in re-categorizing it for myself as a kind of experimental error. However, my time in England included so many interlocking and congruent ordinary and non-ordinary events that it became impossible to rationalize the episode away. Also, my curiosity kept me in the game of trying to "understand."

When a person experiences a contradiction between their beliefs and what is actually happening, the tension is felt as a discordant inner "noise" and pressure that can be highly unpleasant. The more intense the experience of this "cognitive dissonance," the greater the "noise." Therefore, we tend to work to harmonize our experiences with our beliefs—to normalize our perceptions. Our values determine which facts can be admitted. When our direct experience challenges our fundamental beliefs about reality (our ontological frames), the pressure to resolve the discord is even greater. Underlying the inner split are questions like: "If reality is not as I thought it to be, then who am I and what *does* exist?" "Do I exist?" "Have I been missing something in my life, so far?" "What is going on and can I trust anything I perceive?"

The fact is our beliefs and values can dominate so completely as to cause the addition or removal of information from our perception. Accordingly, whether one is a *seer* or a scientist, it is essential to be aware of the values and stories we tell ourselves, if we are to become accurate and true reporters of our direct experience—the "stuff" of which our reality is made. To do good science or be an accurate *seer*, one must stick to the facts and observations and must remain as close as possible to unadorned, uninterpreted phenomenological reports.

I am constantly made aware of the power of ontological bottom-line beliefs and how any pressure to review or revise these "truths" engenders intense and often irrational responses. Over the years, while conducting workshops on *seeing* I have asked participants for a definition of reality. The first time I did this, an immediate reply was, "to each his own." In a broad sense, this is an interesting definition, which, appears to imply that we have an unlimited range of possibilities, but actually hints at the nature of the trap in which we find ourselves. Through the conditioning of past events and our reconditioning of our self-definitions in the present, we keep to "our own" with great determination.

Sometimes we do try to question or change our beliefs, but if this effort in any way threatens our sense of what is real, we resist it and, instead, use our power to create the illusion of change while carefully maintaining the status quo. Underlying this is fear—of being dropped into an existential void where the bottom cannot be found.

Also, we construct personal and cultural myths to reassure ourselves that we stand on solid existential ground. It is like the old story in which a seeker is told that the world rests on the back of a giant turtle. When he asks: "What does the turtle stand on?" he is told, "Another turtle."

"But what does *it* stand on?" the seeker persists.

"Another turtle," comes the response. "It's turtles all the way down."

We fall into this paradox of an infinite regress whenever we attempt to find the story that describes an "unmoved mover" on which everything finally rests.

Whether our final ground of being is a turtle or a Higgs boson (the current "ultimate particle" in physics), once the story is embraced, it becomes the bottom-line truth on which we rest our beliefs and reassure ourselves that we know where we stand. However, when the tale we tell ourselves regarding the ontological ground is disrupted, we then imagine a free-fall into the fearful void "all the way down."

23. Psychological and Philosophical Reflections

The physicist and philosopher Thomas Kuhn once wrote that what drives scientists forward in their various quests is not so much "truth" but the need to find a solution to whatever puzzle has captured their attention.[1] I discovered this was true when I analyzed what happened to me in London. After my initial encounter, it was only my overriding curiosity and unwillingness to abandon the "puzzle" confronting me that kept me engaged, despite the recurring impulse to bolt and run. I was torn and during that time I repeatedly accused Alice of trickery and duplicity, as I struggled to come up with a "natural" explanation for what had happened and to reveal what she was doing to manipulate me and maintain the illusion that I was entering into the world of *seeing*.

Later I learned that there were serious-minded, highly educated people who believed that non-ordinary perception not only existed but understood it to be a normal aspect of human functioning. That summer, in addition to discovering Bendit's book,[2] I met the eminent biologist Sir Alister Hardy, FRS,[3] who at that time was acting head of the British Society for Psychical Research. In spite of the existence of a few eminent thinkers, an open-minded view among the educated seemed to be rare in a world where the majority, including myself back then, responded to reports of such phenomena with cynicism and distrust or by erecting a wall of denial.

As the years passed, I learned how driven, vicious, and irrational some people become when attempting to construct or maintain that wall. Once I was asked by a curriculum organizer for an adult education program at the University of California to give a talk on

---

[1] T. S. Kuhn, *The Structure of Scientific Revolutions* (Chicago: University of Chicago Press, 1962).
[2] L. J. Bendit, *Paranormal Cognition* (London: Faber & Faber, 1945).
[3] A. C. Hardy, *The Divine Flame* (London: Collins, 1966).

parapsychology at one of their campuses. I agreed but immediately after the lecture was announced, a professor from one of the science departments began issuing violent threats to disrupt the talk, on the grounds that it would harm students' minds. The hostility he expressed seemed completely out of proportion to the apparent threat: a simple lecture on parapsychology. He made no attempt to find out exactly what I was offering, or whether I was a threat to scientific rationalism and student well-being. The word "parapsychology" was enough to send him into paroxysms of rage.

Even outside academia there are organizations who put themselves forward as guardians of rational thought and protectors of the "church of science" against the threats of the paranormal. One such group is known as the Committee for the Scientific Investigation of Claims of the Paranormal (CSICOP). This cabal operates much like the religious police in Iran, monitoring the beliefs and activities of groups and individuals, and accusing them of anti-science heresy if they dare to advocate even the possibility of paranormal perception.

A few years ago a highly respected skeptic, Daryl Bem, professor emeritus at Cornell University, conducted a statistical meta-analysis of previous studies of remote viewing that had used the Ganzfeld technique (see Chapter 24 for a description of this research). He concluded in his report that, in spite of opposition to the idea of the paranormal in scientific circles, what he called an "anomalous process of information transfer" merited further careful, scientific examination.[4] As a result of his meticulous and rational work, he lost his status as one of the darlings of CSICOP and the Committee for Skeptical Inquiry (CSI), and became a target of attack and ridicule.

The so-called skeptics who opposed Bem and other open-minded researchers of paranormal perception do not appear to understand the nature of skepticism at all. A true skeptic does not confine his scrutiny to other people's work. He must be skeptical of his own beliefs, methods, assumptions, and conclusions as well—in other words, of his own skepticism. In his explication of the work of second century

---

[4]D. J. Bem and C. Honorton, "Pt.1- Does Psi Exist? Replicable Evidence for an Anomalous Process of Information Transfer," *Psychological Bulletin*, 115(1) (1994), 4–18.

skeptic, Sextus Empiricus, the modern philosopher, Leszek Kolakowski, maintains that a true skeptic must

> ...acknowledge that everything we think we know is in fact uncertain; that the reasons for accepting opposing claims are equally strong (therefore none is really strong)...In order to be convinced of the truth of an opinion or belief, we must have signs with the help of which we can tell if something is true or false; in other words, we need a criterion of truth. But how can we tell if a given criterion is reliable? In order to be able to assess its reliability, we must have another criterion according to which we might judge it. And so on *ad infinitum*. Thus there is no criterion of truth; there are no signs that could tell us what is true and what is false. Similarly, in order to be convinced by a proof, we need proof that the proof is reliable...When Carneades, one of Sextus' great predecessors, declared that knowledge is impossible, he demonstrated thereby that he was not a Sceptic...Furthermore, such a claim entangles us in self-contradiction, for to assert that knowledge is impossible, is to assert that one has acquired the knowledge that knowledge is impossible...the Sceptic does not make such dogmatic claims: he simply suspends judgment. The suspension of judgment is the Sceptic's principal intellectual act...(Scepticism) is, as Sextus gracefully puts it, a medicine that flushes harmful humours out of our organism and flushes itself out with them.[5]

It is my view that when an organization makes its primary purpose the stamping out an idea in order to "purify" the human condition and protect rational (read: "approved") thought, beneath its stated aims lies fear. In the case of belief in the paranormal, this is primarily a paranoid, delusional fear that such a notion might contribute to the downfall of science and Western civilization as we know it. Underlying it is probably a deep apprehension concerning loss of control and inundation by chaotic forces. It is a fear that there really might not be a "final turtle," an ultimate ground of being—a realization that threatens to precipitate a free fall into the ontological void.

What this suggests is that much of the critical trashing of parapsychological and related research is actually an attempt to fend off threats to foundational beliefs and values. Only a small minority of individuals, such as Daryl Bem, have shown the courage to question a

---

[5]L. Kolakowski, *Why Is There Something Rather Than Nothing? 23 Questions from Great Philosophers,* trans. A. Kolakowska (New York: Basic Books, 2007). Kindle edition locations 368–409.

dogmatic stance in the face of growing evidence to the contrary. When his meta-analysis led him to conclude that there was an unexplained "anomalous" communication worth investigating, he published his findings in a prestigious scientific journal in spite of the fact that his co-author, a long-time researcher and supporter of psi-phenomena, Charles Honorton, had died. At that point Bem could have buried the whole business in order to maintain his earlier beliefs and academic credibility, but he did not, which suggests that he felt strongly enough about the subject to persist.

Another type of critic of those who explore the non-ordinary is exemplified by Richard DeMille. In the 1970s, after reading *The Teachings of Don Juan: A Yaqui Way of Knowledge*, which recounts the supposedly real-life encounters between an anthropologist, Carlos Castaneda, and a Yaqui Indian sorcerer in the Sonoran Desert of Mexico, DeMille set out to find the author and question him about his work, only to meet with rejection.[6] After repeated rebuffs, DeMille then launched a campaign to debunk Castaneda's work as "mere fiction." Regardless of whether Castaneda's popular books are partly or wholly fiction, such a blanket condemnation hardly provides a balanced approach and appears to be generated primarily from his frustration with Castaneda's refusal to engage with him.

Another skeptic who suffered similar disappointment is Susan Blackmore, an academic psychologist from the United Kingdom, who is typical of modernist, reductive, academics who actively campaign to undermine any belief in paranormal perception. Blackmore has argued that "psychical research has been under way for more than 100 years, and parapsychology (its more laboratory based counterpart) for more than 50, yet they have made virtually no progress in understanding what, if anything, ESP is."[7] She has admitted that she herself set out on a quest to discover examples of paranormal experiences in her work, using the Ganzfeld technique, but failed and so declared the whole

---

[6]R. De Mille, *Castaneda's Journey: The Power and the Allegory.* (Bloomington, IN: iUniverse, 2000).
[7]S. Blackmore, "Why Do So Many People Believe in the Præternatural?" *New Scientist,* (22 September 1990), 47.

subject null and void after she decided one particular researcher was falsifying his results.[8]

This kind of dogmatic response to research into the paranormal denies the vast body of often successful experiments and exploratory studies of spontaneous events conducted over the past century.[9] As an empirical scientist I am willing to consider any non-ordinary experience as "real," when it pragmatically connects to my daily world with a veracity and power similar to ordinary sensate experiences. That science cannot yet offer a definition or theoretical explanation of *seeing* is irrelevant to whether or not it exists.

***

This was made clear to me during my London experience in 1969—those events happened whether I could explain them or not. Nevertheless, it left me with a theoretical conundrum—how to reconcile the extraordinary events that took place with physical law— particularly thermodynamics.

One way to interpret the apparently collusive relationship between subjective experience in the present and the future objective world is to

---

[8]This admission was made in the early 1990s during an interview on an Australian radio program broadcast on Radio National called the *Science Show*.

[9]A small sample of some of these studies can be found in the following:

A. Greeley, *Ecstasy: A Way of Knowing* (Englewood Cliffs, NJ: Prentice-Hall, 1974).

D. Hay, "Religious Experience amongst a Group of Postgraduate Students: A Qualitative Study," *Journal for the Scientific Study of Religion*, 18 (1979), 164–82.

D. Hay and A. Morisy, "Reports of Ecstatic, Paranormal or Religious Experience in Great Britain and the United States—a Comparison of Trends," *Journal for the Scientific Study of Religion*, 17 (1978), 255–68.

E. Haraldsson, "Representative National Surveys of Psychic Phenomena: Iceland, Great Britain, Sweden, USA and Gallup's Multinational Survey," *Journal of the Society for Psychical Research*, 53 (1985), 145–58.

M. Laski, *Ecstasy: A Study of Some Secular and Religious Experiences* (London: Cresset Press, 1961).

C. M. Macleod-Morgan, "Quantifying the Unspeakable: The Incidence of Numinous Experience in an Australian University Sample," paper presented at the XVth International Association for the History of Religions Congress, Sydney, Australia, 1985.

P. L. Nelson, "A Survey of Mystical, Visionary and Remote Perception Experiences," in *Exploring the Paranormal: Perspectives on Belief and Experience*, ed. G. K. Zollschan, J. F. Schumaker, and G. F. Walsh (Dorset, UK: Prism, 1989), pp. 184–214.

L. E. Thomas and P. E. Cooper, "Incidence and Psychological Correlates of Intense Spiritual Experiences," *The Journal of Transpersonal Psychology*, 12 (1980), 75–85.

L. E. Thomas and P. E. Cooper, "Measurement and Incidence of Mystical Experiences: An Exploratory Study," *Journal for the Scientific Study of Religion*, 17 (1978), 433–37.

say that I was "led" to London by something outside myself. The dream, my powerful compulsion to go to a foreign place I barely recognized, the serendipitous arrival of someone to take me there—all seemed to point to a "guiding hand," sending me messages and "pulling" me toward a future somehow known but yet to be revealed. Perhaps that "pull" was exerted by Alice waiting at the other end. Whatever the case, the conundrum of time, even more than the issue of distance, has demanded my attention over the years. So how can I address this tricky issue?

According to science, the time arrow of thermodynamics points from the past, through a narrow window of the present, toward an indeterminate future. In practical terms, this law implies that it is not possible to see next week's stock results nor un-butcher a lamb should we suddenly develop vegetarian sympathies while gnawing on its cooked leg. In the macro-world of people and objects, cause and effect are considered the result of a transfer of energy or matter from the causal agent to its point of effect. This process is locked into the asymmetry of the time arrow—moving from past to future with direct, objective knowing available only in the window of the present.

However, not all laws of physics oppose the reversal of time. Some formulations of the workings of the micro-world of quantum mechanics allow for time-reversed negentropy, that is, information coming from the future.[10] Some commentators on this subject claim that such negentropic "particles" may be simply a necessary artifact of the equations of quantum mechanics, a conceptual filler required to balance the mathematical description but not an actual possibility in the world of people, lambs, and so on. This remains to be seen. Nevertheless, the confirmation of non-locality in particle physics suggests that negentropy might operate at least in the world of very small, subatomic particles that are "entangled."[11]

For me, in the end, it is the empirical data that speaks most convincingly. Did the precognized event actually occur later, and was it

---

[10]M. Gardner, "Quantum Weirdness," *Discover* (October 1982), 69–76.
[11]B. Hiley, "Quantum Mechanics Passes the Test," *New Scientist* (6 January 1983), 17–19.
J. Gribbin, "The Man Who Proved Einstein Was Wrong," *New Scientist,* (24 November 1990), 33–35.

observed in a reliable manner? When I started to look dispassionately at what was happening in my life during my encounter in London, I had to admit that something real was occurring, even if it did not fit my current model of causality. I gradually came to understand that my way of observing reality was from a top-down position—in effect, I was looking for what I expected to find and rejecting observations that did not fit those expectations. I realized it was necessary to let the data speak and see what it collectively suggested, rather than only letting in facts that fitted my belief system.

I was never able to reconcile the arrow of time with precognitive experiences, other than to understand time as an experiential artifact of the way we store and retrieve memories.

***

As I searched for a conceptual overview that would include *seeing*, it became obvious to me that the experiential world, from a commonsensical point of view, holds primacy for human beings. Our moment-to-moment sense of existence is how we identify ourselves as "being" and what we look to as our source of the "data" that underpins all our knowledge. In other words, whether we are looking at the "inner" (subjective) or the "outer" (objective) stream of phenomena, the ongoing experiential flow is the only "data" that exists for us as human knowers. It is the bottom line. The subjective and the objective are both experiences—each being associated with a different style and combination of perceptions, as William James suggests.

> Just so, I maintain, does a given undivided portion of experience, taken in one context of associates, play the part of a knower, of a state of mind, of "consciousness"; while in a different context the same undivided bit of experience plays the part of a thing known, of an objective "content."[12]

The self-referenced experiential flow is what we tend to call consciousness, and our sense of being is consciousness reflecting on itself. The notion that it is possible somehow to step outside our moment-to-moment experiential worlds to directly know something from a transcendent position is a logical and commonsensical absurdity. It is simply ludicrous to think that we can know anything beyond our

---

[12]W. James, *Essays in Radical Empiricism and a Pluralistic Universe*, ed. R. Barton Perry (Gloucester, Mass: Peter Smith, 1967), p. 10.

experience of it. The experiential world is all we have, no matter what beliefs we hold regarding an objective, ontological "otherness" that our experience seems to suggest. What I am suggesting is that the notions of objectivity and subjectivity are post hoc conceptualizations arising from what we ascribe as being the source of our experiences. Underlying such beliefs about reality are the knowledge-generating operations of attention and consciousness that produce them.

In the latter phase of his life, William James argued convincingly for a recognition of the primacy of experience. In fact, he can be thought of as the first American phenomenologist, pre-dating the emergence of phenomenology as a discipline in Europe.[13] In some ways James' position was close to that of the twentieth century philosopher Jean-Paul Sartre, who, in his reinterpretation of the European phenomenology, argued that there was no reason to see consciousness as a "thing" or "place."[14] Instead he and James both believed consciousness was a construct, born of the nature of human attention and awareness with its capacity to reflect on itself while it simultaneously perceives the world.

Sartre's consciousness is an "object" created from the experience of the "backward-cast shadow" of the reflected memories of multiple previous consciousnesses or experiential states. This notion is reflected in my model shown in the diagram in Chapter 11, which allows us to understand both consciousness and the view of reality we glean from it as processes that operationally construct a "picture of reality" we call knowledge, whether it be ordinary or non-ordinary.

This understanding of the nature of reality underscores the need for an ontologically neutral position, if we are ever going to have a less restricted and more pragmatic science that can include the idea of an experiential world and activities such as *seeing*.[15] To become neutral, we must first recognize our desire to take an ontologically absolute position whenever we try to know something, then subject that

---

[13] J. Wild, *The Radical Empiricism of William James* (New York: Doubleday, 1969).

[14] J. P. Sartre, *The Transcendence of the Ego: An Existentialist Theory of Consciousness*, trans. F. Williams and R. Kirkpatrick (New York: Octagon Books, 1972).

[15] P. L. Nelson, and J. D. Howell, "A Psycho-social Phenomenological Methodology for Conducting Operational, Ontologically Neutral Research into Religious and Altered State Experiences," *Journal for the Psychology of Religion*, 2–3 (1993–4), 1–48.

foundational position to the same kind of scrutiny we reserve for empirical data. The unwillingness of many scientists to do just that is well known to those of us who have been "in the game" ourselves, so to speak. Indeed, a lot of researchers think the sole purpose of their work is to generate an ontological picture of "what is," rather than recognize that what they are doing is just an epistemic, or knowledge-making, activity within a limited frame of reference. I believe that science should not be about declaring "what is" but about building a useful, consistent and hopefully repeatable body of knowledge.

When the notion of objectivity is applied to *seeing,* the salient point is not whether what is *seen* is true in an absolute, transcendent sense, but whether the world of the *seer* is as reliable (i.e., repeatable across multiple inquiries) and pragmatically useful as is the "objective" world of the scientist. I would assert that once the methodology and techniques of *seeing* are mastered and well practiced, they can yield pragmatically useful and repeatable results that properly intersect with events of the ordinary world and therefore can be cross-validated. In this sense, these two ways of knowing, science and *seeing,* are not mutually exclusive. Instead, they complement one another.

A case in point is the way some scientists have experienced unintended acts of *seeing* in the form of dream-visions that have led to important discoveries. For example, in 1936, a German pharmacologist, Otto Loewi, won the Nobel Prize for Physiology or Medicine after discovering that nerves use chemical messengers to regulate heart rates. What few people knew at the time was that his discovery resulted from a vision that came to him in a dream. The famous science fiction writer Isaac Asimov describes what happened:

> The idea for the experiment occurred to him at 3 a.m. on two successive nights. The first night he wrote it down and went back to sleep. In the morning he could not read what he had written. The second night he went straight to his laboratory and got to work. By 5 a.m. he had established the point.[16]

In his dream, Loewi witnessed a lab setup with two hearts suspended, one above the other, with liquid dripping from the upper to the lower. This gave him an idea for an experiment so when he went to

---

[16]I. Asimov, *Asimov's Biographical Encyclopedia of Science and Technology* (Garden City, NY: Doubleday & Company, Inc., 1982), 644–45.

the lab that morning, he set two freshly excised still-living animal hearts in an apparatus that allowed him to drip saline solution over the upper one onto the organ below. As he stimulated the nerve attached to the upper heart, causing its rate of beating to increase, the saline dripping onto the lower heart caused its rate to increase as well. Thus, chemical mediation between nerve and heart muscle was established.

***

If such interesting phenomena are reported by reputable sources, why is psychology not willing to even consider, much less explore non-ordinary experiences? It seems surprising that this discipline is so hostile to knowledge derived in ways other than through a rationalistic, reductive model. Does the notion of reality implicit in mainstream psychology's theory of perception require that there be only one reality, knowable through the ontological model of materialism? If this is so, then psychology is behind the times, still stuck in the realm of Newtonian physics, while physics has long since moved on.

Having embraced the complexities of quantum theory, physicists now seem willing to consider the possibility of more than one reality and other ways of knowing. Some have even interpreted their equations in a way that implies the universe is multi-leveled, an example being the many-worlds hypothesis of quantum mechanics originally expounded by Hugh Everett.[17] In his construction of reality, Everett implies that all possible alternative histories and futures are real, each representing an actual world or universe.

It is important to remember that "reality" does not refer to what ultimately exists and is "out there." In fact, some philosophers have argued that you cannot know directly what is "out there" because all knowing is just human knowing, which, when you think about it, is a translational process. In other words, what you receive from your environment as input is transformed into electro-chemical signals that are compiled into a picture of reality by a large chunk of meat and fat that resides in your skull! Your brain is not transferring the "real world" to your awareness; it is creating an awareness of its own kind (human) from processes that are not direct reproductions of what is "out there." Moreover, this chunk of fatty meat, also known as your brain, uses

---

[17]P. Byrne, "The Many Worlds of Hugh Everett," *Scientific American* (December 2007).

different types of attention and arousal states (consciousness) to generate different modes of awareness.

A few brave psychologists have taken the risk of swimming against their profession's ideological tide. For example, an academic psychologist, Charles Tart, has proposed, in his work on consciousness, the notion of "state-specific knowledge."[18] In his view, different states of consciousness create access to different types of knowing, which open us to the possibility of new knowledge and realms. Perhaps there is a relationship between Everett's quantum states and Tart's states of consciousness—an idea that at times has caught the imagination of some thinkers.[19]

As I see it, psychology's rejection of different ways of knowing may have at least two causes. First, the operational and objective (scientific) psychology, also called behaviorism, that emerged in the early twentieth century has rejected human experience.[20] Instead, it views it as an artifact or by-product of neurophysiological activity—in particular, the electro-chemical activity taking place in the brain. From the behaviorist perspective, the "dialogue" between neurons is driven by the interaction between the human organism and its environment. . In this model there is no conscious experiencer and therefore no one to put differing attentional emphases on what is experienced.

Such a model allows no possibility of variation regarding what is known or how it is experienced, and it becomes difficult, if not impossible, to explain how the physico-chemical communication among neurons and between them and the environment can produce an experience of being consciously aware. This mechanistic, reductive approach leaves a significant gap concerning the transition from the so-called objective world of brains and trains to the subjective world of

---

[18]C. T. Tart, *States of Consciousness* (New York: E. P. Dutton, 1975).
C. T. Tart, "States of Consciousness and State-Specific Sciences," *Science,* 176 (1972), 1203–10.
[19]J. Jeans, *Physics and Philosophy* (Ann Arbor: University of Michigan Press, 1958).
G. F. Chew, "Gentle Quantum Events as the Source of Explicate Order," *Zygon,* 20 (1985), 159–64.
K. V. Laurikainen, "Quantum Physics, Philosophy, and the Image of God: Insights from Wolfgang Pauli," *Zygon,* 25(4) (1990), 391–404.
[20]J. B. Watson, *Behaviorism,* 2nd ed. (New York: Kegan Paul, 1931).
S. S. Stevens, "The Operational Basis of Psychology," *American Journal of Psychology,* 47 (1935), 323–30.

experience (*qualia*), unless, like James, we view all these workings in terms of "raw experience" itself.

The second problem with modern psychology's rejection of the experiential domain involves what philosophers call a "category error." Either no one has noticed it, or those who have simply do not care. When scientific psychology explains consciousness by reducing it to neurological activity, it is attempting to use perceptual or cognitive knowledge originating in sense perception to explicate *qualia*, or the experience of conscious awareness. This reductive approach implies that there is just one physical reality and that all we know is generated by physical processes interacting with each other. The problem with this concept is it leaves out the knower, the one who is viewing that single reality, which, logically considered, dismisses psychologists themselves.

A move away from the phenomenology of early psychologists like William James occurred because, in the early twentieth century, behaviorists (who now call themselves cognitive scientists) found it simpler to do psychology without dealing with the experiential domain as its own category. As a result, they only had to deal with what could be seen and measured with an external device—a not altogether rational attempt to emulate physics, which meanwhile, was going the other way—recognizing the role of consciousness (the observer) in the peculiar behavior of particles in the micro-world. In other words, physics was reintroducing consciousness into its theories just as psychology was removing it.

***

We know from the comparative study of cultures and belief systems that human beings tend to make their perceptions more comprehensible by putting them into a story about what happened that becomes understood as an account of the way things *are*. For the most part, these stories are not recognized as such but are understood to be actual accounts describing the objective world.

There are social, scientific, religious and familial stories that provide mythic structures and explanatory maps by which we understand who we are, what is going on in the world, and the meaning behind how things, people, and events function and interact with each other. What we accept as bottom-line truth has a great deal to do with how the stories associated with our culture and family of origin shape our perceptions of reality.

In addition to what is handed down by families and cultures, people also "narratize" events from their lives and turn them into meaningful stories. As we recall things that have happened, we fill in gaps, manufacture "plots," and reorganize the material into a tale with a beginning, middle, climax, and a morally pleasing end. This helps to make it more meaningful and interesting to us, as well as easier to remember, rather than fragmented bits of experiences. In other words, much of what we think we remember is a constructed narrative and not a strictly factual record of events.

Cognitive scientists as well as some self-proclaimed skeptics have used the fact that people narratize events to dispute the validity of *seeing*, in particular, precognition. They argue that whatever a *seer* thinks he *saw* concerning an event before it happened is just a reorganization in his mind, after the event, in order to make the story of precognition true. He could not actually have *seen* the event before it happened because that would defy scientific law—particularly thermodynamics and the time arrow.

The flaw in such an argument is this: If those of us having non-ordinary *seeing* experiences cannot trust our knowing because of narratizing and potentially faulty ordering of memory, then it is likely that no process of acquiring knowledge will function outside this limitation. The way data from laboratories is remembered and interpreted, as well as the way theories are constructed, would be a product of the same kind of faulty cognitive processes designed to fulfill the need for convenient and meaningful reconstructions and interpretations.

No doubt there is distortion in all of our recollections, but this must be understood as universal to human endeavor—including cognitive psychological research (though scientists rarely see their own theories as stories born of narratization.) Therefore, on logical grounds, we are forced to conclude that if there are sufficient pragmatic correspondences between *seeing* and sensate experiential life, then there is no reason to reject such data as less true than the ordinary sensory kind, which must be corroborated in a similar way.

Recognition of the role of constructive story-making in any attempt at objective information gathering has been growing in recent years. The idea of the "social construction of reality," as Peter Berger and Thomas Luckmann called it in their now-classic treatise, can be understood as an attempt to show that our knowledge arises from our personhood, which filters "reality" according to our beliefs and desires. Summarizing this idea they state that:

> What is "real" to a Tibetan monk may not be "real" to an American businessman. The "knowledge" of the criminal differs from the "knowledge" of the criminologist. It follows that specific agglomerations of "reality" and "knowledge" pertain to specific social contexts.[21]

Building on the Berger and Luckmann notion, social psychologist Kenneth Gergen states that the constructivist position

> begins with *radical doubt* in the taken-for-granted world— whether in the sciences or daily life... Constructionism asks one to suspend belief that commonly accepted categories or understandings receive their warrant through observation. Thus, it invites one to challenge the objective basis of conventional knowledge.[22]

In other words, when we look beneath the cover story of any system of knowledge or belief, we find a human one. This idea is not to suggest that reality is just a figment of our imaginations—rather, it simply recognizes that as human constructors and tellers of stories, we take the beliefs and values that are inextricably woven into the fabric of our stories to be objectively real. Toward the end of his life, Erwin Schrödinger, one of the founders of quantum physics, stated:

> The world is a construct of our sensations, perceptions, memories. It is convenient to regard it as existing objectively on its own. But it certainly does not become manifest by its mere existence.[23]

---

[21] P. L. Berger and T. Luckmann, *The Social Construction of Reality: A Treatise in the Sociology of Knowledge* (Middlesex, UK: Penguin Books, 1971), p.15.

[22] K. J. Gergen, "The Social Constructionist Movement in Modern Psychology," *American Psychologist*, 40 (1985), 266–75.

[23] E. Schrödinger and R. Penrose, *What Is Life? And Mind and Matter* (Cambridge, UK: Cambridge University Press, 1967), *Kindle Locations 1424–1425*.

As I have said before, I remain a practitioner of empirical science and a believer in its pragmatic veracity, yet I have come to view scientific activity as an endeavor that is prone to the same distortions and unconscious malpractices found in all human activities. Humans are "top-down" processors who actively construct order and meaning according to their beliefs and theories from an array of sensory data that would otherwise overwhelm them with a perceptual, emotional and cognitive storm.

The fact that the mind organizes data this way is well established in scientific psychology. However, this appears to be largely ignored by those who advocate for an absolute scientism by denying that there is anything to be considered in the critique of human knowledge-making. I use the term "knowledge-making" since, as I have already stated, knowledge is not an objective fact but, rather, a construction of perceptions, both external and internal, into units of coherence defined by association, congruence and cognitive-emotive charge in relation to an established socio-cultural backdrop.

I agree with the postmodern critique that claims we filter and organize our experiences and give them meaning that is not inherent in them. In the course of making my own conceptual traverse from a reductive scientism to a broader understanding of what is possible through knowing the world as a *seer,* I have witnessed this process of filtering and ascribing meaning in myself. In a very real sense, philosopher Mark Taylor's statement that "the reading of the text is the writing of the text" is true,[24] although I would not go as far as to assert, as some postmodernists do, that there is no ontological bottom line—I just do not know what it is.

In fact, radical deconstructive notions that eschew a bottom line are merely positing another—the bottom line of no bottom line (another form of "turtles all the way down"). In any case, whether one is a scientist or a radical deconstructionist, any attempt to state definitively what underlies the perceived reality in which we all find ourselves embedded would require stepping out of that reality in order to observe it from a meta-position beyond human knowing. Clearly, this is not

---

[24]One of the foremost exponents of the work of Jacques Derrida. M. C. Taylor, "Deconstruction: What's the Difference?" *Soundings,* 66 (1983), 387–403.

possible, even for those who claim they have done so, like mystics, for they "return" only to give us their version of what they encountered filtered through human perception and knowing.

***

The examination of culture and belief probably reached its zenith in postmodernism, especially in the work of the deconstructionists. The attitude associated with the deconstructionist school of thought is a system of critical analysis that probably has its origins in the idea of "bracketing" expounded first by early twentieth century phenomenologists, such as Edmund Husserl.[25] In the bracketing process, the roots of meaning, belief and perception itself are sought by trying to recognize the social, cultural, and psychological contexts that shape our perception. The intention of this philosophical method is to "suspend" the filtering and distorting activities of our cultural and linguistic minds and allow a more "purified" experience of both inner (subjective) and outer (objective) phenomena to appear. In other words, this method seeks to deconstruct the foundation stones of that ontological edifice we call "reality" so we might see how the building of "truth" is accomplished.

From my perspective as a *seer*, deconstructionism takes on an additional meaning. More than an academic mental game played by literary critics and philosophers, it becomes a living process of watching fundamental beliefs about reality come into question and emerge profoundly altered. In the language of deconstructionists, *seeing* engenders a radical recontextualization of the social world in which we are embedded.

From my perspective, without *seeing*, it is easier for most people to maintain their stories about the world. Typically, they walk down a street and take in the scene as a natural and indisputable fact. The associations that come up in their minds and the beliefs they maintain seem perfectly reasonable and unassailable as the true picture of what "is." But if one is a *seer*, then some other picture or knowing, one that is capable of radically undermining the apparent "truth" of the scene, may obtrude at any time. The two perceptual frames that constitute the seer's

[25]E. Husserl, *Ideas: General Introduction to Phenomenology*, trans. W. R. Boyce-Gibson (New York: Collier-Macmillan, 1962).

regular experience of the world can (and often do) contradict one another in striking ways, for example, when someone's verbally expressed intentions are radically contradicted by the *intentionality* they project through their *field*, or when the content of the *field* of what appears to be a bucolic country scene cries out with the sounds of battle and death from another time.

So, how does a *seer* handle the constant deconstructive process that *seeing* entails? One way is to simply manage the contradictions as they arise. Another, perhaps better way, is to directly engage in a deconstructive activity as a daily practice. Instead of taking the series of associated images, feelings, and thoughts from which we construct our usual reality as given, replay all those associations that constitute our usual construction, holding up each in turn and asking, "How do I know this is true?"

The first response is often: "Of course it's true, I have always known it." The deconstructive response then is to ask, "What if it is not that way? What if I only believe it to be so?" By giving ourselves permission to entertain (radical) doubt about the truth of our perceptions and beliefs, we crack open the door to the possibility of something else. For *seers,* this opening is essential because, as human perceivers, we tend to believe and act based only on what we conceive as possible. A deconstructive practice helps develop a flexibility that allows us, when confronted by radical alterations in perception and experience, to engage fully with them by relinquishing old understandings that normally get in the way.

This process is difficult and requires deep concentration, not unlike that necessary for successful meditation. In fact, it is like Buddhist insight meditation, in that one has to follow the chain of associations for any thought, idea, belief, or perception back to its "roots." Intense dedication is required to overcome the temptation to drop the process in the name of comfort. Our "mind"—that constellation of feelings, thoughts and beliefs we usually identify as ourselves—finds this type of deconstructive activity threatening and difficult and therefore resists it. If we persevere, however, eventually a kind of existential suspension occurs, manifested as a profound alteration of awareness of self, time, space, and other. It is at this moment that the true deconstructive act occurs, disturbing what Husserl calls the "natural attitude," and allowing for a shift in awareness and understanding that amounts to nothing less than a discovery of the roots of knowing.

Arthur Deikman's work with experimental mysticism, mentioned in Chapter 14, bears some relationship to the process suggested here.[26] He would instruct his subjects to stare at a blue vase in an unfocused, non-conceptual way that seemed to "unfreeze" (deautomatize) perception. Subjects then had the opportunity to realize that their constructed "picture" of the vase was not absolute; rather, its creation required participation by them as observer, in ways related to the discussion of how saccadic eye movements create visual perception as described in Chapter 10.

As I have also discovered, when deautomatization occurs in relation to looking at oneself, rather than an external object, the effect is more intense and profound, representing a reconstitution of self-knowledge and belief (see Chapter 12). This entire deconstructive procedure is like a meta-scientific investigation—a purposeful and skeptical inquiry into the foundations of perception and belief. In this type of research, unlike ordinary science, the "truth" uncovered reflects aspects of how we may be constructing truth itself.

---

[26]A. J. Deikman, "Implications of Experimentally Induced Contemplative Meditation," *The Journal of Nervous and Mental Disease,* 142 (1966), 101–16.

Over the past century research on psychic and paranormal phenomena has grown into a considerable body of published literature that anyone can now access. This chapter does not attempt a methodical review of these research efforts; instead, it highlights some areas relevant to this book, including my own work.

A great deal of past research has been focused on whether or not psychics' claims can be experimentally demonstrated in a laboratory setting. J. B. Rhine's early work with card-guessing in the 1930s marks the start of these controlled, experimental studies,[1] which led eventually to the more interesting and sophisticated Ganzfeld experiments conducted by Charles Honorton in the 1970s.[2] The Ganzfeld tests were designed to investigate clairvoyance and telepathy, two forms of interpersonal communication across space and time without reference to the usual physical mediators of communication, such as electromagnetism and mechanical energy.

In the Ganzfield approach, an experimental subject would be asked to sit in a comfortable reclining chair in a quiet room. Special goggles, often consisting of halves of a ping-pong ball, were placed over his eyes, a red light was turned on in front of him, and white noise, like the sound of rushing air, was played through headphones. All the subject experienced in this situation was a visual field of diffuse red light and a quiet sound. The subject, who was called the "receiver," was then asked to sit quietly while someone else (the "sender") at a distant location attempted to communicate with him through "force" of thought. In most of these experiments, the sender stared at a randomly

---

[1] J. B. Rhine, *Extra-Sensory Perception* (Boston, MA: Bruce Humphries, 1934).
[2] J. C. Terry and C. Honorton, "Psi Information Retrieval in the Ganzfeld: Two Confirmatory Studies," *Journal of the American Society for Psychical Research*, 70 (1976), 207–17.

chosen picture or movie clip—the "target"—and attempted to send the image, while the receiver was asked to describe the thoughts and images (or dreams, if he happened to fall asleep) that appeared at the same time. In the evaluation phase of the experiment, independent judges determined whether or not the receiver's description bore any resemblance to the target viewed by the sender. If they agreed that the receiver's report resembled the target, it was considered a "hit," or evidence for "anomalous communication" between receiver and sender.

From the start of the early parapsychological studies to the present, the sophistication of the experimental and statistical designs has grown considerably, so that today the published reports conform to the highest standards of research methodology. I would argue that, compared to many studies published in clinical medicine for example, parapsychological research is both more rigorous and better designed. I say this from first hand experience, having taught statistics to undergraduates and in a medical school as well as having served as an external editor for international journals.

Throughout my time in academia I witnessed a lot of research irregularities, including fraud, in papers published in respected medical journals. In contrast, I also witnessed so-called "skeptics" attack credible, rigorous research in parapsychology, such as the Ganzfeld studies, and accuse them of fraud—without even investigating the scientific methodology or inspecting the laboratories involved. These accusations seemed to become more shrill and frequent, as research into the paranormal succeeded.

Not only have respectable researchers been vilified as fraudsters by the "science police," the same treatment has been meted out to those who have reported having spontaneous paranormal experiences. Accounts by psychics, *seers*, and shamans of such encounters have been labeled as "self-delusion" by some skeptics who go on to say that they are driven by "primitive" cultural and pre-scientific irrational beliefs. This is most often seen in mainstream anthropological research on shamanism where a position of cultural superiority prevails in spite of researchers' attempts to treat non-Western cultures with respect.

Typically this is seen when researchers focus on the cultural beliefs and behaviors underlying the shamanistic worldview at the expense of the shaman's actual "other world" experiences.[3] In many cases, the idea of such experiences being real encounters is generally denied or ignored.[4] Despite this, a few lone voices, like the populist author Michael Harner and sociological scholar Julia Howell of the University of Western Sydney, Australia, have advocated for the authenticity of these experiential domains beyond being mere cultural artifacts.[5]

Very little research into *seeing*, shamanism, and psychism is ontologically neutral, that is, starting from the position that such experiences could be veridical for those who have them and therefore they represent a valid way of knowing that is worth studying *sui generis*. Notable exceptions are the works of the transpersonal psychologist Charles Tart[6] and the philosopher Roger Walsh.[7] Although they and others have done important groundbreaking work in exploring the nature of transpersonal experience, most have confounded their explorations by loosely incorporating religious worldviews, such as those of Christianity, Buddhism, and Vedantism, into their work. There has been precious little study of transpersonal experiences in and of themselves.

In the 1970s and 80s, there was a flurry of activity among scholars of religion who attempted to discover how widespread transpersonal

---

[3]P. L. Nelson and J. D. Howell, "A Psycho-Social Phenomenological Methodology for Conducting Operational, Ontologically Neutral Research into Religious and Altered State Experiences," *Journal for the Psychology of Religion,* 2–3 (1993–94), 1–48.

[4]Traditional examples of experiences similar to those reported by *seers* and psychics are found throughout the literature on shamanism. See for example: M. Eliade, *Shamanism: Archaic Techniques of Ecstasy,* trans. R. Trask, Bollingen Series vol. 76 (Princeton: Princeton University Press., 1964).

A. P. Elkin, *Aboriginal Men of High Degree.* 2nd ed. (St. Lucia, Queensland: University of Queensland Press, 1977).

[5]M. Harner, *The Way of the Shaman: A Guide to Power and Healing* (San Francisco: Harper & Row, 1980).

J. D. Howell, "The Social Sciences and Mystical Experience," in *Exploring the Paranormal: Perspectives on Belief and Experience,* ed. J. F. Schumaker G. K. Zollschan, and G. F. Walsh (Dorset, UK: Prism Press, 1989), pp. 77–94.

[6]C. T. Tart, "Consciousness, Altered States, and Worlds of Experience," *The Journal of Transpersonal Psychology,* 18 (1986), 159–70.

[7]R. Walsh, "The Consciousness Disciplines and Behavioral Sciences: Questions of Comparison and Assessment," *American Journal of Psychiatry,* 137 (1980), 663–73.

experiencing was in the general population. The results of their surveys suggested that the potential to be a *seer* must be fairly common.[8] The studies conducted in the USA, Britain, Iceland, and by me in Australia, found that better than 40 percent of the population had at least one spontaneous *seeing*-type experience in a lifetime. However, less than 10 percent reported that these events happened regularly, and an even smaller number—usually only those who identified themselves as psychics, shamans, and/or *seers*—said that they consciously engaged in such activities daily, as a way of life.

In efforts to go further than merely counting how many transpersonal experients were out there, researchers like Ralph Hood and myself attempted to discover what triggered spontaneous paranormal, mystical, and visionary experiences. Using different methods, we each examined these occurrences apart from their usual religious and occult contexts. Hood's work on nature mysticism, together with Tart's model of states of consciousness, suggested a possible technology of consciousness underlying the accessibility of these states.[9] Building on their work, in the early 1980s I developed a model of a psycho-phenomenological technology of altered-state experiencing, based on an in-depth statistical modeling of the

---

[8]D. Hay and A. Morisy, "Reports of Ecstatic, Paranormal or Religious Experience in Great Britain and the United States—A Comparison of Trends," *Journal for the Scientific Study of Religion,* 17 (1978), 255–68.

E. Haraldsson, "Representative National Surveys of Psychic Phenomena: Iceland, Great Britain, Sweden, USA and Gallup's Multinational Survey," *Journal of the Society for Psychical Research,* 53 (1985), 145–58.

P. L. Nelson, "A Survey of Mystical, Visionary and Remote Perception Experiences," in *Exploring the Paranormal: Perspectives on Belief and Experience,* ed. G. K. Zollschan, J. F. Schumaker, and G. F. Walsh (Dorset, UK: Prism, 1989), pp. 184–214.

P. L. Nelson, "Transcending Limitations: Spontaneous Paranormal and Spiritual Experiences in Australian Daily Life," *Australian Parapsychological Review,* 2, 3(18) (1991), 8–12.

L. E. Thomas and P. E. Cooper, "Incidence and Psychological Correlates of Intense Spiritual Experiences," *The Journal of Transpersonal Psychology,* 12 (1980), 75–85.

[9]R. W. Hood Jr., "Eliciting Mystical States of Consciousness with Semi-structured Nature Experiences," *Journal for the Scientific Study of Religion,* 16 (1977), 155–63.

R. W. Hood Jr., "Anticipatory Set and Setting: Stress Incongruities as Elicitors of Mystical Experience in Solitary Nature Situations," *Journal for the Scientific Study of Religion,* 17 (1978), 279-87.

P. L. Nelson, "Personality Factors in the Frequency of Reported Spontaneous Præternatural Experiences," *The Journal of Transpersonal Psychology,* 21 (1989), 193–209.

spontaneous paranormal, visionary, and mystical experiences of several hundred individuals.[10] These days, when I describe my model to people who have had such encounters, they usually agree that it captures the essence of what is going on for them when episodes are triggered.

So, what does research have to say about how *seers,* psychics, and mystics are made? Are they born that way, or do life circumstances cast them into the role? Do they have a unique talent, or are they simply manifesting a normal aspect of human perception available to everyone but more often neglected than not? Here psychological research based on the notion of a technology of consciousness has something to offer.

During the 1980s, noted parapsychologist Harvey Irwin, of the University of New England, Australia, and I conducted related, but separate research on the psychology underlying paranormal experience. Professor Irwin was the first to show that "personality trait absorption"[11] was predictive of the type of people who were more likely to claim to have had out of body experiences.[12] In my research I also found that trait absorption correlated strongly with the frequency of reported mystical, visionary and psychic encounters.[13]

People high in this trait have an enhanced ability to become entranced or absorbed in external sights and sounds as well as their own inner worlds. They can enter into an experience so totally that they lose self-awareness and any sense of time. Although high absorbers often put their attention wholly and completely into a task, their concentration remains relaxed, unforced, and certainly not goal oriented. The focus of these absorption states can be external or internal, though high absorbers tend to spend more time than others wandering through their own inner landscapes. For example, high

---

[10]P. L. Nelson, "The Technology of the Praeternatural: An Empirically Based Model of Transpersonal Experiences," *The Journal of Transpersonal Psychology,* 22 (1990), 35–50.

[11]A. Tellegen and G. Atkinson, "Openness to Absorbing and Self-Altering Experiences ("Absorption"), a Trait Related to Hypnotic Susceptibility," *Journal of Abnormal Psychology,* 83 (1974), 268–277.

[12]H. J. Irwin, "Some Psychological Dimensions of the Out-of-Body Experience," *Parapsychology Review,* 12 (1981), 1-6.

[13]P. L. Nelson, "Personality Factors in the Frequency of Reported Spontaneous Præternatural Experiences," *The Journal of Transpersonal Psychology,* 21 (1989), 193-209.

absorbers are often surprised when a movie ends because they were so "into" it, as if they were actually there. Typically, the child who sits in a classroom and stares out a window at the trees, fascinated by the play of light through the leaves, may be high in trait absorption.

Developmental psychologists tend to agree that some personality characteristics are inborn while others appear to develop in response to circumstances during our growing up. No one is sure whether personality trait absorption is inherited or developed. However, the research done by Irwin and myself strongly suggests that this personality characteristic is a fundamental quality in the making of psychics, visionaries, and *seers*.

I would argue that, in the past, such a personality characteristic might have been highly valued as a talent that could have found its outlet through the trance practices of shamanistic societies and the prayerful life of cloistered religious orders. However, today, such a trait is not so valued. This is because it appears to offer little advantage for getting ahead in our achievement-driven and socially demanding world. Those oriented this way are often shamed for not properly paying attention at school and pressured to engage in outward-directed activities, such as sports. In fact, when the teacher demands of a high absorption child to "pay attention," he likely *is* paying attention, but his awareness is not deployed where it is supposed to be when in class.

Typically, high absorbers have a greater talent than others for experiencing altered states of consciousness such as hypnosis and self-induced trance states. They tend to gravitate toward meditation or mild hypnotic drugs (such as cannabis) that facilitate their preferred states.[14] My research into frequency of cannabis use and its relation to levels of innate trait absorption seems to confirm this view.[15]

There are other personality characteristics that are more prevalent in those who have *seeing*-like experiences than in those who do not. Using a standardized personality assessment scale, I found that,

---

[14]P. L. Nelson, "Cannabis Amotivational Syndrome and Personality Trait Absorption: A Review and Reconceptualization," *Imagination, Cognition and Personality*, 14(1) (1994–95), 43–58.
[15]P. L. Nelson, "Personality Trait Absorption: An Exploratory Study of Opportunity and Capacity in Relation to Cannabis Use," *Imagination, Cognition and Personality*, 15(1) (1995–96), 75–101.

compared with non-experients, individuals who have regular episodes of *seeing* manifest higher levels of feelings of personal well-being, are less emotionally constrained, are greater risk takers, and tend to be more honest in their evaluations of themselves. They are also more emotionally fluid and capable of experiencing a wider range of emotions—both negative and positive.[16]

Overall, my research appears to show that high trait absorption individuals who enter into a relaxed, entranced state in a quiet setting while they are in a positive mood, are more likely than others to have a *seeing* experience. If the positive mood comes at the end of a prolonged period of stress and negative affect, their experiences are more likely to be quite intense and profound, even mystical.

In summary, research done by me and others has shown that higher levels of trait absorption facilitate the ability to engage in altered states of consciousness. This has implications for some parapsychological experimentation. For example, it is possible that the conditions created during the Ganzfeld experiments may have simulated the state that high absorbers create for themselves. To date, no one has sorted subjects in the Ganzfeld experiments according to their level of trait absorption. I believe that if they did, they might find an even higher "hit" rate among high absorption "receivers" and possibly among "senders" as well. Also, because some drugs help to facilitate absorptive states that are conducive to the engagement of the *second stream*, this might explain their use in shamanic rituals.

***

Why, we must ask, do these encounters continue to occur among the general population in spite of society's denial and suppression of them? As part of my research, I examined the processes of consciousness, particularly the deployment of attention, that activate spontaneous *seeing* experiences and found that many individuals, by a fortuitous combination of accident and inclination, simply stumbled upon the "inner technology" that facilitates *seeing*. In fact, there appears to be a natural technology of consciousness (see chapters 10 and 11)

---

[16]P. L. Nelson, "Personality Attributes as Discriminating Factors in Distinguishing Religio-Mystical from Paranormal Experients," *Imagination, Cognition and Personality,* 11(4) (1991-92), 389–405.

available to all of us that high absorbers seem especially able to access at times. So, from my research as well as my personal experience, *seeing* appears to be a natural part of being human and is available in varying degrees to everyone.

My original suspicion about my own *seeing* experiences—that they were linked with some type of neuro-psychological dysfunction—aligns with the prevailing cultural view: that they are delusions or hallucinations caused by mental illness or brain malfunction. Some cognitive psychologists, such as Graham Reed, have attempted to thinly disguise this pathological attribution with a more neutral description, calling such encounters "anomalous experiences."[17]

Reed uses this term in his explanation of déjà vu, a feeling that you have been in a situation or place before, when you know you haven't. He bases his theoretical perspective on Donald Broadbent's filter theory of how information is processed in the brain.[18] According to the filter theory, the nervous system is a single communication channel with a bandwidth too narrow to carry the combined parallel inputs of all five sense modalities and thus bottlenecks arise. To prevent overload of the processing channel, sensory input must pass through a filter that selects input sequentially and also according to its intensity and novelty. Some input can be held up briefly in a short-term store or "buffer" (a model drawn directly from how computers work), which is how reversals in timing can appear to take place. When the delayed information finally appears in conscious awareness, it gives rise to perceptions of an event apparently before it takes place. This view raises a thorny question about our capacity, under any circumstances, to recall the real order of what we perceive and think about an experience.

Following on from this theory, it is possible that *seers* might be especially prone to these temporal reversals of perception, which could originate from a neurological disorder such as "temporal lobe syndrome." The neuropsychologist Michael Persinger has found that the rate of report of spontaneous paranormal experiences is strongly correlated with symptoms such as spontaneous loss of self-control, onset of "strange" feelings, and occurrence of unexplained feelings

---

[17]G. Reed, *The Psychology of Anomalous Experience* (Boston: Houghton Mifflin, 1974).
[18]D. E. Broadbent, *Perception and Communication* (London: Pergamon Press, 1958).

and/or sensations, some of which have been shown to be related to electrical anomalies in the temporal lobe of the brain.[19] As it turns out, these kinds of abnormalities are prevalent in the brains of epileptics, which might suggest that people who claim to be able to *see* are, in fact, mildly epileptic and that their visions, voices and knowing can be interpreted as aspects of mini-seizures.

However, unlike the visions and voices experienced by epileptics, what is perceived by most competent *seers* has strong congruence with what actually happened in the past or will happen in the future. Therefore, the significant difference between epileptics and *seers* may be that unusual temporal lobe development in *seers* creates an exceptional brain rather than a pathologically dysfunctional one that generates seizures, as in epileptics. The temporal lobe anomalies may be related in both, but clearly they lead to different outcomes.

In cases of high creativity and intelligence, for example, too much development in one area of the brain can lead to imbalance in the person's psychological "ecosystem." This is often seen in high achievers who border on being pathologically manic. Similarly, a *seeing*-capable brain could be the result of a temporal lobe variation that is part of the mechanism that allows for the sensitivity required for *seeing*. However, if that variation is of the wrong type, it may cause over-excitation that generates seizures.

As for Reed's delayed-information-processing model of déjà vu, it could be taken seriously if it did not contradict the experiences of so many *seers* I have observed, as well as historical accounts of *seeing*. Déjà vu experiences often occur across long periods of time, even years, so for Reed's information delay model to apply, the brain would have to be capable of information delays spanning years. Also, the reversed order of event and perception that he proposes would occur randomly during ordinary experiencing in a way that would lead to confusion, disorientation, and noticeably dysfunctional behavior for most people. Yet, according to research, most *seers*, trained or not, appear to have well-integrated personalities and function at or above

---

[19]M. A. Persinger, "Propensity to Report Paranormal Experiences Is Correlated with Temporal Lobe Signs," *Perceptual and Motor Skills,* 59 (1984), 583–86.

average in their jobs and among friends and families.[20] In my own case, electroencephalogram recordings show no spike and wave or other electrical characteristics indicative of epilepsy—even when I was put to the standard test with a flashing strobe.

It is possible that, as psychology suggests, some déjà vu experiences are just the echoing of a perception through the nervous system's processing channels, but this does not mean they all are. When we see puddles of water shimmering on the road surface during a hot, dry summer's day, some indeed may be mirages, but others can turn out to be real puddles. I have had many déjà vu experiences which seem to arise out of nowhere, though some seem to be associated with precognitive dreams.

For example, I remember going to a friend's house in Sausalito, California in the late 1960s and being introduced to a couple who were visiting from the Deep South for the first time. As I shook hands with one of them I had an intense déjà vu experience, and straight away I remembered a dream I had about a week earlier. In it, I was standing in the backyard of a large, older house that I knew was somewhere in the South because of its style and the humid heat. I was with a young couple (similar to the people I was meeting), looking away from the house across a downward slope toward a small shack at the back of the property.

Around this building the grass was overgrown, and behind it and to its right were a creek and a wooded area. In the dream I indicated that I wanted to walk toward the shack, but the people I was with warned me to keep an eye out for poisonous snakes, particularly copperheads, which were a problem in the area, they said.

All this was going through my mind as I was being introduced to the young couple in Sausalito. Within a few minutes of our introduction, I found myself asking if they had lived in a building like the one I dreamed of and whether there was such a shack and a problem with copperheads. With surprise, they confirmed it all, and then the subject was abruptly dropped, which, as I have said before, is a typical

---

[20]P. L. Nelson, "Personality Factors in the Frequency of Reported Spontaneous Præternatural Experiences," *The Journal of Transpersonal Psychology*, 21 (1989), 193–209.

response among those confronted by a paranormal perception. I now understand this as an effort to demark an existential "space" between the recognition of a *seeing* event and the accepted reality of our ordinary world, as if the recognition opens a door to something uncontrollable and threatening.

Of course, this has been the same problem researchers into the paranormal encounter—the use of denial to squelch any engagement. If a passive method fails to terminate discussion, more targeted and even virulent criticism ensues. I have observed that there is also a cyclical aspect to this resistance. Attacks by the "science police" tend to intensify as more and more positive results for research accumulate. When funding for research and interest dry up, the attacks cease and there is a quiet period until someone else sticks their head up with interesting findings. Then the campaign starts all over again...

VI. Further Reflections

O Light Invisible, we praise Thee!
Too bright for mortal vision.
O Greater Light, we praise Thee for the less;
The eastern light our spires touch at morning,
The light that slants upon our western doors at evening,
The twilight over stagnant pools at batflight,
Moon light and star light, owl and moth light,
Glow-worm glowlight on a grassblade.
....
And when we have built an altar to the Invisible Light, we may
set thereon the little lights for which our bodily vision is made.
And we thank Thee that darkness reminds us of light.
O Light Invisible, we give Thee thanks for Thy great glory!

T.S. Eliot

Choruses from The Rock

25. The Psycho-Spiritual Dimension of *Seeing*

These days I regard being a *seer* as a wonderful gift. It has opened a panorama of knowing not otherwise available—a view of self and others that has broadened my understanding of life and been deeply spiritualizing. But that is not how I felt about it at the beginning, when I discovered that there was a price to be paid: a prolonged period of confusion, disorientation, paranoia, depression and at times physical illness which only ended when I integrated my new worldview into my daily life and recognized myself as a *seer*.

In his classic book, *Shamanism,* Mircea Eliade called this turmoil the "initiatory illness"—a period of physical and psychological debility that often precedes someone's initiation as a shaman.[1] He said that, in certain traditional cultures, such an "illness" is seen as a sign of an initiate's opening to shamanic power. However, in modern Western societies, it seems to be viewed only as the onset of mental disorder or some neurological dysfunction. This is very much the case when it comes to *seers* undergoing their initiatory turmoil. If they are unlucky, their breakthrough into *seeing* can get them into difficulty and result in them being treated as if they are having a breakdown.

This is because the methods and worldview necessary to facilitate an integration of *seeing* into ordinary life are almost entirely absent in modern, developed societies—apart from a confused mixture of New Age and other spiritual beliefs. In the professional domain, almost no one is available with the technical knowledge required to mentor a person through the "initiatory" process, so often those having non-ordinary encounters turn mainly to psychologists and physicians. And this is where the process often goes wrong. Indeed, I would venture to

---

[1]M. Eliade, *Shamanism: Archaic Techniques of Ecstasy,* trans. R. Trask, Bollingen Series vol. 76 (Princeton: Princeton University Press., 1964).

say that a significant number of individuals being treated for mental disorders are, in fact, "failed" shamans, mystics, and *seers*.

An example is a young woman I met in 1972, a few years after she had been diagnosed as having had a brief but intense psychotic episode. During the course of our conversation she told me that she had been up late studying for a college exam when suddenly, everything she was reading and trying to understand fell together into what she perceived as a wonderful, all-encompassing whole. She felt that she was able to grasp a higher meaning underpinning events and she perceived everything as being connected as one. The experience was expansive, beautiful and exciting, leaving her feeling highly energized and alive.

As I listened to her, it was clear that her "shift" in attention and point of view had led to an altered self-awareness, an encounter with *seeing* traditionally called a numinous experience. She was certain, she said, that during and immediately following the episode, she was unafraid and felt only ecstasy and joy. In her excitement, however, she made the mistake of sharing what she was experiencing with her college roommates. Predictably, they viewed her statements as bizarre and reacted accordingly. The dormitory headmistress was called, followed by medical authorities, and the young woman was hospitalized. Psychiatrists diagnosed her as schizophrenic, and nurses and social workers treated her as if she was no longer sane. It was then that she first felt fear and anxiety, she told me.

Weeks of "therapy" combined with the liberal use of powerful anti-psychotic drugs and a total conditioning program on the part of her friends, family, and hospital staff led her to believe that she was, indeed, insane. She became paranoid about her thoughts and actions, since she was judging them from the social and medical models foisted on her. Whatever emerged into her awareness was experienced as potentially dangerous, possibly leading her into another bout of mental illness. Before long, she had lost her sense of who she was, what was appropriate behavior, and what was "real." In short, her breakthrough into mystical *seeing* had been transformed into a breakdown for lack of appropriate support.

Now I am not arguing that all deviant cognitions and behaviors classified under the umbrella term "schizophrenia" are episodes of *seeing* gone awry, but those who are starting to consciously experience *seeing* sometimes find themselves radically out of time and context in a way that can be confused with mental dysfunction. In such circumstances their "symptoms" may be contextualized medically and psychologically leading to them being treated for a "breakdown." With the onset of *seeing*, some neophytes experience a deconstruction in which their values, meaning structures, and sense of self alter profoundly. This can look like the onset of a mental disorder rather than a reorganization of understanding and a transition into a different way of knowing.

The late Ronald Laing, a psychiatrist notable for his contribution to the anti-psychiatry movement and theories of interpersonal perception, believed that the transcendental aspects of these kinds of ego-disrupting breakthroughs are often missed and sometimes confused with psychotic episodes.[2] What is meaningful and apparently real in a spontaneously altered state of consciousness may be understood entirely differently in an ordinary state—whether by a treating psychiatrist or the patient himself, once he has returned to an ordinary state of consciousness.

Usually, the neophyte *seer* is unconscious of how the line between ordinary and non-ordinary awareness is crossed and finds the apparently haphazard shifting back and forth between *seeing* and ordinary awareness disturbing and disorienting. Statements he makes when he is *seeing* may be unintelligible to a therapist, doctor, or indeed anyone else who hears it in an ordinary state of awareness. When the experient returns from his non-ordinary state and hears the "expert's" opinion on what he has said, he has little choice but to agree.

***

One way to reduce this disorientation and prevent confusion between ordinary and non-ordinary states of awareness, is to have an in-depth psychological knowledge of oneself, which, as I have already said, is essential to learning to *see*. Without understanding our unique

---

[2] R. D. Laing, *The Politics of Experience and the Bird of Paradise* (Middlesex, England: Penguin Books, 1967).
R. D. Laing, "Transcendental Experience," in *The Highest State of Consciousness*, ed. J. White (Garden City: Anchor, 1972), pp. 104–13.

psychological processes—associative chain of thoughts and emotional reactions—we cannot know if what we are experiencing is a genuine episode of *seeing* or just a fantasy. With in-depth psychological work and regular reality testing, the *seer* soon discovers that what is *seen* has not only a unique phenomenological quality and intensity—a "signature," if you like—but also an attached story that can indicate its location in space and time as well as give clues to its meaning. In addition, it might have a direction, by which I mean it can be perceived as coming toward us from a location outside ourselves.

So how should a *seer* approach the task of understanding himself better? The first step might be to begin formulating a map of perceptions and behaviors that we normally hide from ourselves. Sigmund Freud's classic text, *The Psychopathology of Everyday Life,*[3] on how behavioral slips reveal unconscious beliefs and desires, can open the way for mapping aspects of our perceptions and behaviors hidden from ourselves. Since his time, various schools of psychodynamic therapy inspired by his theories have offered ways to explore this further. Of these, I believe the broader and more eclectic schools, such as Gestalt psychotherapy and existential psychoanalysis, are better than systems that are overly attached to a particular founder, who tends to be viewed by followers as the bearer of a transcendent truth applying to all people and situations.

A good indicator of the usefulness of any form of psychoanalysis or psychotherapy is its method of dream interpretation. In my opinion, this should not be overly burdened with a standardized, one-size-fits-all symbolic system for mapping the unconscious as this is usually just a reflection of the founder's own unconscious symbolic process and does not apply to everyone.

Without developing a personalized, detailed map of how we interpret the world, two obstacles will obscure the ability to *see*: denial and projection. Both of these terms originated with Freud but have become widely used by a variety of therapeutic schools. Denial is the mind's capacity to compartmentalize thoughts and perceptions as a

---

[3]S. Freud, *The Interpretation of Dreams,* vols. 4 and 5, in *Standard Edition of the Complete Psychological Works of Sigmund Freud,* ed. and trans. by J Strachey (London: Hogarth Press, 1959).

method of keeping unwanted cognitive content and emotions out of conscious awareness. Projection is seeing characteristics in others that are really aspects of ourselves, particularly ones we have denied.

A typical example of how these two work together is found in someone who loves his parents yet simultaneously feels anger toward them. Because rage directed at a parent is generally unacceptable in our culture, it is often suppressed and denied while feelings of love are allowed to remain. Later some of the repressed hostility is unconsciously projected at others, such as a spouse, employer, friend, lover, or child. The person doing the projecting may be unaware that he has chosen an inappropriate target for his anger and may genuinely believe that the victim deserves it. If he is a *seer*, such behavior will distort his non-ordinary as well as ordinary perceptions. For example, when experiencing someone's *bio-field*, he may "color" his awareness by implicitly (unconsciously) interpreting such a *field*-presence as being evil and even dangerous. On the other hand, if he becomes aware of his projection, he will be more able to separate his personal feelings and judgments from what he perceives, viewing non-ordinary events with a less personalized lens.

Typical of what happens to individuals with little or no psychological self-awareness who have non-ordinary experiences is a woman I once interviewed. She was a well-educated former college professor who had some intense encounters she believed to be psychic and visionary in nature. These experiences led her to adopt a whole range of New Age beliefs and practices. During one conversation, she offered what appeared to me to be an episode of simple road hypnosis as an example of the new and amazing supernatural world she believed she now inhabited. She had been driving home from Los Angeles to Santa Barbara late one night on the freeway—usually a two-hour trip—but had no memory of about 45 minutes of the journey and so decided that she and the car had been instantly "teleported" over the distance.

Her entry into a New Age worldview led her to re-evaluate her beliefs about what was real, but since she had no clear guidelines as to what was possible, she began to see any unusual experience as evidence of paranormal magic. In her attempt to get free of her old limited beliefs and broaden her worldview she went too far and jettisoned many of her former views about what is possible. Needless to say, her new beliefs made for a far more exciting life than what she experienced in the constricted and emotionally tense world of academia.

After studying more than a thousand spontaneous, non-ordinary experiences in people, I have discovered that a significant number of them are not *seeing* experiences at all, and some may be purely imaginary. For this reason, and in the spirit of good scientific inquiry, I recommend that, in addition to engaging in psychotherapy, the budding *seer* should examine all non-ordinary experience for possible congruence with ordinary everyday events. When a radical experience seems to have no counterpart in daily life, judgment concerning its authenticity should be suspended, and if possible, it should be compared with the reports of other, more experienced *seers*.

Seeking validation from those who are more experienced is part and parcel of socialization into any new group or worldview. It is the best way to avoid becoming lost in fantasy and is no different from the methods we use to interpret the input from our physical senses. In my case, the many instances when Alice commented on my *seeing* helped to validate my experiences, and reality testing was a daily exercise during the first years of my development.

In recent years we have seen the arrival and rapid spread of a new system for understanding emotional awareness and behavior, called Emotional Intelligence. The term was popularized by American psychologist Daniel Goleman's in his first, seminal book on the subject.[4] Generally, emotional intelligence, or EQ, refers to the level of awareness of and capacity to manage both one's own emotions and those of others. Most books on the subject emphasize the management aspect for the sake of becoming a more effective player in the workplace and in life. However, this seems limited and I believe that what *seers* perceive through their felt awareness of the *field* can take the concept of emotional intelligence to a whole new level.

Virtually everything written about emotional perception in others refers to what can be understood from vocal, behavioral, and physiological "signaling." In fact, there is a long history of attempting to

---

[4]D. J. Goleman, *Emotional Intelligence* (New York: Bantam Books, 1995).

map emotions in the body from these signals—from the James-Lange theory of emotion to the present-day work on micro-expressions based on Paul Ekman's original research and conceptualization.[5] While this physical map is very useful, from a *seer's* standpoint it offers only an indirect, interpretive approach. Nowhere in the literature have I seen a reference to the idea that emotions might be perceived directly from a person's *field* without having to look at the secondary signaling process. And isn't directly perceiving an object preferable to being given a description of it?

Again, for a *seer* to clearly engage with the emotional content of another's *field* requires a deep self awareness that allows him to experience things more objectively and not just through the filter of his own desires. Such self-knowledge is necessary not only for accurate *seeing*, but in order to prevent the most common and egregious fault I have observed in psychics and *seers*—impenetrable and severe narcissism.

It is easy to fall into the narcissistic trap, especially when individuals are trying to carve out occupational niches for themselves as *seers*. In these cases, practitioners have strong needs to be recognized for their non-ordinary abilities and this can lead them to proving themselves constantly by ever more "amazing" performances. Also, it has been my observation that people with a more severe form of narcissism—a narcissistic personality disorder—are drawn to becoming psychics and *seers* precisely because of the attention, accolades, and special status these occupations offer. The more disordered they are, the more likely they are to exaggerate what they do and incorporate fantasy material into their work, because their narcissism requires that they continually create an ever bigger splash with clients and followers.

Narcissism is a self-reflecting wall that a person inadvertently builds around himself to maintain a self-aggrandizing picture of who he is. It is made of the bricks of judgment cemented together by an underlying paranoia usually originating in an early wounding of a person's self-concept. The only way to deal with this trap is to develop the Watcher's

---

[5]W. James, *The Principles of Psychology*, vols. 1 and 2 (New York: Dover Publications, 1890, 1950).
P. Ekman, *Emotions Revealed: Recognizing Faces and Feelings to Improve Communication and Emotional Life.* 2nd ed. (New York: Holt Paperbacks, 2007).

meditative and de-automatized style of being in the world and observe oneself (as discussed in Chapter 11) not only as a *seer* but in ordinary life.

While psychological clarity and self-awareness are essential for a *seer*, it is also true that no one is perfect. Personal needs and desires leak into perceptions—ordinary or non-ordinary. All I am suggesting is that *seers* must make a supreme effort to become as self-aware and honest as possible, because the clarity and authenticity of what they articulate about their perceptions depend on it.

***

The self-aware, honest, and open way of engaging life as a *seer* can also contribute to a more spiritualized way of being in the world. Being a spiritual person does not make one a *seer*, just as the act of *seeing* does not make one spiritual. However, many practices, such as meditation and contemplative prayer, can facilitate *seeing*, just as the ability to *see* can sacralize our daily world and open one to a deeper spiritual perspective. From my perspective, the perception of the *field* can be understood as an expression of connectedness. *Seeing* the *field* represents an opening of the heart and mind to a larger reality that deepens our awareness of and connection to others and the environment in which we are embedded. It is the *suchness* of the moment, as some Buddhist teaching describe it, that is revealed. This broader and deeper awareness arising from *seeing* facilitates a perspective of dispassion that I understand as the core of compassion and spirituality.

At times, the *field* manifests as a powerful and influential force that appears to irrupt into a person's awareness and can seem like a message from a divine source, especially when the recipient perceives it as offering guidance and meaning. Entire religions have been spawned or changed by such encounters, an example being George Fox's vision at Lichfield, which, no doubt, influenced the Quaker religion he founded (See Chapter 17). I do not believe that an encounter with the *field* puts us in touch with divine forces, however.

I am not attempting to reduce religious experiences such as Fox's to mere acts of *seeing*, but I have little doubt that a great many experiences that have been given religious and spiritual meaning are in fact spontaneous acts of *seeing*. Most commonly for *seers*, the simple sense of connectedness experienced as a result of their perception of the *field* can open them to a greater capacity for spiritual awareness. In this state, a deeply felt compassion may be discovered in a direct, experiential way as opposed to an application of a principle of belief.

In my academic writing I have called the kinds of *seeing* experiences that produce religious or spiritual meanings "ontic," meaning that they are taken as coming from or representing another level of reality or ontological other (such as a god). I differentiate these from purely perceptual experiences, which may have similar content but are generally not viewed as representing a source of "otherness" arising from beyond our human realm.[6]

Also in my academic work I have argued that it is best to maintain ontological neutrality—to suspend judgment about the source of our experiences—and remain just a good observer. It is better to understand such encounters as being *sui generis,* that is, we should attempt to explicate them from within the frame of reference of their occurrence. In this position, we use our human awareness directly as a witness, meeting daily life as we encounter it, in a succession of moments of immediate, experiential apprehension. When we attempt to make sense of these events after the fact, it is important to accept uncertainty and leave the door open regarding what an encounter ultimately is, or what it means.

A case in point is my encounter with the two apparently disincarnate beings in the Back Bay of Boston. My experience was that they said: "You called, what do you want?" Within the experiential frame of the event, I can only say they seemed to construe what I did as "calling" them, although I did not understand it that way. Except for their sudden and unusual entry and departure, they met all the criteria for the type of veridical experience that I usually call real. However, in terms of who they were, where they came from, and whether or not they were "real," I must conclude that I do not really know, in any

---

[6]P. L. Nelson, "The Technology of the Praeternatural: An Empirically Based Model of Transpersonal Experiences," *The Journal of Transpersonal Psychology,* 22 (1990), 35–50; http://www.socsci.biz/resources/PraeterTech.pdf.

ultimate sense. Instead, I can only describe, as neutrally as possible, my direct experience.

Another event that I could be tempted to label as spiritual and possibly ontic occurred at Mt. Tamalpais, in Marin County, just north of San Francisco in 1976. On a beautiful spring day, I went with a group of friends for a picnic on the mountain, where we made camp in an open grassy area close to a large grove of pine trees. After eating and sitting around chatting for an hour or so, I suddenly had an urge to leave my companions and walk into the grove. It was not as if a voice called me, but there was a "pull," nonetheless.

Once I was inside the grove I had another urge to lie down on the ground in front of three tall pine trees. Looking up at the tops of the trees high above me, I saw their *fields* join together, and from that combined *field* a beam of green light emerged and shone down onto my chest, seeming to penetrate and connect directly to my heart. A profound sense of calm came over me, and as I deeply relaxed, I sensed many months of anxiety and stress passing away from me. The sensation only lasted a few minutes, and then the green beam of light withdrew and disappeared. I was left with a sense of peace and well-being I had not experienced in years.

This was a marvelous encounter that left me feeling blessed, but was I? Well, yes and no. I felt "anointed" and helped and I was grateful, but as to who, what, or whether anything was responsible for that sense of being blessed I cannot say, because I do not actually have access to any source for that. Nevertheless, I consider this *seeing* encounter a spiritual event because it sacralized the moment and opened my heart, leaving me with a deeper sense of connection to life and a broader knowledge of what is possible.

As a *seer*, I do not accept the notion that there are higher and lower states of consciousness, some more spiritual than others. Spirituality is simply conscious connectedness, which is both immanent and transcendent. *Seeing* can add to that connectedness, though it is not essential. In fact, *seeing* can be done for quite different reasons such as self-aggrandizement and the manipulation of others. *Seeing* and spirituality are not the same thing, though *seeing* can lead to a deeper spirituality. In fact, I would argue that a *seer* without a spiritual perspective is incomplete and, in a sense, defective and possibly dangerous to others. In such a person, the natural human tendency toward egocentricity combined with the unique capacity to experience the non-ordinary can result in that person creating a narcissistically falsely inflated, grandiose pseudo-self. A *seer* so afflicted believes that he is operating from beyond the human realm—an absurd notion, when you think about it, since human beings cannot know from a position apart from their human capacity for knowing, no matter what is believed to be the supposed source.

I tend to think of spirituality as a way of looking at life that requires both "big mind" and "little mind." The former leads to an understanding of the totality of existence in which we are mere specks, while in the latter view we are the very center of the universe. *Seeing* can facilitate knowing that arises from either perspective. The difficulty for people is in maintaining a dual perspective and self-understanding at all times and about all things. The real danger for *seers* is in conflating "big mind" and "little mind" and acting as if their *second attention* knowledge places them apart from their fellow beings.

A useful technique for *seers* to maintain a balanced view of themselves in relation to others is to attempt to consciously connect to the *field* of the Earth just as you would to any living being—a person, a tree or an animal. While this is not an easy exercise, it can be practiced at the end of a meditation, when the mind is stilled and the observing Watcher is more available. Such an effort facilitates an awareness of the presence of our "big" and "little" natures at once.

Another technique that is useful to reduce narcissism and facilitate the maintenance of a balanced perspective is to connect to the *field* of a place where human suffering happens or has happened. My trip to India in 1974 was just such an opportunity. On the streets of Delhi I found myself immersed in the *field* of the place and its human occupants, almost to the point of feeling overwhelmed.

At one point, I stood on a corner surrounded by people being born as others were living and dying. The air was filled with the noise of wailing babies mixed with sounds of mourning as the bodies of those who had died in the night were carried away. When I connected to the *field* generated by this juxtaposition of life and death, I was forced to be in both perspectives at once. It was like a time-lapse movie, where you see a tiny shoot push through the soil, grow into a mature plant, flower, and die, all in the space of a minute or so. At that moment in India, I was humbled and awed as I witnessed the time-lapse presentation of human birth, life and death.

For me it took an act of *seeing* to have this perception, but in fact such a direct apprehension of the human condition is available for anyone. All it requires is for us to let go of certain prejudices—what I have been calling the fixed point of view. For example, it is easy to think of people in America or Australia as having few problems compared to the sufferings of those in the developing world, yet everyone's struggles are important from their own perspective. Recognizing this and *seeing* suffering directly was the opening of genuine compassion for me. It helped me to realize that all the people of the world are in the same boat. As a *seer*, I now know what that boat is—our planet and its overarching *field*.

26. SOME CAUTIONARY NOTES

When a *seer* offers his perceptions to those who have asked for them, he must keep in mind a sense of responsibility both to himself and to his clients. Is he telling the truth? Is he offering too little of what he *sees,* or, on the other hand, too much? Sometimes I have been overly cautious, but in general, caution is a good idea when touching the lives of other people. At this point it is probably a good idea to talk about what impact a *seer* may have on others and look at some of the common mistakes that are made during acts of *seeing*.

About seven years after my journey to England and my initiation as a *seer,* I started doing what are commonly called psychic readings. My career as a professional reader began in Santa Barbara after a friend organized a talk for me at the local campus of Antioch University. We had thought that perhaps 15 or 20 people would attend, so we were surprised when more than 100 showed up, crowding into the seminar room and overflowing into the adjacent hallway. That evening I told the story of my initiation publicly for the first time and then described psychometry and what it was like to perceive the world as a *seer*. During the presentation, I made my contact details available, thinking that a few people might want to meet with me afterward. The next morning the phone rang off the hook, and the calls did not stop until I returned to Australia several months later.

The readings I did back then usually began with a psychological "mapping" of the person, after which I would relate their personality and behavioral patterns to key events in their past, call attention to any major health issues, and finally report on anything I might *see* coming up. However, as I soon learned, doing readings for the public as a professional *seer* can be fraught.

As in any business, a *seer* doing readings is under a great deal of pressure to give the customer what he wants. Despite my intentions to be honest and forthright, I found myself, on occasions, feeding clients what I perceived they wanted to hear, leaving out parts that I was aware might frighten or displease. My clients did not have to verbalize what they wanted; I would perceive it directly from their *fields*. As a "reader," I felt pressure to turn in a good performance and be supportive, as most psychic practitioners try to do. After all, only happy customers come back or tell their friends about you. Sometimes, when I did not sugarcoat my message or make it fit the client's desire, the outcome was negative—such as the time I told the mother of a famous Hollywood personality that she was an alcoholic and needed help. Although I had been speaking to her regularly and had a social relationship with her, after "telling it like it is" I never heard from her again.

Over time, I have learned that just as we can misperceive the color of an object, misremember what was in a room, or misconstrue what was said to us, we can make those mistakes with what we think we perceive as *seers*. Psychological research shows that social situations can pressure us into believing what is not true and coerce us into ignoring perceptions that are unacceptable. This was demonstrated in a "life reading" I did during my days as a professional *seer*.

In 1983 I had a session with a powerfully built man, over six feet six inches tall, who was sent to me by mutual friends. As soon as he arrived I *saw* that there was something physically wrong with him, even though he appeared energetic and in good health. While doing a body or medical "scan" for clients in those days, often I would get a quick flash of an inner picture of the physical organ system involved. However, with this client I could not pinpoint any particular location or organ in his body even though I felt certain that something was wrong. The contrast between his apparent well-being and my *seeing* left me confused, so I rationalized away my initial perception, telling myself that something was a bit strange about his coloring and I was probably just projecting because of that.

In retrospect, I understood that my decision not to pay attention to what I *saw* was exacerbated by a pressure I felt from him. I had a perception that he was a bit of a "health nut" and really wanted to be told that he was going to live to a ripe old age. So I told him what he wanted to hear. I felt his longing, which hooked into my desire to please, so I reassured him about his longevity while ignoring my initial reading of him.

This turned out to be a terrible mistake. He died two years later of AIDS. To this day, I still feel unhappy about what happened. His friends told me that because of my reputation as a *seer*, he never came to terms with the fact that he was dying. While in the hospital in the final stages of his disease, he kept saying: "I can't be dying because Peter said I am going to live to old age." My intention had been to help people with my *seeing* ability. Yet what I did was one of the worst things I could have done for him, because he remained in denial and did not have the opportunity to properly come to terms with his death. The event deeply unsettled me and was part of the reason I eventually stopped doing "life readings" commercially.

It is easy to see how it happened. My inexperience and desire to please had combined with the pressure of his yearning. I had no experience of AIDS (it was 1983) so I did not know how to make sense of what I *saw* in his body scan. I had perceived a similar, generalized sense of illness with no specific cause in other clients, perhaps due to them having an ordinary viral infection, and rashly assumed it was the same with him.

My error in attempting to please was a mistake I have seen in other *seers* and psychics, particularly those who give public readings and "healings" where they can get caught up in the idea that a dazzling performance is the same as a powerful and accurate reading. In reality, it can be just the opposite—all show and no substance. Some psychics and mediums do this quite cynically, turning on a great show while babbling out a standard set of lines, a kind of psychic patois. Others appear to be unconscious of their attempts to impress and please their audience, but the net effect is the same.

As a mentor of *seers,* I attempt to correct this behavior, insisting that the information should always be presented as an impartial phenomenological report, the way a social anthropologist might recount what he witnessed at a tribal ceremony, for instance. Sometimes this falls on deaf ears however, especially when the trainee has such powerful narcissistic needs that it is impossible to get him to self-reflect enough to change his desire to dazzle and "give 'em a good show."

After encountering a number of such individuals while training *seers*, I have learned to stop working with them as soon as it becomes evident that they will not explore their distorted fixed point of view or recognize and make an effort to change their narcissistic behavior. Nevertheless, this will not stop charismatic individuals who are both narcissistic and sociopathic from putting themselves forward as *seers*. Some famous cult leaders, like Jim Jones, operated in this way.

***

Since the early twentieth century Freud, Jung, and their professional offspring have called our attention to the importance of the inner landscape of our dreams in relation to the process of psychological exploration. Generally, and especially among psychoanalysts, the "messages" embedded in dreams are considered signals from the unconscious, whether personal or archetypal; only rarely are they viewed by psychologists and psychoanalysts as acts of *seeing*.

No doubt symbolic interpretations done by analytic psychologists lead to useful therapeutic insights, but from my direct experience, I would argue that some dreams are oracular—they point to events yet to unfold in our life streams. Oracular dreams are a reminder of what to do, where to go, and what is coming. They help us to recognize that our life direction is created not only by the push of the past and the contingencies of the present but also by a future into which we are inexorably drawn.

The materialist ethos of reductive science seems to have infected the analytic psychologies and society in general to the extent that we no longer recognize the divinatory power embedded in some of our dreams and visions. The same ethos has been used to disempower those who would utter prophecies, so that any prognostication that they might offer is viewed just as a sign of their psychological or neurological dysfunction. Indeed, the current over-concern with psychological "processing" and its inevitable focus on personal self has left some of us inhabiting a disembodied and disconnected pseudo-self obsessed with performance and "mental health."

In ecological terms, we have been psychologized right out of our psychic and spiritual worlds, a context that once helped us gain a sense of connectedness and wholeness. In fact, our links to others and the broader environment through our *fields* are aspects of the greater ecological matrix of which the physical world is just a part. In a profound sense, oracular activity sits at the heart of our psycho-social evolution because it opens the self and society to a wider vision and hence new possibilities. From my standpoint as a *seer*, it is only through the process of *seeing* that the spiritual dimension can be fully reintroduced into our lives.

Psychotherapy's other major failing is its lack of recognition of *seeing* and therefore, any useful guidance for the psychological development of a *seer*. Therapy's focus on victimization, woundedness, and entitlement suggests that its primary concern is "fixing" dysfunctional individuals so that they become "useful" in society, grist for the social and corporate mills as contented professors, accountants, and bulldozer drivers. It is a rare therapist, indeed, who can recognize, much less acknowledge, that a client's existential battle may be about finding room for his *seeing* capacity in an awareness-challenged society. For this to change, it is essential that more *seers* educate themselves to become psychotherapists and more therapists get some useful and realistic training by *seers*.

***

Just as a genuine experience of *seeing* can be missed by explaining it away, there is the equal danger of misconstruing ordinary occurrences by giving them visionary meaning and divine significance. The sixties saw the rise of hip, "psychic-speak," and the New Age spawned some well-known practitioners of this self-deceptive discourse. In the context of New Age and other forms of religious magical thinking, certain thoughts and imaginings are taken to be acts of genuine *seeing* and are interpreted as directions from a higher power—for example: "My spirit guide instructed me to take more beta-carotene," or "The Lord spoke to me and He wants you to make a donation to His cause."

Instances of imagined "cosmic" connections between ordinary events result in similar ascriptions made about the action of supernatural forces directing one's life. The best example is what social anthropologists call an "emic" (insider) statement, like the one signifying a special connection with "higher forces" often heard in New Age circles: "Your presence here is no coincidence…it was meant to be." The language and symbolic systems employed in such cases are often confused with the genuine knowledge gained through *seeing*. It is the old problem of the roadmap being confused with the territory. Indeed, many New Age beliefs seem to be floating on the same imaginary naive-real river of "truth" upon which the materialist religion of science sails.[1]

What we must conclude from this is that the line between projected fantasy and true *seeing* is rather fine, which can make discriminating the facts of *seeing* from the fiction of imagination difficult. Such borderline issues arise around any experience that is fleeting and cannot be revisited easily, leaving the mind and imagination to fill in the details. In a sense, *seeing* is sometimes like being a witness to an accident or a crime. One is caught up in the contingencies and suddenness of the event and cannot take in its entirety, so that only part of what happened is remembered and articulated by the *seeing* reporter.

With *seeing*, we cannot return physically to the scene but can only evoke an internal replay of what we experienced, so there will be some filling in of gaps and narratizing associated with these, as well as with memory of ordinary events. With *seen* episodes, one can partially reconnect across time and re-experience the event, but some parts will still be lost in the replay and possibly elaborated. Only with a great deal of experience can a *seer* learn to trust the validity of such replays. Of course, some people are better observers than others and those who are more familiar with the workings of their perceptual processes will likely show greater skill when sorting the relevant from the spurious when making sense of an unfamiliar scene.

***

All the requirements and proscriptions I have been discussing with regard to becoming a reliable *seer* suggest the importance of having a mentor, or what some Buddhist traditions refer to as a "spiritual friend."

---

[1]The late Oxford philosopher C. D. Broad used the term naive-real to describe the false ontological beliefs that science tends to ascribe to its knowledge.
C. D. Broad, *Perception, Physics, and Reality* (Cambridge: Cambridge University Press, 1914).

For *seers* this does not mean a guru or a spiritual figure in the traditional sense. Rather, the teacher should be simply a *seer* who has been down the road before us, someone who can point to the terrain and make us aware of the lay of the land, so to speak, just as Alice did for me.

For *seers* there are no gurus or exalted teachers out there waiting to receive us if only we can climb some mystical mountain and get them to pay attention to us. There are only people who can demonstrate, by example, abilities and traits that we are trying to develop in ourselves. It is important to remember that these guides are not perfect, and they make no pretense at being so—or if they do, they should be avoided.

Unfortunately, as I have often observed, many "seekers," especially in the USA, seem to be obsessed with perfection. Americans appear to have a drive to strip themselves down to some final, purified form—an impulse that probably derives from our cultural grounding in puritanical religion developed in a frontier context where austerity, self-denial, and being "pure" constituted a path to virtue and success. In this way, many on the path to spiritual awareness become fanatics, seeking pure food, pure lives, and perfect gurus. This is despite the well-observed fact that a teacher often comes in an unexpected form and may appear at first sight quite ordinary, as happened to me in my journey to a Buddhist retreat in the Indian Himalayas.

In August 1973, after a rather difficult trip overland from Turkey to India, I found myself in New Delhi, nursing a nasty case of dysentery. I was sitting in a vegetarian restaurant off Connaught Place when I looked up to see a young Asian man seated alone at a table, staring at me with a broad grin on his face. He was dressed completely in white and just kept staring and grinning, so I smiled back—rather weakly, I might add, considering the state of my innards. After a few minutes, the young man, who turned out to be Vietnamese, came over to my table and started talking about his guru, Goenka-ji, a former Burmese businessman who had become a Buddhist monk and for years had traveled around India offering teachings. It turned out that he had acquired a considerable reputation and following as a result.

In reverential tones and with a sense of awe, the young devotee told me my karma must be incredibly good, since I had the opportunity to be guided by him to the guru, who was about to start a retreat in

Darjeeling, in the eastern foothills of the Himalayas. At that point I was not particularly interested in a meditation retreat, nor had I heard of the guru, but, caught by his enthusiasm, I agreed to go with him, though my traveling companion was not at all interested and later declined.

About a week later, I found myself in Darjeeling at a former tuberculosis sanitarium, left over from the days of the British Raj, with a group of devotees and Goenka-ji, who turned out to be an ample-bellied former businessman. On this occasion he sat cross-legged on a dais in front of us, talking about the Buddhist notions of suffering, the four Noble Truths, the Eightfold Path, and so on. I was bored. There was nothing new in this for me because of my previous years of Buddhist practice and study. Also, my *seeing* did not reveal anything about him that set him apart. Despite this, his followers treated him like some kind of radiant being. What I *saw* was just a very dedicated man who was offering Buddhist teachings in a yearning, devotional way. It was disconcerting for me to *see* that his *seeing* was not operating.

On the second day of the retreat a new person wandered into camp—a young American who had been in India about five years. He looked like a thin, blonde-haired California surfer. He was dressed only in a dhoti (men's cloth skirt) and had walked to Darjeeling from some distance because he had heard that a great Buddhist teacher was going to be there. Evidently, after a stint in the Peace Corps in Africa, he had arrived in India and studied with a guru in an ashram in the South. When, after a few years, the teacher died, he started his pilgrimage around India on foot, which he had been doing for about a year.

From what I was *seeing,* the young man had a real presence. He was "there" in a fundamental, unannounced yet incredibly clear way—his *field* was intense, warm, large, and aglow. Straight away it was clear to me that he was the only truly "radiant being" in that place. I was quite drawn to him, and we started to hang out together. He told me about his travels around India, and we each talked about our plans—his was to make a pilgrimage around India on foot.

After we talked for a while, he suggested that I would probably be more comfortable if I wore a dhoti during the humid heat of the Indian monsoon, so we set off to the local marketplace, where he taught me how to haggle with a Tibetan trader for a piece of cloth. We walked, talked, and laughed a lot, in spite of my cramped and painful lower gut, and gradually made our way back to the retreat site.

He then told me that he had hoped to join the Goenka retreat, but he had no money because he was a mendicant monk, which was why he had walked hundreds of miles to get there. All he owned was a begging bowl, and he lived on people's handouts. I was very keen to have him in the group, so I presented his case to a "committee" of Western follower-overseers and asked if he could be let in without charge. They seemed embarrassed that I would even ask such a question and retreated to hold a meeting.

As one of the payees, I let them know that I had no objection to him being admitted gratis and expressed my belief that his presence would be an asset. However, for the committee, the important issue was whether or not other participants would feel cheated if someone attended for free. After much deliberation, they decided not to let him attend the retreat, though he could remain at the site and participate in less important events.

That moment in Darjeeling was a turning point for me. I *saw* the wandering monk and I *saw* the followers who had just made the decision to exclude him and I realized that the followers were blind, they could not *see* at all and did not have a clue as to what was important. With the departure of the surfer-monk a day later I decided that there was nothing further to learn, so I left. I also realized at that moment that I was finished with gurus and their followers. Today I believe they are two aspects of the same phenomenon—you cannot have a guru without a true believer and vice versa.

***

The process of relinquishing the need for an ultimate parental authority figure, like a guru, and taking responsibility for oneself as a *seer* brings us to the notion of fate, or karma. Eastern ideas, such as karma, tend to get deconstructed by the Western mind and rewritten as a form of crypto Judeo-Christianity. In its original Eastern frame of reference, karma is more like spiritual gravity—events "fall" according to their karmic "mass." However, in its Western reconstruction this concept has been transformed into a notion of punishment—"sin, retribution, and death"—becoming the basis of highly judgmental beliefs concerning personal goodness or badness and spiritual worth. Many believe that unless we evaluate ourselves this way, we will not learn the required "lessons" and will therefore miss the boat (or the guru) either for eternity or this life, depending on the mythology of their particular religious club.

My trip to India and my encounter in Darjeeling were key events in the process of learning how to let go—a fundamental capacity required on the path of acquiring the skills to be a *seer*. Letting go is akin to accepting that you are living your life and, simultaneously, your life is living you (karma). That is, we tend to see ourselves as being active participants in our lives who make things happen but the life we are living is also a stream that is moving and carrying us along. In a sense, my karma brought me to the moment where I could make the leap by letting go of my need to find a teacher, but I still had to choose to participate by acting to move with what the current offered.

Our personal stream throws up obstacles, opens doors, gives and takes away. We are traveling in its direction whether we like it or not. Our choice is to either move within those constraints or spend a great deal of time and energy fighting the current. The only way out appears to be to leave the corporeal stream altogether (and that might not be a way out, either). The causal stream, which is our karma, is not something to be endured as punishment. It is a valuable learning opportunity—a chance to deepen understanding, open new doors, and glimpse other realities by meeting it consciously.

We may hear "tales of power" concerning others' lives and wish such events would happen to us. But those particular events cannot happen to us because they belong to the life streams of others. Only by attending to the events and moments in our own stream can we find openings to new awarenesses and a deeper reality. It is amusing to recall that in the 1960s and 70s, many inspired seekers were roaming Mexico's Sonoran Desert looking for Castaneda's Don Juan.[2] They never found him because that story and those events belonged to Castaneda, just as our stories belong to us and no one else.

In the end, it is up to us to overcome fear, follow our *seeing*, and persevere with the twists and turns of our life stream with a faith that

---

[2]C. Castaneda, *Tales of Power* (New York: Simon and Schuster, 1974).

this life, whatever it brings, is our only true path—our karma. The journey of becoming who we are always depends on an act of letting go—ceasing to grasp after fantasies and illusions while being present with all our energy and attention. This is what I call *the way of a seer*.

Bringing It All Back Home

Throughout this book I have been attempting to take you on a journey into the world of the *seer*: firstly with the story of my own entry into that realm and, secondly, by exploring what a *seer* experiences and how *seeing* works as intentional awareness. If you have stayed with me, then you have begun to understand the role and importance of attention in opening this perceptual gateway. In *seers* attention is uniquely deployed in that it is always moving fluidly between two streams—the world of ordinary knowing and that of the non-ordinary, *second stream*. As I have said before, a *seer* is a person who is always "on" and engaging both streams.

In telling my story, I have highlighted the more dramatic instances of *seeing* in my life, ones that opened new vistas for me. However, I have to say that my day-to-day life is filled with many smaller, nondramatic acts of *seeing*, and these remain at the heart of my interactions and relationships with others and the world around me. *Seeing* governs what I do, who I live and work with, where I live, my plans for the future, and much more. Of course, with my training in science, I still evaluate and make decisions in what I like to think is a rational fashion—I watch events, listen, read, discuss, experiment, and logically analyze. But my knowledge of the world is built just as much on the information my *second stream* provides and, for interpersonal decision-making, the most important "raw" data I use is what I glean through *seeing*.

Because *seers* are constantly in touch with the *field*, its *tone* and *contents*, aspects of the emotions and lives of those around them are continually available to a *seer's* awareness. This is both pleasant and unpleasant. For example, I am conscious of people who radiate beauty into the *field*, but I also *see* those who wear a mask of positivity yet underneath are deeply conflicted, hiding anxiety, depression, and rage.

Most people who carry the burden of a great discrepancy between their personas and their subjective worlds—pretending to be something they are not—are usually unaware that their inner struggles and lack of integration play out in front of a *seer* like a movie. In my experience, such people are the most difficult for me to be around because they highlight for me the dilemma of living in the prevailing social conspiracy that holds that *seeing* is impossible and, therefore, we must act like what we perceive through the *second stream* does not exist.

As a result of this social requirement, a great deal of my life is spent not acknowledging or commenting on what I experience in my immediate social world, because doing so can be very upsetting and decentering for most people. It is like traveling incognito and living like a spy, even though there is no secret and no one to report back to.

***

In my view, all perception—ordinary and non-ordinary—is a chain of creation originating from a nexus of external inputs mixed with memory and associations that underlie our emotional and cognitive knowing. The *second stream* is one of those inputs, just like vision, hearing, and so forth. A *seer* attends to the physical world, like everybody else, but he is also paying attention to the *field*, its *tone*, and *contents*. In order to do this successfully, he must have a degree of mastery over his total epistemic process in order to successfully integrate the two streams. In other words, he has to have a deep understanding of the internal process of his knowledge-making that allows him to access how he "maps" who he is and participates in the creation of his reality. A *seer* is both a witness to the present moment around him as well as to the process of his knowledge-creation that emerges from the totality of his perception and participation.

Having said this, the picture of the *seer's* world I have presented is not going to be exactly the same as ones experienced by other *seers*. The lack of consensus and acceptance around acts of *seeing* and what it is to be a *seer* means that descriptions of our perceptions tend to show greater diversity than those of ordinary experiences. The variability is due, in part, to the lack of social norms for navigating the non-ordinary world. We each have a unique perspective, whether it arises from *seeing* or from ordinary perception, and the variability between these perspectives should be acknowledged in the non-ordinary domain as much as it is in the ordinary.

Nevertheless, *seeing* and related experiences seem to be part of the fabric of the lives of many ordinary and honest people, as various surveys and scientific studies, including ones carried out by me, show. Such research clearly reveals that a majority of people are willing to report paranormal episodes that they believe are real and genuine as long as they do not have to do so publicly.[1] During the course of collecting data on non-ordinary experiencing at two Australian universities, I was struck by how often individuals prefaced their story by stating, "I have never told anyone this before, but...."

***

It is an ongoing challenge for all of us that *seeing* and experiences of telepathy, clairvoyance, and precognition are regarded by the world of science as unreal—merely the outpourings of a benighted, self-deluding minority. This negative view has not been helped by the fact that psychic, visionary, and mystical experiences have been used by cranks for less-than-honest purposes and many so-called psychic practitioners have been exposed as frauds.[2]

However, the biggest obstacle for a broader acceptance of the capacity for *seeing* is the religious, dogmatic form of science, dubbed "scientism" that now dominates the modern world. As far as I am aware, science in itself, as a collection of empirical research methodologies, is not threatened by what reasonable *seers* claim. The condemnation of research into the paranormal seems to be the result of paranoia and irrational prejudice on the part of those claiming to defend what is mistakenly believed to be "true science." Adherents of scientific fundamentalism not only make it difficult to explore "anomalous communication," they actively campaign against

---

[1] P. L. Nelson, "Transcending Limitations: Spontaneous Paranormal and Spiritual Experiences in Australian Daily Life," *Australian Parapsychological Review* 2, 3(18) (1991), 8–12.

[2] A good account of the history of psychical practice and research can be found in Harvey Irwin's textbook on the subject. H. J. Irwin, *An Introduction to Parapsychology*, 2nd ed. (North Carolina: McFarland, 1995).

researchers who study the paranormal and denigrate their efforts, no matter how rigorously the research is conducted.

Today, science seems to have become the intellectual alter-ego of the individualist ethos that dominates the *weltanschauung* of modern, Western societies. Within this framework, progress has come to mean the human mastery of nature. We command our environment with a whip, and it obeys, or so we like to think. The belief held by many pre-literate societies that nature can and does speak back apparently has been lost to us in our rush toward progress over the past 300 years. Yet, whether or not we hear the message from our environment (the life stream) ultimately will not matter in terms of its effect on us. Aware or not, recognizing our fundamental connectedness to nature or not, we are still subject to its power. What we need now are open minds and I believe that will only come about if we gain greater access to the more fluid type of attention that is part of *seeing*.

In my opinion the failure to recognize *seers* and *seeing* is part of our disconnection from nature, which has negative spiritual ramifications for all of society. In our current educational practices it seems we would rather produce anxious, depressive, disconnected, high achievers than empathic, deep experiencers, whose natural gift is the capacity to open to expanded consciousness. By short-circuiting these potential visionaries—those who connect us to what the Australian Aborigines call "the Dreaming"[3]—we are losing our connection not only to each other but to the sacred as well.

This is a profound loss to our society. In effect, it removes the conduits to both our creative roots and our spiritual center. Traditionally, we have looked to organized religion to connect us to the "big picture" of who we are and where we are going. But most religions, too, have been methodical in their efforts to eliminate any spontaneous irruption of visionary experience, insisting instead that we adhere simply to the stories we have been told.

Before their exposure to European colonization, many tribal societies defined community primarily through kinship, which was both

---

[3]The Dreaming, or "Tjukurrpa," can mean to "see and understand the law" as it is translated from the Arrernte language. http://australia.gov.au/about-australia/australian-story/dreaming.

a biological and a social concept. There were no national boundaries as we understand them today, yet there was a sense of cohesiveness, and I am sure this root-level social connection was maintained in part through a shared awareness of the communal *field*. Today, it is still true that members of social groups who directly experience their connectedness through any form of *seeing*-like consciousness know themselves both as individuals and as a larger organism—a kind of collective psycho-social "self."

When we directly perceive our connection to another, I know you as part of me and you know me as part of you. Therefore, we know each other and our commonality in a way that transcends our apparent physical separation and the social structures in which we are embedded. I believe that through an awareness of the *field*, we are capable of understanding ourselves as part of a larger self—what the American aboriginals of the Iroquois Nations referred to as the "long body," the psycho-spiritual-somatic body of the group.[4] I also believe that we are still capable of the same kind of connection today, if we can reclaim it.

In his book, *Speaking of Sadness,* sociologist David Karp argues that the 11 to 15 million Americans who suffer from depression do so in part because they are fundamentally disconnected from any meaningful social group.[5] Suggestions for fixing this problem and recreating community in order to promote social cohesion and more satisfying living have included projects like cohousing and the reinvigoration of cultural and religious networks. However, in my view, these do not go far enough.

Overcoming the deep sense of isolation and alienation present in most industrial societies will require much more than just a bit of social engineering. I believe it will take nothing less than the rediscovery of the psycho-emotional links existing among all living creatures, and between us and our environment that can only take place when we expand our awareness to include direct perception of the *field*.

---

[4] C. M. Aanstoos, "Psi and the Phenomenology of the Long Body," *Theta,* 13–14 (1986), 49–51.
[5] D. A. Karp, *Speaking of Sadness: Depression, Disconnection, and the Meanings of Illness* (New York: Oxford University Press, 1995).

Ultimately, our future survival will depend on developing a deeper capacity for connectedness—a level of communication with each other that transcends our highly developed verbal and physical signaling. In this sense, *seeing*, as a more profound act of interpersonal awareness and knowing, is at the heart of spirituality, communion with others, our connection to the broader social ecology and, ultimately, compassion.

About the Author

Dr. Peter Nelson is a registered psychologist and social science researcher who consults with individuals and organizations in the USA, Australia and New Zealand. For the past 30 years he has also conducted research into non-ordinary experience and published his findings in academic journals and books in several countries and has been the subject of numerous interviews in the popular media.

A native of New York City, he began his career in neurophysiology with research programs in the USA, England and Denmark. Then, in the 1980s, he switched to social science, focusing on how people create and experience reality. In the late 1980s he conducted ground breaking research into non-ordinary experiencing, for which he gained a Ph.D. degree from the University of Queensland in Australia. For the next decade he taught psychology and conducted research at universities in Australia, New Zealand and the US. Since then he has worked for governments, non-profits and businesses as a research consultant on projects including statistical surveys, usability research, end-user ethnography and corporate cultural analysis. He also has been a counselor, life coach and a psychological consultant, including working as a forensic psychologist for the Australian criminal courts.

Made in United States
Orlando, FL
20 July 2022

19983458R00154